CONTENTS

Joining in with the Spirit

Connecting World Church and Local Mission

Kirsteen Kim

EPWORTH

British Library Cataloguing in Publication data

A catalogue record for this book is available
from the British Library

978 0 7162 0658 3

This edition published 2009
by Epworth Press
Methodist Church House
25 Marylebone Road
London NW1 5JR

Typeset by Regent Typesetting, London
Printed and bound in Great Britain by
CPI Antony Rowe Chippenham SN14 6LH

PREFACE

Ten years of my adult life have been spent outside these shores: five years in South Korea, a year in the USA and four years in India. In these years I encountered different expressions of Christian faith and – particularly in Korea, my husband's home country – had deep exposure to other ways of living. In the places in which I lived, taught and studied, the churches were very much aware of their mission context and were motivated to share their faith widely. Our presence with them was a reminder that they were not alone in this but were connected in one Spirit with other Christians around the world. Korean churches especially had a great sense of God's blessing coming to them by the agency of foreign missionaries. They felt a corresponding responsibility to be a light to the nations and to 'repay the debt of the gospel' by evangelistic and social work wherever in the world they thought it was needed. We trained and did our best to prepare enthusiastic volunteers to use their skills and spread the gospel message, often in very challenging situations. Then we ourselves were sent by the Presbyterian Church of Korea, supported by Choongshin Church in Seoul, to serve by teaching missiology at Union Biblical Seminary in India. Our students there were mostly presbyters and pastors who were working cross-culturally within the subcontinent.

After four years in India our designation was changed as the Korean Church thought it desirable that we obtain doctoral degrees, and was prepared to support that. So it was that in 1997 I found myself returning to my home country as an overseas student. I came as a migrant with a foreign husband and two children born overseas, struggling to find a place in a crowded island. When I returned to Britain it was again as if I had entered a foreign country as I saw my homeland through the eyes of my husband and children. Beyond my immediate family and close friends, there was little welcome. In fact rather the opposite: I found my British nationality and heritage questioned by complete strangers who wanted to know where I was from. And I was constantly reminded that it was only my economic status and connections with the UK which were relevant. Because I had been out of the country I had no credit rating, my past was suspect, and my loyalties were questioned. To cap it all I qualified to study at a British university only at the overseas student rate. I felt alienated from my own people for whom my experience in Asia, and the connections I had there, were not seen as an asset but as a liability.

Our local church at that time, Bar Hill Church near Cambridge, was an exception among British institutions. There we did feel at home and were accepted, especially by those with overseas experience themselves, as part of the church family. However we had arrived at a time when the British churches, like the wider society, were focused on local affairs. We ourselves got caught up in mission to Britain and have remained here till now, contrary to our original intention to return to India. And all the while I have been trying to work out what is the connection of the churches in India, Korea and the USA to those in Britain, and how local mission in Britain is related to world mission. In 2001, a tutor post in Selly Oak at the United College of the Ascension (UCA) presented a wonderful opportunity to explore this in an international setting in the UK. And the closure of the college in 2006 only underlined the urgency of the question.

The origins of this book lie in the mission programme that I coordinated at UCA, Selly Oak, the core of which was a ten-week introduction to mission studies. Students were drawn from many different countries, and European students usually found themselves in a minority in the classroom. We also taught ordinands and clergy undergoing continuing education, who came to UCA for some 'world church' experience, mission and development executives, and clergy and church workers arriving to minister in Britain. Over the five years (2001–06), there were a number of changes of staff but I worked with four throughout: Israel Selvanayagam, now Principal of the United Theological College, Bangalore; Val Ogden, who went on to direct the Selly Oak Centre for Mission Studies in the Queen's Foundation in Birmingham; Chad Gandiya, now Bishop of Harare, and Ruth Tetlow, several times Chair of the Birmingham Council of Faiths. Other colleagues included John Corrie, Gary Hall, Emmanuel Jacob, Colin and Maureen Marsh, and Jørgen and Ann Skov Sørensen. Interaction with students and colleagues was immensely stimulating and has greatly enriched this book. The chapters follow the outline of the UCA core course which we designed together and co-taught but the content is largely my own, and I have made my own theological framework for it explicit: a mission theology of the Holy Spirit.

UCA courses were highly acclaimed but reached relatively few, and it was always our wish that the material and approach should be more widely disseminated. The establishment of the Selly Oak Centre for Mission Studies was one way of doing this; this book is another. Its writing has been generously supported by the Formation in World Mission fund of the Methodist Church. I also wish to thank the editors at Methodist Publishing House – Natalie Watson and Angela Shier-Jones – for their hard work and encouragement.

Kirsteen Kim
York, May 2009

1

ONE SPIRIT

Mission beyond Global and Local

> Christian mission is 'finding out where the Holy Spirit is at work and joining in'.[1]
> Rowan Williams

This book explores what the Archbishop's suggestion (above) that we start with the Holy Spirit might mean for the theology and practice of Christian mission. In particular, it attempts to show how the unbound nature and unpredictability of the Spirit's presence and activity (John 3.8) cuts across human expectations and confounds our sense of geography. The most striking example of this in recent history took place in the twentieth century when European Christians found their mission to bring all the other peoples of the world into their churches resulted instead in what we call 'world Christianity', in which Europe becomes a relatively small part of a much larger movement. The realization that Christianity is not (and never was) a European religion, and that the Spirit is moving in ways far beyond our control, poses the new challenge in mission that will be the main subject of this book: How does our local experience of the Spirit connect with the Spirit's global work? And conversely, what is the relationship of what we sometimes call 'the world church' to ministry and mission in Britain?

1.1 Seeing ourselves from outside

Kwame (not his real name) came to Britain recently from a large Methodist church in Ghana on a scholarship programme.

At home his church is made up predominantly of young people who are upwardly mobile and believe that the blessing of Jesus is responsible for their success. On his first Sunday morning in the UK, a middle-aged woman member took him across the city where he was staying to a Methodist church. As they drove there Kwame was struck by the quietness of the streets. No-one seemed to be up yet and no one else was on their way to church. The building was a turn-of-the-twentieth-century chapel. The gallery was closed off and the grey-haired congregation was scattered among the pews on the ground floor. There was no bustle, no singing or dancing, and no children and no young people were to be seen. The service proceeded with a predictability that seemed to Kwame to imply that there was no expectation that God could intervene. At home the power of God would be called upon to help the congregation overcome what was holding them back and achieve success. The woman minister spoke eloquently but there was no loud exhortation, fervent prayer, or insight into details of the lives of the congregation that would lead to healing. There were no signs of the Spirit here as he understood them. At home a woman minister would usually be the wife of a successful pastor but this woman seemed to be alone – a status that raised his suspicions about her sexuality. There were other questions too. If God was present among this congregation why was it not flourishing like the ones in Ghana? Perhaps, he pondered, there was some curse on these people – a judgment maybe for their enslavement of black people and plundering of Africa? In view of this it was appropriate that something was being given back to Africa in the shape of his scholarship, Kwame thought. On the way back home he saw a large mosque on the skyline. How was it, he wondered, that when missionaries had come from Britain to halt the spread of Islam in West Africa they had not been able to do that at home? Kwame had the contacts for other Ghanaians in the city and as soon as he got a new mobile phone he called them up and joined them for worship. The thriving church community was led by a pastor who shared many of Kwame's worries about British churches and believed that African congregations could be God's gift to deliver the British people from what was binding them.

Lee is a junior pastor in a thriving Presbyterian church in Seoul, South Korea, who has come to England as a postgraduate theology student, supported by his home church, bringing his wife Heejin and young family. As a Presbyterian he went first to the United Reformed Church that happened to be quite close to where he was staying. It was a relatively large congregation by British standards, almost entirely white. Lee expected that his children would go to the kindergarten for the duration of the service and was surprised at the pattern of all-age worship. He appreciated the inclusion of the children but felt it was rather at the expense of the solid preaching of the Word that he was accustomed to. After the service an invitation was made to join the rest of the congregation for coffee in the church hall. Lee and Heejin followed others there and took the coffee which was offered, dropping some change into the box provided. They stood together in the hall, the children around their legs, hoping that someone would talk to them. As a pastor, Reverend Lee expected that the minister would ask him to preach on some near occasion and his wife was looking forward to joining a women's bible study group, where she could improve her English. The minister, however, was deep in conversation with other members of the congregation and no one else talked to them. The children were restless so they went back home. The next Sunday they tried again – and the Sunday after that – but they never got beyond, 'Hello', 'Where are you from?' and, 'How long are you staying?' As he and his wife observed the congregation, it seemed like a close-knit, supportive community but its informality seemed to indicate that it did not take itself very seriously as an institution. Lee's presbyterian church in Seoul regarded itself as a mainstream denomination, whereas this seemed more like a sect. He realized that to belong to the mainstream in Britain he would have to worship at the large Anglican church in the centre of town. There the Sunday morning service was formal, as he thought appropriate, although he also thought there must be local cell groups and prayer meetings during the week where people could pray aloud and sing new worship songs. But he found it difficult to take his family to the Anglican church because it appeared to be Roman Catholic, and therefore highly suspect in his Calvinist tradition. The Anglicans he knew, from the cathedral in Seoul, called their ministers 'priests', took communion weekly or even daily, and had idolatrous-looking statues in their church. Other Koreans would be suspicious if he went there, and his wife especially would not be comfortable with it. He asked his supervisor at the university for advice but was shocked to discover that this professor of theology did not attend church at all. What, Lee wondered, was he going to learn about Christian theology from someone who was an atheist?

June is a Chinese academic visiting a British university as part of an exchange programme. Her research topic is English literature but, since she recently became a Christian in China, she wants to use the opportunity to study Christian literature in particular. Her conversion to Christianity was through academic friends who belong to a small prayer group, but she and they have never attended an institutional church, and she is not baptized. As a member of the Communist Party she risks losing her job if she declares her faith openly – although she knows many other members who are Christian – but here in Britain she would like to attend church. The obvious place to start is the Anglican cathedral in the city where she was staying but when she went to have a look they treated her like a tourist and expected her to pay for entry. She asked several of her academic colleagues if any of them went to church; either they looked embarrassed and vaguely guilty or they laughed and made it clear they would not want to be thought religious. Eventually she found out the times of a local church service through the internet – the website was out of date but when she turned up at the stated time worship was about to begin. She went timidly inside and was handed two books and a service sheet. She sat down on her own right in the back corner and wondered what she was supposed to do. She tried to follow the rest of the congregation but found it very confusing and rather embarrassing. She slipped out as soon as she could when the service ended. She continued her reading of Milton and Bunyan but their writings did not seem to bear much resemblance to what she had seen of British Christianity. In the end she met some Chinese students and they invited her to their meeting where she could feel at home but, since none of them had any contact with the indigenous church, June remained puzzled as to the meaning of British Christianity.

David came to the UK as a lecturer at a theological college. A presbyter of the Church of South India, he had many years' experience of Christian ministry in situations where congregations are full of young people but resources are extremely limited. His grandparents were outcastes or 'untouchables' who converted to Christianity as part of a mass movement, understanding that the gospel would enable them to break out of caste oppression. Although the majority of Indian Christians are from outcaste backgrounds – or dalits as they designate themselves – David is exceptional in having received postgraduate education and in becoming a leading theologian. Here in a predominantly white college and church setting, he and his family feel welcome and appreciated, and they are often asked to talk about the church in India. They speak warmly of the colonial missionaries who brought them the gospel and gave them an education to help them uplift themselves socially and come out from under the yoke of the high castes. In the church and college they have also felt a new freedom, and believe they are accepted for who they are rather than being regarded prejudicially. David is overwhelmed by the wealth of the churches here and the huge number of resources available to relatively few people. When he feels a bit homesick, his acute sense of justice makes him rather cynical about Christians who live luxurious lives and whose efforts to share their resources with the poor of the world amount to so little. As well as attending the local Anglican church, David is a member of a local Tamil Christian fellowship and through this he has become aware of some of the needs of the local Tamil community. However, in seeking to address these he comes up against a problem: the local authority relates to the different communities through a council of faiths. The Indian representatives there are high caste Hindus and the organizers of the council seem to have little or no understanding that these people may not be representative of or sensitive to the needs of the whole Indian community. David is also rather hurt that Christians anxious to build relations with other faiths seem more interested in Hindus than in Indian Christians.

The above case studies are fictitious but based on real-life examples of the varied experiences of Christians from Africa and Asia in Britain and British churches.[2] Seeing ourselves as others see us is sometimes encouraging and sometimes disconcerting but if we are open to such scrutiny it can be a life-changing experience.

1.2 Colonial mission and the legacy of empire

Until we are challenged, we humans are 'ethno-centric'. We tend to regard our own homeland as the centre and standard of the world and others as eccentric or 'remote'. The name Mediterranean literally means 'the centre of the earth' and for the Romans the British Isles were a far-flung outpost. The Chinese name for China is 'middle kingdom' or 'central empire'. Looking from China, Britain is at the very far end of the earth, the 'Far West'. But maps produced in the imperial period in Britain position the British Isles in the upper centre, as the 'mother country' presiding over her sons and daughters across the world. The old Mercator projection tends to minimize the size of her dominions and enhance her own. However, there are maps in East Asia in which Japan is in the mirror position to the British Isles, reflecting her erstwhile imperial role in Asia and the Pacific. North American maps often have the USA in the dominant position and split the Eurasian landmass in two. As author Bill Bryson has shown us, looking at Britain from the USA, it is just a 'small island' off the edge of a continent.[3]

Many, perhaps most, nations look back to a classical period in which they made a significant contribution on the world stage. Today it is sparsely populated and struggling economically as it comes out from the under the domination of the Soviets and builds a new relationship with China, but Mongolia was once the centre of the largest contiguous empire ever, covering much of Asia from Vienna almost to Vladivostok. Mexicans can recall the splendour of the Aztecs; the Shona people the power of Great Zimbabwe; the Danes the Viking era; and so on. Although it has done much to shape the modern world (for good or ill), in the grand sweep of history Britain is not unique in having past glories to justify a superior position. In the UK the memory that we once ruled a quarter of the globe, and the legacy of our colonial past, bolsters our confidence in varied ways. It is the reason for our strong economy and high standard of living, for the high volume of international traffic through Heathrow and the movement of global capital through our financial systems, and for the use of English as the international lingua franca. The colonial legacy continues to inform our view of the world so that we can still talk about going 'out to Kenya' (for example), as if it were far from civilization, whereas in fact it is the hub of activity for a different region of the world. In fact, many Kenyans today are less concerned about the old colonial links and much more interested in other global powers such as the United States or China.

Empires are made when expanding nations draw other peoples into their sphere of influence. The European empires, beginning with the Spanish and Portuguese in the late fifteenth century, set up trade relations with others around the globe. As Iberian power waned, first the Dutch, then the French, and then the British took over their trading posts and continued this process. The trading posts expanded into colonies or plantations and the expanding nations of Europe began to control the world's labour markets. As their power grew, the colonial powers reached further into the lives of people in other lands, attempting to shape aspects of their cultures to suit their purposes. Their need to secure their investment led them gradually to take over the government of other peoples and the management of their lands through the local elites. The British Empire in particular built up and controlled a global system of capital in which its colonies were inextricably linked together and which extended even beyond the empire to most of the other countries of the world.[4] The legacy of empire has had many effects on British church life, especially on those denominations which thrived in imperial times. These churches have inherited links with churches across the globe with which they once had a mother–daughter relationship. Most of these were in countries with which Britain had strong colonial links – the Indian subcontinent and Malaya, Palestine, Egypt and Sudan, large parts of East, West and southern Africa, much of the Caribbean (but few countries of Latin America), many islands of the Pacific, and of course Canada, Australia and New Zealand – and even churches in the present United States – were once in such a dependent relationship too. In fact superimposing a map of British church links with one of the old empire yields a very high measure of correspondence.

Even though, largely because of two world (or imperial) wars, the British and other imperial powers (including Japan) became bankrupts, the economic system they had created survived but its centre was shifted at the end of World War Two to the United States. US post-war policies of economic development encouraged other nations to conform even more to the Western pattern and further strengthened the global markets which it now controlled. The US eventually overcame the rival political system and economic bloc led by the Soviet Union, to become the strongest imperial power ever, exercising extensive control over the economics and politics of almost the whole planet and wielding enormous cultural influence as well in the process known as 'globalization'. Some enthusiasts for globalization see it mainly in economic terms as a self-regulating and universal economic system, which also facilitates liberal democratic political systems.[5] But the balance of opinion is that it heralds an unprecedented transformation which affects all areas of life. The globalized world is connected through a network of communications: especially air and shipping links and the media of satellite TV, the phone system and the internet, using the lingua franca of English. In this way, new products and ideas (which do not necessarily originate with the most powerful) as well as problems and diseases, are rapidly disseminated around the world. The changes brought about are varied, not uniform across the globe, and some are excluded, or exclude themselves, from aspects of globalization, but no-one on the planet is unaffected by it.[6]

1.3 Global mission or local mission?

Christians have born witness to Jesus Christ since the very beginnings of the early Church at Pentecost, and understand that they are 'sent' into the world as Jesus himself was sent in the power of the Spirit from the Father (John 20.21–2). The term 'mission' derives from the Latin 'I send'. It carries the sense that God needs emissaries to make the good news of Jesus Christ heard (Rom. 10.14–15) and that those who witness to Christ are ambassadors (2 Cor. 5.20). However, in the sixteenth century when the members of the Society of Jesus (Jesuits) began to be sent by popes to do their bidding in any part of the world, the term acquired the technical meaning of the overseas division of the established church, a mobile 'force' to establish and build up the church abroad. Missions became the foreign arm of churches based in powerful countries, who took advantage of their global connections to carry the message further afield. The established churches, naturally, were expected to follow their governments in imperial expansion, at least to provide for the spiritual needs of the expatriate communities. In practice their work often embraced the local community as well. So, for example, the missionaries of the Society for the Propagation of the Bible (SPG), founded in 1701 to send clergy to minister to the needs of the colonists, were soon ministering to American Indians as well, and Henry Martyn, chaplain to the East India Company (1805–12), translated the Bible into Urdu and Persian. The Spanish and Portuguese governments expected that missionary priests and nuns would settle and Christianize the local people in the Americas, although this often conflicted with the interests of traders. Later imperial powers, such as the British, welcomed missionary medical, educational and other contributions to the welfare and 'civilization' of colonized peoples but often discouraged their religious conversion. European Christians nevertheless soon began to take advantage of the opportunities afforded by the empire to complete the command of Jesus Christ to 'make disciples of nations' (Matt. 28.19).[7]

The great European movement of social Christianity, which began with the Pietist and Methodist movements in the seventeenth and eighteenth centuries and was stimulated by a series of Evangelical revivals, embraced a huge range of activities both at home and abroad.[8] Because of the legacy of Christendom, organizationally the domestic agenda and work abroad were represented by different bodies, and a distinction was made between 'home' and 'foreign' missions. This mirrored the distinction in the Roman Catholic Church between 'evangelization' and the mission *ad gentes*. The former is the work in Christian or Christianized lands, and the latter is directed beyond. It was assumed that the 'home base' was Christian or already evangelized, whereas 'overseas' was heathen and in need of missionaries for conversion to Christianity for the first time. In the late nineteenth century, William Booth, founder of the Salvation Army (1865), shocked the nation when he turned the language of foreign missions such as 'darkest Africa' back on his homeland, describing it as 'darkest England' and arguing that salvation was as much needed here as anywhere else.[9]

The distinction between home and overseas reflected the imperial relationship of the mother country and her dependent children, the one Christian the other non-Christian. However, in the post-colonial world this distinction began to break down. In the churches it was eroded from both ends: on the one hand, the 'younger churches' overseas were growing fast and, on the other hand, the 'older churches' were finding themselves in increasingly non-Christian societies. By 1961 the World Council of Churches declared an end to the distinction between the older and younger churches. Furthermore, mission was now understood to be 'in six continents'.[10] No longer was it assumed that mission was uni-directional from the West to 'the rest' but churches were encouraged to engage in mutual sharing and receiving of personnel and gifts. Now that churches were present in most countries of the world, and mindful of the danger of 'sheep-stealing' between churches, the emphasis was on the local church as the agent of mission in its locality, rather than on foreign agencies coming in.

This new situation put the former mission agencies in a difficult position. In the retreat from empire some Christians and agencies such as Christian Aid dropped the word 'mission' from their vocabularies and espoused instead the post-war Western agenda of 'development', which they saw as altruistic service to other nations (although the concept of development is not without ideological baggage either). While many mission societies struggled, Christian development agencies were well supported. With the growing social emphasis on respect for others' cultures and religions, British churches were no longer sure about proclaiming the gospel overseas in word but were comfortable with doing so in deed, and in order to raise funds some mission agencies so played down the evangelistic and pastoral aspects of their work overseas that they became almost indistinguishable from secular relief and development agencies.[11] Many Evangelical agencies, in contrast, continued to urge that the task of world evangelism was not yet complete. These agencies did not have a close relationship with the British government but were close to North American churches. Since the USA was not undergoing the same experience of post-colonialism but was growing as a world power, they perceived the world differently. Their mission strategists argued that there was an ongoing need to share the gospel, especially by verbal proclamation, in sections of the world where there were far fewer Christians, and where the name of Jesus Christ was not heard.[12] Although churches overseas continue to grow, researchers can still point to 'people groups' among whom there are no known believers or congregations, or language groups who do not yet possess a translation of the Bible in their own language.[13]

In rethinking their *raison d'être* in the new situation, some agencies bravely concluded that there was no longer any justification for their existence. For example, the London Missionary Society (Congregational), formed instead the Council for World Mission at which all the churches founded by the society were equally represented together with the founding body (now the United Reformed Church), and the funds of the society were managed by all.[14] In the British Methodist Church, the missionary calling of the local church and each Christian was taken very seriously so the logical step was that the Methodist Missionary Society be expanded to be co-extensive with the whole church membership. 'Missionaries' are no longer sent from Britain but instead there are 'mission partners' coming in both directions.[15] Other agencies such as the (Anglican) Church Mission Society, USPG, now Anglicans in World Mission, added projects in the UK as well as overseas and invited overseas personnel to be involved in them.[16] For those which had a more specific interest in a particular part of the world, such as OMF International, formerly the China Inland Mission, working in the UK was easily justified on the grounds that, as a result of migration, these communities could now be reached through diaspora communities as well.[17] The Church Mission Society in the UK has a focus on 'interchange', especially enlisting the help of partners in its former mission churches for mission in Europe.[18]

As evidence of the decline in traditional churchgoing in the UK began to mount up in the late twentieth century, and as the older denominations particularly began to feel financial strain as a result of this, maintaining relations with churches overseas began to seem like a colonial hangover and the costs of sending personnel became increasingly difficult to bear. The rapid erosion of Christian practice in a country which had exported Christianity worldwide, together with the aggressive secularism which ridiculed faith or pushed it into the private sphere, and the blame that was heaped on missionaries for the evils of empire in the academy and the media, had undermined the confidence of many British Christians in the Christian faith and their ability to witness to it. The basic maintenance of the church was as much as many Christians thought they could manage. But at the same time, faced with the closure of churches, mission to Britain gained ground as a way of increasing and reviving the local church.[19] Interest in mission methods – personal evangelism and discipleship such as Alpha and Emmaus courses, church growth strategies such as cell groups, and new ways of being church such as Fresh Expressions – increasingly rose to prominence. Lessons in inculturation or contextualization learnt from experience overseas were pressed into service at home to try and reverse the tide. In this process British churches became increasing parochial. Contact with churches in the rest of the world was conducted mostly through development projects.

In the space of about 20 years the meaning of the word 'mission' in British churches seems to have changed from being used almost exclusively for overseas work to referring to the outreach work of local churches in Britain. The British and Irish Association for Mission Studies (BIAMS) was founded in 1989 to study the history, theology and practice of mission and to encourage awareness of the major issues in contemporary mission. BIAMS was to serve a consortium of churches and mission agencies, which were known for their activities overseas, so when the constitution was approved the following year no one thought to specify that the study of mission should have a global dimension – that was a given. Yet only 15 years later, at its conference in 2005, BIAMS found it necessary to change the Constitution by inserting the word 'worldwide' because the use of the word 'mission' in Britain had become so focused on the local context that a global interest could no longer be taken for granted. It is the aim of this book to show the integral connections between global and local mission.

1.4 Christianity as a world religion

As we saw at the beginning of this chapter, Christians from Asia, Africa and the Americas may be bewildered by the loss of confidence of many of the churches of Europe who, in a previous era, had brought the gospel message to them with such conviction. Although some in these continents felt that their churches were tainted by association with colonialism, Christians did not believe that this invalidated their faith but that it needed rethinking in their context.[20] People who had made a conscious decision to turn from their previous way of life and embrace the Christian faith, or whose recent ancestors had done so, naturally resented the aspersions cast on their motives by those who portrayed Christian expansion as part of the imperial project. The argument that conversion was the result of imperial pressure must be questioned in light of the fact that churches in the former mission fields grew more rapidly after independence than they had done before.[21] Former mission churches flourished under local leadership and new indigenous denominations sprang up. In Africa these were known as African Independent, or African Initiated, Churches; in India various different groups grew, such as the bible-centred Bakht Singh movement and Pentecostal-type churches; in China the 'underground churches' mushroomed in size.[22] Christians in the independent churches did not feel they were the result of Western imperialism; they took the gospel for their own and saw themselves as belonging to a local church, not an arm of a church centred elsewhere. The churches of Africa, Asia, Latin America, the Caribbean and the Pacific gradually developed new ways of reading the Bible and new theological thinking. New practices of worship and service to the community arose that incorporated (consciously or unconsciously) aspects of local culture and religious practice. Similarly, former colonial churches are locally rooted in their contexts, together with other indigenous forms of Christianity.[23]

In the 1970s and 1980s the eminent Scottish mission historian Andrew Walls drew attention to a remarkable fact: there were now more Christians outside the West than within it. Walls regarded this as the latest of a series of shifts in Christian history, which he saw as proceeding by 'serial expansion' beginning with the paradigmatic movement of Christianity from the

Jewish cultural milieu in which it was born into the Hellenistic world. In succeeding centuries the 'centre of gravity' of Christianity shifted again to the Barbarian tribes of Europe, and now in this latest phase to the 'non-Western world'. Walls and his colleagues did much to draw attention to the strength and vitality of the churches of Africa and Asia especially.[24] But his theory of 'serial expansion' is sometimes misleading. Although Walls himself has drawn attention to the spread of early Christianity from Jerusalem in all directions – including to Syria, Persia, India and China in the East and to Egypt, North Africa and Ethiopia in the early centuries – it is easy to get the impression from the phrase 'centre of gravity' that in any one period there was only one centre of Christian faith, whereas in fact throughout Christian history there have always been multiple centres. Even when European Christianity was at its height, there were many Christians whose allegiance was to Orthodox patriarchs in Asia and Africa. And within Europe Christianity was polycentric, with Catholics looking to Rome, Protestants to the German heartlands of the Reformation, and Orthodox Christians looking to Athens, Moscow, or another national capital depending to which autocephalous church they belonged.

The fact that the 'centre of gravity' of Christianity is now in the global South might also be taken to imply that there is a unified body of 'Southern Christians' setting up a 'new Christendom' there. Such is the thesis of Philip Jenkins. He shows that Christianity is by far the world's largest and most influential religion, with about one-third of the world's population, and he believes that its dominance is far from declining but is set to increase in this century, due largely to its rapid growth rate in Africa, Asia and the Americas. Biological growth alone, he argues, is enough to continue the shift of Christianity southwards while, even within Europe and North America, Christians are increasingly 'brown' due to migration of Christians from the South. Europe still has more Christians than any other continent but by 2025, if we extrapolate current trends, Latin America will have the most Christians, Africa will be next, Europe will be pushed into third place and the number of Christians in Asia will not lag far behind. Today, Jenkins points out, a 'typical Christian' is a woman living in a village in Nigeria or in a Brazilian *favela*.[25] But Jenkins regards Southern Christianity as a new bloc that evokes ancient Christendom, which is engaged in a new struggle against Islam and generates widespread intolerance. He describes the Christians of the global South as poor, conservative in morals and theology, tending to fundamentalism in their reading of the Bible, and having a strong belief in a spirit-world and spiritual powers. But Jenkins's generalized statements should not be allowed to obscure the tremendous variety in Christian faith and practice in every part of the world. His application of the terms 'Christendom' and 'Medieval' to Southern Christianity are pejorative and unhelpful. 'Southern' Christianity is not unified or uniform. It has multiple centres – Nairobi, Seoul, Sao Paulo, to name just a few. It is a mosaic of churches and communities within which transcontinental patterns are traceable but which is becoming ever more complex as Christian faith spreads from multiple centres across the globe.[26]

The initial effect of the end of empire was to gradually cut British people off from their former overseas colonies, despite the continued existence of the Commonwealth. Britain had become strongly bound to the United States as a result of World War Two, and then since the 1970s gradually moved closer to the developing union of European nations. In the 1940s and 1950s thousands of citizens returned from serving in the empire to a country that was much more homogeneous and racially 'white' than today.[27] As a consequence much knowledge of the outside world was lost and interest declined. However, the trade links continued and the flow of personnel actually increased – but mostly in the opposite direction. For many reasons people have been migrating to Britain in larger numbers than ever before from former colonies and elsewhere. As a result new relations with 'overseas' are being established through communities settled here. Although many migrants follow other faiths, many of those who find their way here – especially from the Caribbean, from sub-Saharan Africa, Latin America and

East Asia – are Christians and have set up their own churches in Britain. Not only here but across Europe, migration of Christians both within and from outside the continent is adding to an already complex picture[28] and further confounding efforts to distinguish 'home' from 'overseas'. The presence of migrant churches has heightened awareness that Christianity is truly a world religion and that, despite its long Christian tradition, European Christianity is not central to Christianity any more. Since the 1970s, ease of travel from these islands to other continents has also led to new cross-cultural encounters. British churches can no longer control their overseas links through mission agencies, official denominational links and international offices. They are linked with churches around the world in myriad ways: through the members of their congregations, visits overseas and overseas visitors, and through Christian neighbours who belong to 'migrant churches'. It is no longer obvious – as it once seemed to be – who has a mission to whom.

Notes

1 Quoted on the Fresh Expressions website, <www.freshexpressions.org.uk>, front page (September 2006).

2 For a real example see Jonathan Gichaara, 'A Look at the British Church and Society from a "Third Eye"', *Rethinking Mission* online journal, <www.rethinkingmission.org> (2006).

3 Bill Bryson, *Notes from a Small Island* (London: Doubleday, 1992).

4 Niall Ferguson, *Empire: How Britain Made the Modern World* (London: Allen Lane, 2003).

5 For example Francis Fukuyama, *The End of History and the Last Man* (New York: Free Press, 1992).

6 Anthony Giddens, *Runaway World: How Globalization is Reshaping Our Lives*, 2nd edn (London: Profile Books, 2002), pp. 6–19; David Held, Anthony McGrew, David Goldblatt and Jonathan Perraton, *Global Transformations: Politics, Economics and Culture* (Stanford, CA: Stanford University Press, 1999).

7 For a good starting point to the discussion of the relationship between mission and empires, see Brian Stanley, *The Bible and the Flag: Protestant Missions and British Imperialism in the Nineteenth and Twentieth Centuries* (Leicester: Apollos, 1990).

8 See D. W. Bebbington, *Evangelicalism in Modern Britain: A History from the 1730s to the 1980s* (London: Routledge, 1989), especially pp. 10–12; Mark A. Noll, *American Evangelical Christianity: An Introduction* (Oxford: Blackwell, 2001), pp. 9–28.

9 William Booth, *In Darkest England and the Way Out* (London: Funk and Wagnalls, 1890).

10 Timothy Yates, *Christian Mission in the Twentieth Century* (Cambridge: Cambridge University Press, 1994), pp. 165–6.

11 For a well-informed discussion of the issues around this see, Michael Taylor, *Not Angels but Agencies* (London: SCM Press, 1995).

12 Donald McGavran, 'Will Uppsala Betray the 2 Billion?', *Church Growth Bulletin* 4/5 (May 1968), pp. 292–7.

13 See the Joshua Project, <www.joshuaproject.net>.

14 Bernard Thorogood, *Gales of Change: Responding to a Shifting Missionary Context – the Story of the London Missionary Society, 1945–1977* (Geneva: WCC Publications, 1994); Kai M. Funkschmidt, 'Partnership between Unequals – Mission Impossible? Mission Structures Revisited', *International Review of Mission* 91 (2002), pp. 395–413; 'New Models of Mission Relationship and Partnership', *International Review of Mission* 91 (2002), pp. 558–76.

15 See Methodist Church website, <www.methodist.org.uk> and Methodist Missionary Society History Project at the University of Edinburgh, <www.div.ed.ac.uk>.

16 Daniel O'Connor (ed.), *Three Centuries of Mission: The United Society for the Propagation of the Gospel, 1701–2000* (London: Continuum, 2002), pp. 382–94.

17 See <www.omf.org>.

18 See <www.cms-uk.org>.

19 Compare Craig L. Nessan, *Beyond Maintenance to Mission: A Theology of the Congregation* (Minneapolis, MN: Fortress Press, 1999); Robert S. Rivers, *From Maintenance to Mission: Evangelization and the Revitalization of the Parish* (New York: Paulist Press, 2005).

20 For a classic example, see G. V. Job, P. Chenchiah, V. Chakkarai, D. M. Devasahayam, S. Jesudason, Eddy Asirvatham and A. N. Sudarisanam, *Rethinking Christianity in India* (Madras: A. N. Sudarisanam, 1938).

21 Dana Robert, 'Shifting Southward: Global Christianity since 1945', *International Bulletin of Missionary Research*, 24/2 (2000), pp. 50–8, at p. 53.

22 Allan Anderson, *African Reformation: African Initiated Christianity in the Twentieth Century* (Trenton, NJ: Africa World Press, 2001); Roger E. Hedlund (ed.), *Christianity Is Indian: The Emergence of an Indigenous Community* (Delhi: ISPCK, 2000); F. Hrangkhuma (ed.), *Christianity in India: Search for Liberation and Identity* (Delhi:

ISPCK, 1998); Tony Lambert, *China's Christian Millions*, revd edn (Oxford: Monarch, 2006).

23 Sebastian Kim and Kirsteen Kim, *Christianity as a World Religion* (London: Continuum, 2008).

24 Andrew F. Walls, *The Missionary Movement in Christian History: Studies in the Transmission of Faith* (Maryknoll, NY: Orbis Books, 1996); Walls, *The Cross-cultural Process in Christian History: Studies in the Transmission and Appropriation of Faith* (Maryknoll, NY: Orbis Books, 2002) – for 'serial expansion', see pp. 27–48.

25 Philip Jenkins, *The Next Christendom: The Coming of Global Christianity* (Oxford: Oxford University Press, 2002), p. 2.

26 Kim and Kim, *Christianity as a World Religion*.

27 Andrew Marr, *A History of Modern Britain* (London: Pan Books, 2008), pp. 40–2.

28 Darrell Jackson, 'Pax Europa: Crux Europa', in Timothy Yates (ed.), *Mission and the Next Christendom* (Sheffield: Cliff College, 2005), pp. 85–106.

2

THE HOLY SPIRIT IN THE WORLD

Biblical and Theological Perspectives

> The wind blows where it chooses, and you hear the sound of it, but you do not know where it comes from or where it goes. So it is with everyone who is born of the Spirit.
> John 3.8

About a century ago in 1910, about 1,200 mission leaders gathered in Edinburgh for what was called the World Missionary Conference. This event turned out to be so significant that its centenary has also attracted worldwide interest.[1] Although the conference brought together representatives from across the spectrum of denominations in a way unprecedented before this time, the delegates were almost all (white) European and North American Protestant men.[2] The watchword at Edinburgh in 1910, inherited from the Student Volunteer Movement, was 'the evangelization of the world in this generation' and the bible verses most commonly used to justify mission were Matthew 28.19–20, often referred to as the 'Great Commission'. This was used to support an understanding of mission as the church's obedience to Christ's command to make disciples of all nations.[3] The impression was of Jesus Christ on the mountain top directing the apostles (representative of the institutional church) to take the gospel into the nations laid out below in a top-down, organized and systematic way.

To be attended by a majority of delegates from the 'global South', the theme of the 2010 international conference in Edinburgh, 'Witnessing to Christ today', calls to mind the promise to the disciples, according to Luke, that when the Holy Spirit came on them they would become witnesses to Christ (Acts 1.8). This was first fulfilled at Pentecost when 120 of Jesus' followers – men and women – suddenly found themselves speaking boldly of what they had seen and heard, and gathered a community of people from across the world into a sharing community (Acts 2.1–11, 41–7). The emphasis of the conference theme in 2010, which may be said to represent a broad consensus in Western mission thinking at the present time, is on God's initiative in mission and the spontaneous, joyful participation in it of grassroots Christians. So it is in line with Rowan Williams's definition of mission as 'finding out where the Holy Spirit is at work and joining in'. In this chapter we will follow the process of rethinking mission that went on in Europe between 1910 and 2010, through the traumatic events of the twentieth century, and the more recent development of mission theology which makes it possible to understand mission in this new way.

2.1 Rethinking mission

Two Germans – Protestant and Catholic respectively – are usually credited with founding mission studies as an academic discipline: Gustav Warneck (1834–1910), who from 1896 occupied the first chair of mission studies, at the University of Halle, and the Catholic Joseph Schmidlin (1876–1944), who was appointed to a chair in missiology at the University of Münster in 1914.[4] They argued the superiority of the Christian religion and showed historically how the expansion of Christianity had been going on from earliest times. Warneck used the language of military conquest to describe the Christian mission and this was carried over into the discourse and reports at Edinburgh in 1910,[5] but he thought the slogan, 'the evangelization of the world in this generation' was superficial and naïve. His own project was one of Christianization of whole people groups. The Scottish missionary educator Alexander Duff (1806–78) also has a claim to occupy the first chair of mission studies. His work represented another strand of thinking at Edinburgh: Western education as preparation for the gospel.[6] This priority was shared by Henry Venn (1796–1873), Secretary of the Church Mission Society, although where Duff insisted on an English medium for education Venn argued for use of the vernacular. Venn, whose grandfather had been spiritual mentor to the leaders of the 'Clapham sect' who campaigned for the abolition of slavery, had much greater confidence than many of his contemporaries in the ability of Africans and Asians to lead and organize their own churches, advocating the 'three-self principle' that churches ought to be self-supporting, self-governing and self-propagating, leading to the 'euthanasia of a mission'. But by 1910, as SPG missionary Roland Allen complained, most Anglican missionaries seemed to envisage a more-or-less permanently paternal relationship between the European churches and those in Africa and Asia. Although they occasionally challenged aspects of colonial policy, as people of their time, missionaries rarely questioned the colonial system itself.[7]

However, events in twentieth-century Europe made this perspective from the high point of European imperialism untenable. First, two world wars undermined the claim of white supremacy and the moral superiority Europeans claimed. The optimism of the social gospel was replaced by a much more pragmatic approach to mission work – influenced especially by the public theology of Reinhold Niebuhr in America – and a greater awareness of the depth of human sinfulness and separation from God, under the influence particularly of the neo-orthodox theology of Karl Barth in Europe. Dietrich Bonhoeffer's letters from a Nazi prison and other writings portrayed the local church in a costly mission of service of others, in contrast to the self-aggrandizement that had seemed to characterize so much colonial missionary effort.[8] Second, decolonization and the growth of the churches in the global South necessitated a partnership and reciprocal approach. Most of the missionaries at Edinburgh proclaimed a 'social gospel', seeing themselves as involved in building the kingdom of heaven on earth in a way that was inseparable from the advancement of Western culture and science. There were perhaps 20 native Christians present in 1910. One of these, V. S. Azariah, later an Anglican bishop in South India, made an impassioned plea for a more equal relationship between the missionaries and their converts. While acknowledging the sacrifices made by the missionaries, he called on them to offer friendship. Some missionaries received this implied criticism by an Indian Christian very badly indeed, grunting their disapproval in the conference hall.[9] Third, complaints of proselytism from Orthodox Christians, Hindus in India and others meant a change in attitude was called for, in order to be more sensitive to and respectful of the other. Military metaphor was prevalent in 1910; for example, the conference organizer, John R. Mott, declared at the close that 'the end of the Conference is the beginning of the conquest'.[10] Such insensitivity to its political implications has been extremely damaging to Christian mission and continues to lead to the suffering of Christians in many parts of the world where they are seen as supporting Western imperialism.

The twentieth century was a learning process for mission theologians and practitioners. British mission theologian Timothy Yates has produced a particularly fine study of the way the theory and practice of mission was rethought from 1910 to about 1990.[11] One way of following the changes is to look at the series of mission conferences that continued throughout the twentieth century after Edinburgh 1910, at first organized by the International Missionary Council (IMC) and later by the Commission for World Mission and Evangelism of the World Council of Churches.[12]

When the IMC met at Jerusalem in 1928, they described mission as the 'the task of the Christian Church . . . both to carry the message of Christ to the individual soul and to create a Christian civilization',[13] revealing a growing tension in mission priorities between those who emphasized the verbal proclamation of the message about Jesus Christ and those who stressed the social implications of the gospel.

The conference at Tambaram, India, in 1938 expressed in another way the tension between liberal theologians and the Barthian theologians who emphasized the uniqueness and finality of Jesus Christ. Two books were part of the preparatory material for the conference: The first, by W. E. Hocking, was the result of a wide-ranging survey of mission work by a group of prominent lay people and non-missionaries, which raised profound questions about what was being done in the name of Christ.[14] One question was why missionaries spent such a lot of energy opposing the other religions of the world, instead of seeing them as allies in a shared struggle against rising secularism. The second book, by Dutch missionary-theologian Hendrik Kraemer, took quite the opposite approach. Entitled, *The Christian Message in a Non-Christian World*, Kraemer contrasted the Christian world-view with that of each of the other major religions and stressed the importance of proclaiming the gospel in mission.[15] A third publication, less often referred to, was offered by a group of Indian Christian leaders from Madras, who called themselves the Rethinking Group. They were led by Pandipeddi Chenchiah who, on the one hand, criticized Kraemer's approach for being unnecessarily antagonistic to other religions, and especially Hinduism to which, although a Christian, he felt indebted as a child to a parent. On the other hand, Chenchiah did not share Hocking's pessimistic view of rising secularism, believing that it was the 'new cosmic energy' released into the world by Jesus Christ that was reviving Hindu society and transforming India for the better, as well as leading to the growth of the church.[16]

Reconvening after World War Two in 1947 in Whitby, Canada, the mood of the International Missionary Council was sombre as delegates focused on the need for reconstruction, and a much more humble approach to mission prevailed. They now regarded themselves as mere 'partners in obedience' in a mission that belonged not to the church but to God. In this partnership the old distinctions between the 'older churches' and the 'younger churches' now established in different parts of the world were discarded since all were sharing in God's worldwide mission. This new perspective was consolidated at a landmark conference in Willingen, Germany in 1952, where mission was defined as 'witness' to Christ in the form of proclamation, fellowship and service. Witness is not something optional but integral to the life of the whole Church and every church; so delegates at Willingen confessed that, 'When God says to the Church: "Go forth and be my witnesses", He is not giving the Church a commission that is added to its other duties; but a commission that belongs to its royal charter (covenant) to be the Church.'[17] At Achimota, Ghana, in 1957/8, the new paradigm of *missio Dei* (the mission of God) was explicit in the conference declaration: 'the Christian world mission is Christ's, not ours'.[18]

Meeting for the first time as part of the World Council of Churches, the next conference in Mexico City in 1963 was described as a conference on 'mission and evangelism'. These terms, which had previously tended to separate work overseas and at home, were now treated together. Mission, it was recognized, was taking place not only from the West to the rest but in 'six continents' that is, everywhere in the world, including the so-called Christian nations. So, as summarized by Stephen Neill, the conclusion of the conference was that 'the age of missions is at an end; the age of mission has begun'.[19] From this time on, the mission conferences represented not just Western missionaries but more and more leaders of the churches in Africa, Asia and the Americas. These had been the recipients of Western missions and were often critical, forcing mission theologians to recognize the colonial attitudes of much past enterprise, and also to appreciate the role of local evangelists and churches in world evangelization.

The focus on 'mission', rather than 'evangelism', and the criticism of previous mission work alarmed the resurgent Evangelical movement. The split in the missionary movement between social action and evangelism became more apparent as Evangelical leaders expressed their alarm that in its concern with social issues and its criticism of earlier mission activity the World Council of Churches was neglecting proclamation and the call for conversion. Their fears were partly confirmed in 1972/3 at the conference in Bangkok, when 'salvation today' was redefined as comprising economic justice, human dignity, solidarity and 'hope in personal life', without any explicit reference to Jesus Christ or eternal life. Activists argued that 'the world sets the agenda' for the mission of God, which was identified as taking place in contemporary revolutionary social movements and seen as bypassing traditional churches which did not move with the times.[20] At their own conferences, Evangelicals condemned such language and accused the World Council of Churches of 'betraying' those who had never heard the message of Jesus Christ.[21]

The Second Vatican Council, 1962–5, changed the way the Roman Catholic Church perceived itself from being a hierarchical institution to being 'the people of God'. It also led to greater interest on behalf of Catholics in reading the Bible, and more openness to co-operation with other churches. Therefore, though it was not officially a member of the Council, the influence of Roman Catholic thought in ecumenical circles increased. This came about especially through liberation theology (see Chapter 6), which brought Catholics and Protestants together in a mission of 'good news to the poor'. Justice for the oppressed was very much the topic of the next conference in 1980 in Melbourne, Australia, under the theme, 'Your Kingdom Come'. The biblical basis of liberation theology helped some Evangelicals to re-engage with the ecumenical movement and their involvement increased from the next conference at San Antonio, Texas, in 1989, which focused on 'mission in Christ's way' and reintroduced the word 'proclamation' into the understanding of mission. The widespread acceptance of David Bosch's summary mission textbook, *Transforming Mission*, published in 1991, showed that the theology of *missio Dei* was acceptable across a broad Christian spectrum, including Evangelicals, liberals, traditional Protestants, Orthodox and Roman Catholics. It also introduced to a very wide audience the idea that mission constantly needed to be refined according to the context in which it was being done, and therefore should be understood as multi-dimensional. So Bosch defined mission in 13 different ways, including mission as 'the church-with-others', as 'mediating salvation', 'the quest for justice', 'common witness' and 'action in hope'.[22]

New Pentecostal-charismatic and other indigenous movements, especially in Asia, Africa and Latin America, meant the World Council of Churches found it increasingly difficult to be representative, and the decline of church-going in Europe undercut its funding base. At Salvador, Bahia in Brazil in 1996, the next conference recognized the difficulties posed by the increasingly multi-cultural nature of the churches and the challenges to Christian authenticity and identity of pluralism and diversity in society. The most recent conference at Athens in 2005 followed this up by focusing on healing and reconciliation.[23] In choosing this topic, the conference recognized the increasing global importance of Pentecostal and indigenous churches in which the gifts of the Spirit are emphasized, and invited their participation. The Athens conference was the first mission conference since 1910 to look at mission from the perspective of theology of the Holy Spirit (pneumatology). This was particularly appropriate not only because of Pentecostal participation but also because the event was hosted by the Greek Orthodox Church, in which pneumatology as a discipline has traditionally attracted greater attention than in Western theology. The conference theme 'Come, Holy Spirit' made explicit what had only been implied: that mission as *missio Dei* means participating in the work of the Holy Spirit in the world.

2.2 Mission as a Trinitarian activity

At the mission conference in Willingen, Germany, in 1952 the theology of mission of the Protestant churches underwent a decisive shift, which Roman Catholic theologians followed a decade later. The first missiologists, Warneck, Schmidlin and others had treated mission under ecclesiology, understanding it to be an activity of the church. The new paradigm articulated at Willingen was prompted by the radical rethinking of theology of the great German theologian Karl Barth. Barth's work, which was stimulated by reading the fathers of the Eastern church, was mediated to mission thinkers chiefly through the German mission leader Karl Hartenstein. In his *Church Dogmatics*, Barth placed his discussion of mission under the heading of the Trinity because it is dependent on the first sending, the sending by the Father of the Son and the Holy Spirit into the world.[24] Barth's reclassification recognized that mission was an activity at the heart of God. In 1952, in the context of the missionary withdrawal from China, now in Communist hands, mission was no longer seen to depend on the church's endeavour but was redefined as participation in the sending activity of the Triune God.[25] As Lesslie Newbigin later described it, mission is 'proclaiming the kingdom of the Father', 'sharing the life of the Son' and 'bearing the witness of the Spirit'.[26]

Basing theology of mission on the Trinity had a number of profound theological effects. First, it shifted the ownership of mission from the church to God: hence this approach came to be known as *missio Dei*, or 'the mission of God'. A *missio Dei* approach to mission theology in this sense was endorsed by the Roman Catholic Church in 1965 in the Decree on the Mission Activity of the Church by the Second Vatican Council, known as *Ad Gentes*, which stated,

> Missionary activity is nothing else and nothing less than an epiphany, or a manifesting of God's decree, and its fulfilment in the world and in world history, in the course of which God, by means of mission, manifestly works out the history of salvation.[27]

Second, *missio Dei* put mission at the heart of God, the Trinity. The report of Willingen declared, 'The missionary obligation of the Church comes from the love of God in His active relationship with [humanity] . . . For God sent forth His Son . . . God also sends forth the Holy Spirit . . .'[28] Whereas in the West reflection on God as Trinity had tended to be on the nature of God as loving communion, the Willingen statement was closer to the view of the Orthodox churches, whose understanding of the Trinity had always emphasized what Irenaeus, one of the fathers of the church, called 'the two hands of the Father', that is, the Trinity's engagement with the world through the dual economy of Son and Spirit. *Missio Dei* thus encouraged a more dynamic understanding of God as outgoing and missionary. Third, the Church was also seen to be missionary by its very nature and its mission was seen as a participation in the greater mission of God, 'a "programme" of the Holy Trinity for the whole of creation'.[29] Such a view was endorsed by *Ad Gentes*: 'The pilgrim Church is missionary by her very nature, since it is from the mission of the Son and the mission of the Holy Spirit that she draws her origin, in accordance with the decree of God the Father.'[30] Or, as Orthodox theologians have expressed it: 'The mission of the church is based on Christ's mission . . . Christ's sending of the apostles is rooted in the fact that Christ himself is sent by the Father in the Holy Spirit (John 20.21–3)'.[31]

This view of mission assumed something of a consensus in the late twentieth century. Mission as God's mission implied a move from the periphery of church and theological concerns – as the activity of enthusiasts in far-away places – to establish mission as an intrinsic part of what it means to be Christian and to be church. At the same time it implied a change in the nature of mission activity from a series of tasks commanded by God to the realization of God's promise of the gift of the Holy Spirit (Acts 1.8) and eternal presence (Matt. 28.20). These new insights were the result both of reflection by Western theologians on the church fathers and also of increasing dialogue with the Orthodox churches. So that, in regard to mission, most Christians in the Western traditions could agree with contemporary Orthodox theologians that mission is a participation in the life of the Trinity: 'Trinitarian theology points to the fact that God is in God's own self a life of communion and that God's involvement in history aims at drawing humanity and creation in general into this communion with God's very life.' So that mission aims primarily at the transmission of the life of the communion that exists in God.[32]

Therefore mission is not an external activity imposed by

church leaders on top of all the other demands on church members. Mission is a heartfelt but the spontaneous outworking of the inspiring, transforming, life-giving work of the Holy Spirit:

> The mission of God (*missio Dei*) is the source of and basis for the mission of the church, the body of Christ. Through Christ in the Holy Spirit, God indwells the church, empowering and energizing its members. Thus mission becomes for Christians an urgent inner compulsion, even a powerful test and criterion for authentic life in Christ, rooted in the profound demands of Christ's love, to invite others to share in the fullness of life Jesus came to bring (John 10:10). Participating in God's mission, therefore, should be natural for all Christians and all churches, not only for particular individuals or specialized groups. The Holy Spirit transforms Christians into living, courageous and bold witnesses (cf. Acts 1:8).[33]

2.3 The church in the power of the Spirit

If mission belongs to God, and all Christians are empowered by the Holy Spirit, what is the role of the church? This was the obvious question raised by the theology of *missio Dei*. The traditional view was that the church is both the means and the aim of mission because God works in and through the church and the church is the only place where salvation may be found. In the twentieth century theologians recognized that the empirical church on earth is not to be completely identified with the kingdom of God, which is something greater and yet to be fully realized.[34] In ecumenical discussion a great deal of importance was attached to the church, especially at the 1938 mission conference at Tambaram, where Kraemer emphasized that the church had a duty and a right to call for conversions because of its missionary obligation.[35] However, by the Willingen conference the new mood of humility had led to a shift from 'church-centred mission' to 'mission-centred church'. Now that *missio Dei* was the overriding paradigm, the church was seen as a servant of God's mission in the world. The church changed from 'being the sender to being the one sent'. In 1968, at the Uppsala assembly of the World Council of Churches, the Dutch missiologist J. C. 'Hans' Hoekendijk, who like many of his contemporaries was embarrassed by the institutional churches of his day, went even further in saying that we should not think in terms of God–church–world. Since God is at work directly in the world independently of the church, he argued, the world, not the church, is the centre of God's plan. The church could not assume it was part of God's mission but should actively seek to discover its role in what he saw as a secular process.[36]

Hoekendijk's view was too radical for most, who held that the church was constituted by the Spirit (Acts 2.41–42), but the discussion led to the development of what David Bosch calls a 'creative tension'. In this the church is called into being by God as an instrument, a sign and even a sacrament of God's mission but at the same time she is always mindful of her imperfections and her need of renewal.[37] The German theologian Jürgen Moltmann expressed the church's provisional nature in a pneumatological framework. Moltmann's practical concern was the reform of the church in Germany, a need which he viewed all the greater as a result of seeing the life of churches in Asia, Africa and Latin America.[38] In his theological trilogy he recognized that the church's Christian hope based on the resurrection and identification with God's suffering on the cross would be incomplete without the experience of the Holy Spirit.[39] The church is the community which knows the Spirit as the giver of life, sees the Spirit's messianic history and experiences the Spirit's charismatic power. Therefore, the church everywhere is a missionary church which participates in the mission of God, sent into the world 'in the same framework as the Father's sending of the Spirit'. The church lives in the presence and power of the Spirit of God but does not separate the Spirit of life from the Spirit of Jesus Christ which he gave up on the cross and which descended in resurrection power on the first apostles.[40]

Of the four classical marks of the church – unity, catholicity, holiness and apostolicity – Moltmann singled out the last as the mark of the church's messianic mission. To say the church is 'apostolic' is not simply to legitimize the church on the foundation of the apostolic teaching or the apostolic succession.

'Apostolic' has a dynamic meaning; the apostle is the messenger and the apostolic ministry refers to the church's action – and suffering – in history.[41] Between 1984 and 1990, the Anglican Consultative Council elaborated on the meaning of apostolicity when it developed the 'five marks of mission': to proclaim the good news of the kingdom; to teach, baptize and nurture new believers; to respond to human need by loving service; to seek to transform unjust structures of society; to strive to safeguard the integrity of creation and sustain and renew the life of the earth. These should be understood not as a list of tasks the church is obliged to perform but characteristics of the church which is alive in the Spirit. They were evaluated again between 1996 and 2000 and remain a valued guide which Anglicans around the world have used for their reflection on mission praxis.[42] There is widespread agreement today, in churches as well as mission organizations, that mission is of the essence of what it means to be church.[43]

2.4 The Holy Spirit as 'the chief agent of mission'

We have seen that, since it is by the Holy Spirit that God is at work in the world, mission as *missio Dei* is a pneumatological paradigm of mission. As Orthodox theologians have expressed it, 'The "sending" of mission is essentially the sending of the Spirit (John 14.26), who manifests precisely the life of God as communion' (1 Cor. 13.13).[44] In his encyclical on mission, *Redemptoris Missio*, promulgated in 1990, Pope John Paul II declared that the Holy Spirit is 'the principal agent of mission'.[45] He described the missionary mandate of the church as 'a sending forth in the Spirit' (John 20.22; Acts 1.8), which applies to the whole church. He reminded his readers how the Spirit directs the church's mission. The coming of the Holy Spirit at Pentecost makes the apostles witnesses and prophets (cf. Acts 1.8; 2.17–18), giving them 'a serene courage' to bear witness to Jesus. Throughout the book of Acts, the Spirit guides the apostles in theological decision-making (Acts 10.19; 11.12; 15.5–11, 28) and travel plans (Acts 13.1–4, 46–8; 16.6–10). It is the

Holy Spirit who leads the believers to form a community (Acts 2.42–7; 4.32–5) in which there is no distinction between Jew and Gentile alike (Acts 11.15–16), and who 'makes the whole church missionary'. As David Bosch has summarized, the Holy Spirit initiates, guides and empowers the Church's mission.[46]

Redemptoris Missio recognizes that 'the Spirit is present and active in every time and place'.[47] According to the biblical record, the Holy Spirit does not first appear at Pentecost but the Spirit of God was present and active from the moment of creation (Gen. 1.2), and is breathed into us to make us human (Gen. 2.7). The Spirit is the Spirit of life (Ezek. 37.10), who creates and renews all things (Ps. 104.30). Pondering on the relationship between the Holy Spirit and mission, Bishop John V. Taylor, former general secretary of CMS, described the Holy Spirit as 'the Go-between God' who makes everything in the universe present to everything else and holds the whole together.[48] The Spirit blows where s/he wills (cf. John 3.8), has filled the whole world and 'with marvellous foresight directs the course of the ages and renews the face of the earth'.[49] In the Old Testament, the Spirit of God inspires leaders (e.g. 1 Sam. 16.13) and prophets (Neh. 9.30) but there is an expectation that the fullness of the Spirit is yet to come, when the Spirit will be poured out on all flesh (Joel 2.28–9), and this is what is understood to happen at Pentecost (Acts 2.16–21).

As Taylor explains, the mission of God by the Spirit is at once very wide but also focused in Jesus Christ.[50] Jesus Christ was conceived by the Holy Spirit (Luke 1.35), anointed by the Holy Spirit at his baptism (Mark 1.10–11 and parallels), led by the Spirit in his ministry (e.g. Matt. 4.1). In the power of the Spirit, he proclaimed good news to the poor, release to the captives, sight to the blind and liberation to the oppressed (Luke 4.18–19). When he died Jesus gave up the Spirit (John 19.30), but then he was raised in Spirit (Rom. 8.11). Since then when Christians talk about the Holy Spirit they mean the Spirit of Jesus Christ, whom Jesus breathed into the disciples (John 20.22) and who was poured out on the church (Acts 2.17). According to John, Jesus promised to leave the Paraclete, another Helper like Jesus himself, who would be in and with the disciples for ever (John 14.16–17). The Spirit will convict the world of sin and judgment (John 16.8). Each individual needs to be reborn by the Spirit (John 3.5–6) and to be led by the Spirit into the truth that Jesus Christ taught (John 16.12–13). Paul describes the Spirit in the church as an earnest or foretaste of the life to come (2 Cor. 1.22; 5.5; Rom. 8.23; Eph. 1.13–14), a life which will eventually renew the whole creation (Rom. 8.22–3). The Spirit is the Spirit of love (Rom. 5.5), life, freedom and peace (Rom. 8.2, 6). Pope John Paul II stated, 'This is the same Spirit who was at work in the Incarnation and in the life, death and resurrection of Jesus, and who is at work in the Church.'[51] In her life in the Spirit the church is continuing the mission of Jesus Christ which is directed through the power of the Spirit not only at the church but also at the reconciliation of all things.

2.5 Discernment as the first act of mission

The *missio Dei* paradigm that the church participates in the activity of the Holy Spirit in the world has found widespread acceptance in the different churches. However, difficulties have been caused by the suggestion that the Spirit of God can somehow bypass the church, as if the left hand of the Father does not know what the right hand is doing. Hoekendijk's secularization of mission in the 1960s was an example of this. He was prepared to endorse all sorts of social revolutions as movements of the Spirit, and urge therefore that the church should support them. Another instance is the theology of dialogue of Stanley Samartha, who came from India to set up the World Council of Churches' unit on dialogue in the 1970s. He argued that 'the two hands of the Father' had a certain independence, and therefore we should not imagine that in any dialogue the Spirit of God was only speaking through the Christian participants.[52] It is true that the Holy Spirit is at work in changing society and among people of all faiths, and that all good things are the work of God. However, the danger in such approaches is that the church fails to discriminate and allies itself too closely with movements or religions which do not share the Spirit of Christ. What the church has to offer to the world is not the endorsement of other movements but its own unique life, which is centred upon Jesus Christ.

John Paul II was prepared to recognize a general presence of the Spirit in all humanity but he asserted that this Spirit would always lead toward Jesus Christ. Furthermore, he insisted that 'the universal activity of the Spirit is not to be separated from his particular activity within the body of Christ, which is the Church'.[53] The recent Commission for World Mission and Evangelism statement on mission explained that a Trinitarian approach to the *missio Dei* is important if the separation of the Spirit from the Son of God is to be avoided. On the one hand, the doctrine of the Trinity 'promotes a more inclusive understanding of God's presence and work in the whole world and among all people, implying that signs of God's presence can and should be identified, affirmed and worked with even in the most unexpected places'. On the other hand, the doctrine of the Trinity clearly affirms that 'the Father and the Spirit are always and in all circumstances present and at work together with the Word'.[54]

These cautions should not be read as trying to restrict the work of the Spirit. It would be foolish indeed if the church was trying to stop the 'violent wind' and fire of the Spirit (Acts 2.2–3). The Spirit of God is present and active everywhere but not every development is the work of the Holy Spirit. Although on one occasion the Psalmist declared that he could not escape from God's Spirit in heaven or on earth or under the earth (Ps. 139.7–10), on another he is contemplating the absence, or the withdrawal, of the Holy Spirit (Ps. 51.11). Furthermore, the biblical writers are aware that there are other spirits abroad: evil spirits (Matt. 10.1), cosmic powers and spiritual forces (Eph. 6.12). Much discussion of the presence or activity of 'the Spirit' assumes a common understanding of what is meant but which is in fact very vague. When Christians talk about 'the Spirit' they refer to a particular Spirit; the Holy Spirit, which is revealed in the New Testament as the Spirit of Jesus Christ.

This is not because Christians are narrow-minded but because it is this Spirit which makes them Christians, and it is Jesus Christ to whom they have pledged their allegiance. The Christian confession is that the life-giving Spirit of God, co-creator of the universe, is the Spirit who indwelt Jesus Christ and who, as Chenchiah wrote in India, is released into the world through the church by the risen Christ as a new energy infusing everything. It is possible for churches not to receive Christ or do what the Spirit is saying (Rev. 2—3). But in so far as the church joins herself to the Spirit of Jesus Christ, she has the gift of discerning the spirits (1 Cor. 12.10) and a duty to test them (1 John 4.1) to identify where the Holy Spirit is, or is not, at work.[55] Christ gave his Spirit in order to guide the church into all the truth (cf. John 16.13).

British New Testament scholar James Dunn has remarked that if mission is defined as 'finding out where the Holy Spirit is at work and joining in', then 'discernment is the first act of mission'.[56] Discerning the Spirit or spirits is a complex process about which much more could be written.[57] However, the criterion for Christian discernment is clear; the Holy Spirit is the Spirit of Jesus Christ. The Holy Spirit is not present only where there is explicit Christian confession but where there is a likeness of Christ. This likeness may be in character or characteristics, the 'love, joy, peace, patience, kindness, generosity, faithfulness, gentleness, and self-control' which are the fruit of the Spirit (Gal. 5.22–3; cf. Rom. 12.9–21). Or it may be in action or activity, where the gifts of the Spirit are being exercised in love for the building up of the body (1 Cor. 12—14) and where people are being liberated, healed, helped, forgiven and reconciled (e.g. Luke 4.18–19; John 20.21–3; Rom. 8.22–6). These are the marks of the Spirit of God shown in Jesus Christ. This Christ-likeness is what we look for when we identify where the Spirit is at work in order to join in God's mission.

Notes

1 See <www.edinburgh2010.org>.
2 For a history of the conference see, Brian Stanley, *The World*

Missionary Conference: Edinburgh 1910 (Grand Rapids, MI: Wm B. Eerdmans, 2009).

3 David J. Bosch, *Transforming Mission: Paradigm Shifts in Theology of Mission* (Maryknoll, NY: Orbis Books, 1991), pp. 340–1.

4 For short biographies of the figures in this paragraph, see Gerald H. Anderson, Robert T. Coote, Norman A. Horner and James M. Phillips (eds), *Mission Legacies: Biographical Studies of Leaders of the Modern Missionary Movement* (Maryknoll, NY: Orbis Books, 1994).

5 Timothy Yates, *Christian Mission in the Twentieth Century* (Cambridge: Cambridge University Press, 1994), pp. 31–2.

6 Andrew F. Walls, *The Cross-cultural Process in Christian History: Studies in the Transmission and Appropriation of Faith* (Maryknoll, NY: Orbis Books, 2002), pp. 27–8.

7 Bosch, *Transforming Mission*, pp. 302–13.

8 See Dietrich Bonhoeffer, *The Cost of Discipleship* (New York: Macmillan, 1966).

9 V. S. Azariah, 'The Problem of Cooperation between Foreign and Native Workers', in World Missionary Conference, *World Missionary Conference, 1910: Vol. 9, History and Records of the Conference* (Edinburgh: Oliphant, Anderson & Ferrier, 1910), pp. 306–15; W. H. T. Gairdner, *Edinburgh 1910: An Account and Interpretation of the World Missionary Conference* (Edinburgh: Oliphant, Anderson & Ferrier, 1910), pp. 109–10.

10 John R. Mott, 'Closing Address', in World Missionary Conference, *World Missionary Conference, 1910: Vol. 9*, pp. 347–51, p. 347.

11 Yates, *Christian Mission in the Twentieth Century*.

12 Cf. Jacques Matthey, 'History of World Mission and Evangelism' – available at <www.oikoumene.org>.

13 Yates, *Christian Mission in the Twentieth Century*, p. 69.

14 William Ernest Hocking, *Re-thinking Missions: A Laymen's Inquiry after One Hundred Years* (New York: Harper and Brothers, 1932).

15 Hendrik Kraemer, *The Christian Message in a Non-Christian World* (London: Edinburgh House, 1938).

16 G. V. Job, P. Chenchiah, V. Chakkarai, D. M. Devasahayam, S. Jesudason, Eddy Asirvatham and A. N. Sudarisanam, *Rethinking Christianity in India* (Madras: A. N. Sudarisanam, 1938).

17 Norman Goodall (ed.), *Missions under the Cross* (London: Edinburgh House Press, 1953), p. 241.

18 Quoted in Bosch, *Transforming Mission*, p. 370.

19 Stephen Neill, *A History of Christian Missions* (Harmondsworth: Penguin, 1964), p. 572.

20 See Bosch, *Transforming Mission*, pp. 382–6.

21 Donald McGavran, 'Will Uppsala Betray the 2 Billion?', *Church Growth Bulletin* 4/5 (May 1968), pp. 292–7.

22 Bosch, *Transforming Mission*.

23 See Jacques Matthey (ed.), *'Come, Holy Spirit, heal and reconcile': Report of the World Council of Churches Conference on Mission and Evangelism, Athens, May 2005* (Geneva: WCC Publications, 2008).

24 See Bosch, *Transforming Mission*, pp. 389–90.

25 For a reflection on Willingen 50 years on, see Jacques Matthey's 'Reflector's Report', at <www.oikoumene.org>. Papers of the 2002 consultation on Willingen 1952 are published in the *International Review of Mission* 92/367 (October 2003).

26 Lesslie Newbigin, *The Open Secret: An Introduction to the Theology of Mission* rvsd edn (Grand Rapids, MI: Wm B. Eerdmans, 1995).

27 Vatican II, *Ad Gentes* ('Decree on the Mission Activity of the Church'), para. 9 – available at <www.vatican.va>.

28 Goodall, *Missions Under the Cross*, p. 241.

29 Ion Bria (ed.), *Go Forth in Peace: Orthodox Perspectives on Mission* (Geneva: WCC Publications, 1986), p. 3.

30 Vatican II, *Ad Gentes*, para. 2.

31 Bria, *Go Forth in Peace*, p. 3.

32 Bria, *Go Forth in Peace*, p. 3.

33 World Council of Churches, Commission for World Mission and Evangelism, 'Mission and Evangelism in Unity Today' (2000), para. 13. Published in Jacques Matthey (ed.), *'You are the Light of the World': Statements on Mission by the World Council of Churches 1980–2005* (Geneva: WCC Publications, 2005), pp. 62–89; also available at <www.mission2005.org>.

34 See discussion in Bosch, *Transforming Mission*, pp. 368–9, 371–2.

35 Kraemer, *Christian Message in a Non-Christian World*, p. 294.

36 Bosch, *Transforming Mission*, pp. 370, 382–5.

37 Bosch, *Transforming Mission*, pp. 374–6, 381–9.

38 Jürgen Moltmann, *The Church in the Power of the Spirit*, 2nd edn, trans. Margaret Kohl (London: SCM Press), 1992, p. xiii.

39 Jürgen Moltmann, *Theology of Hope: On the Ground and the Implications of a Christian Eschatology*, trans. James W. Leitch (London: SCM Press, 1967); *The Crucified God: The Cross of Christ as the Foundation and Criticism of Christian Theology*, trans. R.A. Wilson and John Bowden (London: SCM Press, 1974); *Church in the Power of the Spirit*.

40 Moltmann, *Church in the Power of the Spirit*, p. 11; see also, Jürgen Moltmann, *The Spirit of Life: A Universal Affirmation*, trans. Margaret Kohl (London: SCM Press, 1992).

41 Moltmann, *Church in the Power of the Spirit*, pp. 357–61.

42 The five marks of mission are available at <www.anglicancom-

munion.org>. See also Eleanor Johnson and John Clark (eds), *Anglicans in Mission: A Transforming Journey* (London: SPCK, 2000); Andrew Walls and Cathy Ross (eds), *Mission in the 21st Century: Exploring the Five Marks of Mission* (London: Darton, Longman and Todd, 2008).

43 See, for example, World Council of Churches, Faith and Order Commission, *The Nature and Mission of the Church* (Geneva: WCC Publications, 2005).

44 Bria, *Go Forth in Peace*, p. 3.

45 John Paul II, *Redemptoris Missio* ('On the permanent validity of the Church's Missionary Mandate') (1990), paras 21–30 – available at <www.vatican.va>.

46 Bosch, *Transforming Mission*, p. 114.

47 John Paul II, *Redemptoris Missio*, para. 28.

48 John V. Taylor, *The Go-between God: The Holy Spirit and the Christian Mission* (London: SCM Press, 1972), pp. 17–23.

49 John Paul II, *Redemptoris Missio*, paras. 28, 29.

50 Taylor, *Go-between God*, p. 83.

51 John Paul II, *Redemptoris Missio*, para. 29.

52 Stanley J. Samartha, 'The Holy Spirit and People of Various Faiths, Cultures and Ideologies', in Dow Kirkpatrick (ed.), *The Holy Spirit* (Nashville, TN: Tidings, 1974), pp. 20–39.

53 John Paul II, *Redemptoris Missio*, paras. 28, 29.

54 World Council of Churches, 'Mission and Evangelism in Unity Today', para. 12.

55 Cf. John Paul II, *Redemptoris Missio*, para. 29.

56 James D. G. Dunn, *The Christ and the Spirit: Collected Essays Vol. 2: Pneumatology* (Edinburgh: T&T Clark, 1998), p. 72.

57 For example, Timothy J. Gorringe, *Discerning Spirit: A Theology of Revelation* (London: SCM Press, 1990); *Furthering Humanity: A Theology of Culture* (Aldershot: Ashgate, 2004); Amos Yong, *Discerning the Spirit(s): A Pentecostal-charismatic Contribution to Christian Theology of Religions* (Sheffield: Sheffield Academic Press, 2000); Kirsteen Kim, *The Holy Spirit in the World: A Global Conversation* (Maryknoll, NY: Orbis Books, 2007).

3

DISCERNING THE SPIRIT

Among Peoples and Cultures

> The Spirit is the initiator of fresh movements, the one who guides the course of history, sustains the life of the church, and warms the hearts of all peoples.[1]
> Samuel Rayan

Not only the Scots, the Welsh and the Irish but also the English share identifiable national characteristics. So argues cultural anthropologist Kate Fox in her popular book, *Watching the English*. Fox rather unflatteringly describes the core of Englishness as 'social dis-ease' which veers between over-politeness ('English reserve') on the one hand and loutish behaviour ('hooliganism') on the other, and rarely touches the middle ground. It is countered, she writes, by English humour – not necessarily good humour but the banter, satire, understatement, self-deprecation and sarcasm, which Fox finds pervades 'vitually all' conversations between the English. This is accompanied by other reflexes of 'moderation' and 'a dose of hypocrisy', by 'down-to-earthness', 'eeyorishness' (like the donkey of A. A. Milne's stories) and class-consciousness in outlook, and by values such as fair play, courtesy and modesty. It may surprise the English native to learn that they can be studied in this way but anyone from outside entering England is in no doubt that its people have their own distinctive ways of doing things, whether it be in social systems such as government and education, in family life, television choices, dress styles, beliefs, values, or modes of personal interaction. Generalizations about cultures are filled with pitfalls and need to be carefully nuanced.

For example, not all English people drink tea but it is true that 'tea' has a special significance in England. Nevertheless, there are identifiable shared behavioural patterns and symbols which make up what is known as English 'culture', and this is remarkable considering that this is a nation which is multicultural, whose language is no longer peculiar to its people, and which has seen high levels of contact with the rest of the world for several centuries. Quite what causes this shared behaviour Fox is at a loss to explain – the weather perhaps? Or history? Or geography? However she maintains that what the English share is not nature but culture – 'a set of unwritten codes' which, although at first confusing, can be 'deciphered and applied' by any person who might wish to join English society.[2]

As the apostles travelled around the ancient world they noticed some of the different cultural characteristics of the locals, and found that they responded to the gospel in different ways. The people of Samaria were impressed by the frightened response of the evil spirits to the ministry of Philip, apparently regarding him as a great magician like Simon Magus. Since magicians demanded payment for their services, Simon himself tried to buy Philip's power (Acts 8.5–24). In contrast, the Ethiopian courtier to whom Philip was sent next was an educated man accustomed to reading sacred texts, and who came to Christ in quite a different way as a result of Philip's explanation of how Jesus fulfilled the role of the suffering servant of Isaiah (Acts 8.26–38). When the apostles Paul and Barnabas healed a lame man in their town, the Greek-speaking people of Lystra thought Barnabas must be the Olympian god Zeus in human form and, since Paul did all the talking, they thought Paul must be Zeus' interpreter Hermes. They tried to worship them both by offering oxen and garlands according to their temple customs (14.8–18). Similarly, the native people of the – in those days remote – island of Malta came to the conclusion that Paul had godly powers and showered him with gifts (28.1–10). However the upright Roman citizens of the city of Philippi in modern-day Greece had little time for magic and a Jewish preacher advocating non-Roman customs (16.19–24), and the Romans of Thessalonica and Corinth were easily persuaded that he was politically subversive (17.5–9; 18.12–17). Paul faced little opposition in the pluralistic atmosphere of Athens, where the people loved to discuss new religious and philosophical ideas (17.21) but the Ephesians owed their allegiance to one particular goddess, Artemis, on whom the prosperity of the city depended, and the growth of Christianity there caused a major riot (19.23–41). Even the diaspora Jewish communities differed from city to city, sometimes being jealous, as in Thessalonica, and on other occasions being very open, as in Beroea (17. 5–7, 11–13). Yet according to Luke's account, in every place where they went the apostles were aware that they were guided by the Holy Spirit who testified to them in every city (20.23) through these events and by whom the power of God was displayed over the other gods and spirits they encountered. The book of Acts is less about the acts of the apostles and more about the acts of the Holy Spirit in the people who responded to the gospel.

The gospel is never encountered, and the Holy Spirit is never at work in human lives, except within a particular cultural setting, so the Spirit can only be discerned in and through human culture. In the course of this chapter we will consider the meaning of culture and its significance for Christian mission. We will see how culture both shapes our experience of the Spirit and at the same time offers creative possibilities for defining Christian identity. We will also discuss how the Holy Spirit is at work in different cultures – and in their interaction – transforming culture and challenging cultural oppression.

3.1 Spirit and cultures

Nowadays Western Christians often expect that the expression of Christian faith should vary according to culture; and when visiting another part of the world, they are inclined to be disappointed if the Christianity there appears 'very Western'. However, in the imperial era, for all but a handful of missions, 'Christianization' was virtually synonymous with 'civilization', with particular reference to European achievements in knowledge, the arts, law and so on. Such a perception encouraged colonial missionaries to disregard and even despise the local way of life and see themselves as 'uplifting' native peoples. Converts were often expected to reject their heritage and their families, to live in the mission compound, change their name and dress, and embrace what was understood to be the only Christian way of behaving. Concessions to local feeling were referred to as 'accommodation' or 'adaptation' in Catholic circles, or 'indigenization' among Protestants. Officially any accommodation to culture was forbidden by the *Roman* Catholic Church and 'Christianity in its Latin form was deemed to be the perfection of this culture of humanity'.[3] However, many Catholic missionaries on the ground did have a 'radical vision' of inculturation, but this was suppressed by the authorities.[4] So Catholics and Protestants generally made only a superficial modification of the Christian package to make it more acceptable to local manners or aesthetics,[5] without engaging with other cultures in a way that would challenge their own expression of the Christian faith. In the high imperial period, Roland Allen put this down to the impartation of the law not the Spirit. His fellow missionaries, he believed, failed to respect native Christians as fellow recipients of the Spirit of Christ: 'We believe that it is the Holy Spirit of Christ which inspires and guides us: we cannot believe that the same Spirit will guide and inspire them.'[6]

Contemporary discussions of gospel and culture often begin with H. Richard Niebuhr's five possible models of the relationship: Christ against culture, Christ of culture, Christ above culture, Christ and culture in paradox, and Christ as the transformer of culture.[7] The British theologian Tim Gorringe shows that these are helpful as a starting point for discussion but of limited usefulness in practice because, although derived from history, the models are highly conceptual, and also because Niebuhr is vague as to what is meant by 'Christ' and by 'culture'. On the one hand, he does not distinguish 'culture' from 'civilization', ignoring popular culture, cultural plurality and the relationship of culture and identity. On the other, he works with a Christ concept and it is unclear how this corresponds to Christianity or churches. In Gorringe's view, the models are so slippery that 'At any given point any Christian might want to invoke all of Niebuhr's categories to describe their relation to the dominant culture.'[8]

Starting from the contemporary practice of Christian mission, Stephen B. Bevans has identified five models for the relationship between gospel and diverse cultures which are both more concrete in starting from the practice of faith (gospel) rather than a concept of Christ, and also recognize different understandings of culture itself.[9] The models – translation, anthropological, praxis, synthetic and transcendent – will provide the framework for this chapter. Bevans recognizes all five approaches as valid and authentic examples of the relationship between faith and culture, although each works from a different definition of culture and implies a different understanding of the relationship. Bevans makes a further contribution in showing that the 'faith and culture' question is not just a question for missionaries crossing cultures but for churches and theologians within any culture because no theological statement is culture free. Moreover, by embodying 'gospel' and 'faith' in spiritual life and also communally, socially and politically in the church or churches and Christian community, Bevans demonstrates that in discussing culture we are talking about community relations and this is part of a wider question of the role and place of the church in the world. This is not only an evangelistic question. It may be a question of community survival in many parts of the world. It may also be a very delicate political question as governments try to balance power between communities. In succeeding chapters we will discuss this with reference to Latin American society (Chapter 5), Indian politics (Chapter 6), Western culture (Chapter 7), African mission (Chapter 8) and North-East Asian society (Chapter 9).

Gorringe further points out that Niebuhr's models of 'Christ and culture' lack a Trinitarian perspective.[10] This prompts the question what discussion of 'Spirit and culture' could add to the debate. In his book, *Discerning Spirit*, Gorringe tries to answer this question by being open to the Spirit's work in human cultures beyond religious and church boundaries, in art, human love and human community, for example. At the same time he recognizes the danger that the Holy Spirit is identified with the best of the human spirit, human self-consciousness and self-realization, whereas in fact the Holy Spirit is free and culture is the human response to God's initiative.[11] The Spirit of God cannot be confused with any human or worldly spirit, such as the spirit of a particular culture, and not every aspect of human culture can be attributed to the Holy Spirit; there are other spirits at work. The Holy Spirit does not just affirm and encourage what is good in human culture; the Spirit also transforms culture and liberates it from what is bad. Stimulated particularly by his experience of living and teaching in India at Tamil Nadu Theological Seminary, where Indian Christians were relating the work of the Holy Spirit with the liberation of the poor and downtrodden (cf. Luke 4.18–19), Gorringe sees signs of the Spirit in political life where freedom and justice produce a new society, and Christ-likeness, which as the measure of truly human behaviour, is identified with hope, 'the virtues of Christ' and 'the option for the poor'.[12]

From the perspective of pneumatology, the expression of the gospel in different cultures begins – like all mission activity – with discerning the Spirit, or finding out where the Spirit is at work according to the criterion set by Jesus Christ. The absence of the definite article before 'Spirit' in the title of Gorringe's book, *Discerning Spirit*, allows for a double meaning. Not only is it about 'discerning the Spirit of God' but it is also about the gift of discernment, which, he repeatedly points out, is a function of the Spirit. The Holy Spirit is the Spirit of discernment, who reveals God's will to us in and through cultures. Gorringe develops these ideas in later work to produce a dynamic view of the movement of the Spirit over and through culture, 'furthering humanity',[13] in place of the rather static models of 'Christ and culture'.

The terminology of 'gospel and culture' or 'faith and culture' can lead to dualism: that is the view that gospel and culture are equal and opposing, as if there was a battle between the two.[14] From the perspective of the Spirit, they are interconnected. The Spirit is on the inside of human culture, bringing it to maturity, as well as on the outside, enabling us to discern what is Christ-like in it. We cannot separate 'Spirit' and 'culture' because the Holy Spirit creates culture and realizes the human spirit. Furthermore, in a plural world, it is more appropriate to talk about 'cultures' than 'culture'. So, as we consider each of Bevans's models, we will look at them in pneumatological terms as models of 'Spirit and cultures'.

3.2 Translating the Word

As its name suggests, the translation model of the encounter between the Spirit of Christ and a particular culture uses the analogy of language to express what happens. The translation process began at Pentecost when the Jews visiting Jerusalem from different parts of the world understood the message of disciples in their own mother tongues (Acts 2.11) and has been repeated ever since as the gospel message has spread around the world and been translated into many languages. Prominent advocates of the translation approach are Andrew Walls and Lamin Sanneh, Professor of Missions and World Christianity at Yale Divinity School, both of whom are inspired by patterns of gospel reception in West Africa, where they find a striking difference between Christian and Muslim missionary activity: Christians have translated the Bible and the name of God into local languages, whereas the Qur'an and the name of Allah remain always and everywhere in the original Arabic.[15] They argue that Christianity's ability to spread around the world and take on different cultural forms can be explained by its 'translatability'.[16] However, if considered in an ecumenical perspective, this contrast may be overdone. Historically Christian missionaries have not always translated the Bible or the liturgy. The Roman Catholic Church resisted the translation of the Bible and the liturgy in the name of unity for the better part of 1,500 years.[17] Theologically, the comparison between the Bible and the Qur'an is problematic because the dynamics of the two religions are very different and, although Islam retains Arabic for the Qur'an and for worship, it takes on local cultural forms in other areas of life.

The need and impulse to translate the message was a major insight of the Reformation, and after Vatican II this was recognized by the Roman Catholic Church as well. The translation of the Scriptures into vernacular languages continues to be pursued particularly by the Bible Societies and Wycliffe Bible Translators. Reflection on translation can be instructive in considering the relationship between the Spirit and cultures. Translation is a complex process. It is not a matter of matching one word in one language to an equivalent in another. There are few one-to-one correspondences between words in different languages because meaning is shaped by culture. A literal translation sounds very stilted and can be almost meaningless. Translation websites like Babel Fish can yield some very odd results. A good translator is one who understands both cultures involved and can produce a 'dynamically equivalent' translation[18] which captures the spirit of the original and expresses it fluently in a different language form. The dynamic equivalence approach is reflected in radical bible translations such as the *The Word on the Street*[19] and in experiments with inclusive language.

There are two reservations about the translation model. It may suggest that there is an original, fixed text to be translated, whereas the Holy Spirit and the living Word cannot be captured in any particular formulation and there is no normative Christian culture.[20] Second, the translation model tends to take the perspective of the missionary, who sees him- or herself as bringing the gospel from one place to another. Although the story of Jesus Christ may be new and need translating, the Holy Spirit is already at work in any culture, and so the Christian faith is not imported but emerges out of local experience. There is a sense in which Jesus Christ is foreign to all cultures but Christianity need not be a foreign religion. For Christianity to be an indigenous religion, the emphasis must be not on the translation but on the local interpretation, by the Holy Spirit. In any communication, the message the communicator thinks they are sending is different from what is heard by the receptor. Successful communication is not one-sided proclamation but a two-way process involving feedback from the receptor, which must be 'read' by the communicator until eventually there is agreement about meaning.[21] Professor Kwame Bediako has compared the reception of the gospel in Africa to the very first spread of Christianity from a Jewish to a Gentile milieu.[22] After the initial translation, there is a deeper level and long-term interaction between the new faith and its new cultural surroundings which results in fresh expressions of the Christian gospel. This long and complex process of spiritual and cultural interchange is repeated every time the gospel crosses cultural boundaries.

3.3 Rooting the gospel in culture

The translation model takes culture seriously, but its emphasis is on the integrity of the Christian gospel: there is one Truth in different contexts and one Bible in different languages. Those who are most concerned that Christians should retain their cultural identity, focus on their response to the message, and may prefer the second, anthropological model. Theologically this model begins not from Pentecost but from creation, with the affirmation that what God has created by the Spirit is good, and this includes human cultures.

The anthropological model draws on the insights of cultural or social anthropology. Beginning with US American Franz Boas in the early twentieth century, anthropologists rejected the nineteenth century use of the word 'culture' to mean 'civilization', the final stage on an evolutionary ladder from 'savagery' through 'barbarianism', which Europeans had attained and to which all humanity was expected to aspire. They preferred instead to talk about many different and varied 'cultures', and began to use the word 'culture', like Kate Fox above, to refer to all patterns and symbols of a particular society, including language, art, manners, customs, beliefs, law and morality at both elite and popular levels.[23] At first the cultures studied by the anthropological model were mainly isolated from modern society. More recently the model has also been applied to subcultures within Western societies, such as housewives, bikers or university students. 'Consumer culture' and corporate and business cultures have also been the subjects of anthropological investigation.

For the purposes of research, anthropologists introduced the principle of 'cultural relativism', which means that beliefs and behaviours of a culture are not evaluated but rather interpreted in terms of the rest of that culture. Cultural anthropologists do not judge cultures by any presumed norm but treat all cultures as equally valid so long as they function in human society. The principle of 'cultural relativism' raised profound questions about the universal claims made by modernists, scientists and religious leaders. It also explained the pitfalls of cross-cultural communication not as due to the ignorance of others but to misunderstanding due to cultural difference. Recognition of and sensitivity to culture made moving from one culture to another both thrilling and also awkward, and led to the recognition of cross-cultural understanding as part of missionary training. Furthermore, cultural anthropology was applied to Christian mission to argue that all cultures could be worthy vehicles of the gospel and show how the Christian gospel could be introduced into different cultures while preserving their integrity.[24]

A prime example of a Christian anthropological approach to culture is the Lausanne Covenant, drafted by the Evangelical Anglican John Stott and endorsed in 1974 by a wide gathering of Evangelical leaders.[25] On the basis of the beginnings of human culture after the Fall (Gen. 4.21, 22), the Lausanne Covenant recognized the ambiguity of culture as a human creation, admitting that some of it 'is rich in beauty and goodness', while 'all of it is tainted with sin and some of it is demonic'. It asserted that 'The gospel does not presuppose the superiority of any culture to another', insisting that all cultures are judged only according to 'the criteria of truth and righteousness' and 'moral absolutes' attested to in Scripture. Recalling the example of the Apostle Paul, who became 'all things to all men' (1 Cor 9.19–23), it called for 'imaginative and pioneering methods' to facilitate churches both 'deeply rooted in Christ and closely related to their culture', which 'transform and enrich it' for the glory of God.

Evangelicals are generally optimistic about the possibility of cultural change and very flexible about forms of worship and community which may result from the introduction of the gospel into a new situation.[26] In their view, the task of the evangelist is to reduce the 'barriers to conversion' by stripping away anything that is culturally threatening and making the moral and doctrinal claims of the gospel as friendly to the culture as possible. But perhaps the most well-known example of this approach is not from an Evangelical missionary but from Catholic priest Vincent Donovan, who has reflected on his work among the Masai in Tanzania.[27] Donovan began from a high regard for Masai culture and attempted to minimize the Western cultural accretions of the gospel he preached by living close to the people. He introduced what he called 'the naked gospel' and then accompanied the tribesmen and women as they worked out its implications in their context and developed their own unique way of being church.

The approach bears some resemblance to the 'demythologizing' of the twentieth-century German theologian Rudolf Bultmann, who attempted to strip the gospel of the culture of the New Testament in order to help 'modern man' appreciate its principles better.[28] This 'kernel-and-husk' image implies that there is a core gospel to be passed on, divested of its wrapping and then rewrapped for the new situation. Evangelicals have generally used the terms 'contextualization' (and 'decontextualization') for this process. So conversion should not 'de-culturize' a convert but only cause him/her to reject certain aspects of culture deemed incompatible with Christian morality and doctrine. However, in reality, it is impossible to identify the 'core gospel'. As soon as we have done so, we have already reduced it and expressed part of it in the form of our own culture. Evangelicals in particular are likely to see the core gospel in terms of certain non-negotiable statements of faith and by a heightened sense of human sinfulness, not always recognizing that questions of truth, righteousness and 'moral absolutes' are culturally defined. Roman Catholics such as Donovan regard the core gospel as the celebration of the Eucharist and what Protestants would regard as distinctively Catholic ideas about priesthood. However, if instead of the 'core gospel', we think of the Holy Spirit, then the Spirit cannot be reduced to either of these but is identified with the whole witness of the missionary and/or the life of the church.

A second criticism of the anthropological approach is that it may tend to idealize or romanticize a culture and not challenge the culture with aspects of the Christian message which may be unpalatable. In nineteenth-century Germany the different cultures which nurtured and nourished different peoples or *Volk* were each seen as the expression of a national 'spirit'.[29] On the one hand, this encouraged respect for culture by German missionaries, who encouraged in different lands the development of *Volkskirche*, or a church of the people, which was indigenous in its expression and locally led. On the other hand, it encouraged the disastrous link between religion and nationalism, which at home in Germany produced the infamous 'German Christian' movement which attempted 'to fuse Christianity with Germanness and purge it of Jewish influence'.[30] Too much emphasis on the integrity of culture can encourage policies of separate development on the basis that cultures so shape the lives of individuals that people of a particular culture think and reason differently from those in another. Such an idea contributed to the justification of Nazi racism and to the system of apartheid in South Africa. It leads to pessimism regarding the possibility of human co-operation, such as expressed in Samuel P. Huntington's influential 'clash of civilizations' theory, in which he painted a picture of a new division of the world into religio-cultural blocs, including Western, Chinese, Indian and Islamic, which have irreconcilable differences.[31] This leads to a defeatist view that neglects common humanity and is contrary to the gospel, according to which it is the nature of the one Spirit of Christ to break down the dividing wall which separates different peoples (Eph. 2).

Finally, the anthropological approach can be decidedly secular in that it tends to see 'cultures' as separate from 'religions' and religiously neutral. In this model the reason any culture can play host to Christianity is either because religious elements can be subtracted from it and replaced by Christianity (the Evangelical view) or because Christianity is assumed to be able to fulfil whatever religious inclinations are already present (which tends to be the Roman Catholic view). While affirming of cultures, the Lausanne Covenant was decidedly negative about other religions but, as we shall see, cultures cannot be so easily separated from religions (see Chapter 6).

3.3 Transforming society

The third model, which Bevans calls praxis/transformation, is not inspired by linguistics like the translation model or the study of traditional cultures like the anthropological model but by social and development studies, which are influenced by a Marxian view of culture as social, political and economic structures. Whereas anthropologists generally affirmed culture, Italian Marxist Antonio Gramsci drew attention to the controlling power of culture and its use by the ruling class to exercise power without the use of force. Such cultural 'hegemony' may be seen as the main means by which the USA holds power today.[32] As well as drawing attention to questions of power and cultural dominance, sociologists also gave greater attention to the culture of modernity and the cultural change brought about as it impacts societies in Africa, Asia and the Americas.

The model begins from the conviction that the gospel is an agent of change, and takes its scriptural point of departure from the transforming power of the Spirit of the Lord (Luke 4.18–19). In contrast to the anthropological model, it does not seek to preserve culture, which it understands primarily in terms of social structures, but challenges the status quo. It aims to produce practical results in people's lives and social transformation. Liberation theology (see Chapter 5), which regards the gospel as a message of liberation for the poor and engages in social and political action, comes under this heading. Under the influence of liberation theology, the term 'contextualization' (in a different sense to above) was introduced in the ecumenical movement in the early 1970s to replace the term 'indigenization', which tended to be used for 'responding to the Gospel in terms of traditional culture' and is therefore 'past-oriented', as shown by the accompanying metaphor of 'taking root in the soil'. The new term was intended to include questions of the socio-economic forces of change, modernity, inter-ethnic politics, inter-cultural relations and globalization.[33]

The socio-economic dimensions of culture are also to the fore among Evangelicals at the Oxford Centre for Mission Studies, for example, which has a particular agenda to promote Christian work for personal and social development in the Majority World and to encourage grass-roots initiatives to bring about change.[34] The concern for the ethical imperatives of the kingdom of God and for social justice may mean that the praxis/transformation model advocates solutions from a particular culture, or universal solutions, without necessary sensitivity to local culture or religion. 'Justice' and 'development' are not absolute terms; they are both culturally defined. The division between cultural-anthropological approaches to culture and sociological ones is exacerbated by the fact that missionaries relating to the cultural elite tend to favour the former and those relating to the poor prefer the latter. There is often a tension between theologies which start from traditional culture and those which start from liberation. Liberationists are accused of being preoccupied with the socio-economic situation to the neglect of tradition; whereas those who focus on culture are said to lack social and political concern.[35]

The theological argument for contextualization usually begins from the incarnation: as Jesus Christ was incarnate in the world so the gospel must be incarnated into every culture and society. Theology of the incarnation starts from above, from the pre-existent Word with God who comes down and dwells on earth (John 1.1–18). Verses commonly cited to explain the meaning of inculturation as incarnation are those describing the self-emptying (*kenosis*) of Jesus Christ, who took the form of a servant (Phil. 2.5–8; Mark 10.45). There is considerable variation in the understanding of what it meant for Jesus Christ to be incarnate. How human was he and how divine? What did he give up and what did he retain? He was in the world but how much was he of it? So, for example, the Evangelical *Willowbank Report* (1982) suggested that for the foreign missionary contextualization should include mastering the local language, understanding and empathizing with the people and following local custom, but argues that economic identification (of Western missionaries with the poor) would not be authentic.[36] Whereas for a Roman Catholic missionary order such as Mother Teresa's Missionaries of Charity, for example, voluntary poverty is the first step in inculturation.

Furthermore, the difficulty with all these discussions about *kenosis* is the assumption that contextualization/inculturation is carried out by someone coming from a position of power that can be given up.[37] Not all Christian witness is from the powerful to the powerless. Biblical examples include the Israelite slave girl who testified to her master Naaman about the God of Elisha (2 Kings 5.1–27), the women who visited the tomb and first told their brothers the good news of the resurrection (Matt. 28.1–10; Luke 24.1–12, 22–4), and Peter and John at the temple who had no silver or gold to give the lame man but offered healing in Jesus' name (Acts 3.1–10). As the Apostle Paul explained to the Corinthians, the treasure of the gospel is 'in clay jars, so that it may be made clear that this extraordinary power belongs to God and does not come from us' (2 Cor. 4.7). For many, Christian mission is not about divesting oneself of power but an experience of empowerment (see Chapter 5); not of emptying but of being filled with the Holy Spirit, who gives gifts for the furtherance of the gospel (1 Cor. 12.7; Rom. 12.4).[38] This is because they encounter the underside of the incarnation:

the movement of the Holy Spirit in the world, which subverts earthly power structures and challenges hegemony.

3.5 Inculturation

Model four, the synthetic model aims to balance the gospel message or church tradition, on the one hand, and the culture and society on the other. US Roman Catholic theologian Robert Schreiter aimed to achieve this in his widely known book *Constructing Local Theologies*. Rather than seeing cultures in terms of tangible products and actual practice, Schreiter is influenced by the view promoted by Clifford Geertz and others that culture is a complex web of symbols, signs or signifiers.[39] In the 'semiotic model', which comes from the philosophy of language, these signs carry meaning when they are used according to shared rules. Schreiter makes the point that the gospel message and church traditions are themselves cultures. Each church or denomination emerges from a particular historical context and develops its own language (theology) and cultural system, with distinctive ways of worship, moral codes and so on. The Eucharist is a prime example of a sign which, having deep resonances within church culture, is only really understood from within, and even between different denominations carries different shades of meaning. So the synthetic model envisages a dialogue between the two cultures: one being a particular testimony to Jesus Christ and the other being the heritage of the particular locality. Like other theologies of dialogue which we shall meet in Chapter 6, the synthetic model assumes that the Holy Spirit is moving on both sides of the dialogue. Both partners in dialogue are transformed by the process as the church also is renewed by the encounter.

In the Roman Catholic Church the term 'inculturation' is preferred for the relationship between Christian faith and human cultures. After the Second Vatican Council (1962–5), Pope Paul VI insisted on a 'synthesis between faith and culture', and the term 'inculturation' to describe this came into common currency among Jesuits in the 1970s.[40] In the encyclical

Redemptoris Missio (1990), John Paul II defined inculturation as a dual activity of 'the intimate transformation of authentic cultural values through their integration in Christianity and the insertion of Christianity in the various human cultures'. It is seen as a 'slow journey', or 'incubation', bringing about a new form of life that is marked by both 'compatibility with the gospel and communion with the universal Church'.[41] Although the emphasis has tended to be on culture in the sense of tradition, 'inculturation' was intended to include modernity and social change.[42]

Inculturation is understood as a dialogical process between the church and local culture. Maintaining a middle way is always difficult and others may accuse protagonists of the synthetic model of compromising the gospel by too strongly emphasizing the local context, or the syncretistic mixing of the gospel with other world-views. There are major tensions within the Catholic Church, between the official teaching and those putting inculturation into practice in non-Western local churches particularly.[43] For example, despite the rhetoric of inculturation, heavy restrictions are placed on the translation and adaptation of the liturgy,[44] to which many African and Asian theologians object, wondering why liturgical texts have to be translated from Latin (a local language), and why they cannot be composed directly in the vernacular languages in the first place.[45] The British anthropologist and Catholic missionary to Africa, Aylward Shorter, saw that the emergence of an African form of Christianity, which takes up African symbols and values, was hampered by the belief in some circles that church tradition constitutes a single Christian culture – a view which he regarded as Euro-American cultural domination or imperialism. For Shorter, inculturation 'denotes the presentation and re-expression of the Gospel in forms and terms proper to a culture', processes which result in the reinterpretation of the gospel as well as the culture, but 'without being unfaithful to either'.[46]

If inculturation is a dialogue, a recurring question is whether we start with faith or culture or, as Schreiter poses it, are we discussing 'inculturation of faith' or 'identification with culture'? He comes to the conclusion that we are doing both at the same time: 'they represent two moments in the inculturation process which, depending on circumstances, require greater or lesser emphasis'. Therefore either faith or culture may be an appropriate starting point for the process of inculturation, depending on the circumstances. Sometimes faith may be required to be in solidarity with a culture suffering oppression and at other times faith needs to challenge a corrupt culture or inspire a failing one.[47] Schreiter also argued that a certain degree of syncretism, the mixing of Christianity with other faiths, is an inevitable part of a healthy inculturation process. He was strongly criticized for this view even though, as Shorter pointed out, 'syncretism is present to a greater or lesser degree in every form of Christianity from New Testament times'.[48]

Accusations of syncretism in contextual expressions of the gospel were made at the assembly of the World Council of Churches, which took place in 1991 in Canberra, Australia, when, on the opening day of the conference, a young Korean theologian, Chung Hyun Kyung, chose to express her message of the liberating work of the Holy Spirit by means of a shamanistic exorcism in the Korean tradition.[49] Many condemned Chung's presentation for overstepping the boundary of valid inculturation so that it no longer constituted authentic Christian theology. Chung's presentation precipitated the World Council of Churches into a theological crisis in which the relationship of gospel and cultures was identified as the key issue.[50] This was taken up as the theme of the next World Council of Churches conference on world mission and evangelism, organized by Indian theologian Christopher Duraisingh at Salvador, Brazil, in 1996. The conference yielded many interesting examples of the different models of gospel and culture. An Aborigine theologian reported how, before the missionaries came, certain of his ancestors had visions, which were later realized to be of Jesus Christ. This had encouraged him to 'recognize the gospel of our cultures' as the anthropological model might do. A Brazilian wondered if evangelists could 'sensitively accept a culture rooted in belief in the supernatural' while also demonstrating the liberating quality of Christian faith, suggesting a synthetic approach. Similarly, an African American pointed out that her slave ancestors 'forged an African American Christianity which was a blend of the Bible which they believed and their African world-view and spirituality mediated through the experience of slavery'. Metropolitan Kirill of Smolensk and Kaliningrad argued that the survival of Christianity through decades of Soviet oppression was evidence that over centuries the gospel had become embedded, or translated, into Russian culture. In contrast, Musimbi Kanyoro, a Lutheran theologian from Kenya, found little hope in African cultures riven by ethnic wars but only in the churches where the liberating gospel is lived – suggesting a liberation approach.[51]

The Salvador conference succeeded in broadening the discussion of culture beyond the anxieties about syncretism, pointing out that accusations of syncretism (like heresy) are often linked to power imbalances between churches.[52] Salvador also showed that 'Culture is not a marginal issue appended to the gospel, but touches the very core of the church's identity and mission.'[53] It is not a theoretical discussion for missionaries but a central issue in the life of local churches.[54] However, underlying the Salvador discussion were the questions Chung was raising in her presentation at Canberra about recognizing the work of the Holy Spirit beyond the boundaries of Christian confession. The report of the Salvador conference declared, 'The Christian faith affirms that God is one, and therefore the spirit present in the cultures and religions of humanity *in mercy and judgment* may be said to be none other than the Holy Spirit, that is, the Spirit of God who is eternally united to the Son and to the Father.' The presence of the Spirit among human cultures affirms them as vehicles of the gospel and at the same time judges them (John 3.17–20). Cultural diversity within the one church should be affirmed as the work of the Spirit and a reflection of the Triune God. But in view of the presence of evil as well as good in human cultures, the report advocated a process of 'discerning the Spirit at work in all cultures' and suggested criteria for recognizing the Spirit's presence and activity.[55] The use of the plural 'cultures' deliberately called attention to 'both the inseparable relatedness and the relativity of all cultures in the perspective of God's reign' and opened them up to one another.[56]

3.6 Cultural formation of identity

Bevans's final example, the transcendental model, is based on the model of perception developed by Immanuel Kant and applied to theology in the twentieth century particularly by Catholic theologians such as Karl Rahner and Bernard Lonergan, which assumes that knowledge is subjective rather than objective. This more psychological approach attends to self-understanding rather than to the externals of cultural behaviour in the belief that our inner life is shaped by the culture in which we live, and that it is only by recognizing this that we can understand ourselves and ultimately transcend our cultural limitations.[57] The transcendental model of gospel and cultures draws on the theology of baptism, which in the case of Jesus himself was the occasion of his self-realization, when by the Holy Spirit he came to knowledge of himself and his relation to the Father (Mark 1.9–11 and parallels). By a spiritual immersion, we come to know Christ and ourselves in a new way, and we are then able to reach a new and authentic expression of gospel in culture. An example of this is the contemplative spirituality of Abhishiktananda and his followers who see meditation in the Hindu tradition as a way of transcending religious difference and living the 'Christ-life' in an Indian way.[58] The model is criticized – especially by advocates of the praxis/transformation approach – as too introspective, individual and elitist.[59] In response, advocates argue that, although attending to their own experience, the result is culturally conditioned, and the method allows the possibility of transcending culture to discover deeper knowledge of the divine.[60]

An advantage of the transcendental model is that it highlights the experience of those within a particular culture, and shifts attention away from the missionary or development worker who sees the culture from the outside. Those who live within are not conscious of their culture or of the process of contextualization, unless an outsider points it out to them. Yet in each context, Christians and churches unselfconsciously choose from what is available to them to express the gospel in the way they see fit. Christians construct their Christian identity in relation to the other religious and secular identities in their context. The overseas visitor who expects to see 'indigenous churches' will be disappointed if local Christians choose to express their Christian faith in a modern way, or sing the nineteenth-century hymns the colonial missionaries brought. But such freedom to defy the expectations of people from other cultures is the sign of an authentic local church.

Since the 1970s much of the initiative in the study of cultures has passed from anthropology to the emerging disciplines of critical and cultural studies.[61] In these disciplines, the emphasis is shifted from culture as an external system in which we live to culture as 'constantly being constructed by those who participate in it', like a performance or a conversation.[62] Then the focus is on questions of identity, and only secondarily on the cultural context which fixes it in a specific time and place. French philosopher Jacques Derrida encouraged students of culture to recognize the extent to which it is constructed and representational, rather than an expression of any objective reality. If this is so, then any culture is merely 'a snapshot of the play of discourses within a given time and space'.[63] Culture is not understood as 'tradition' – in the sense of something monolithic and unchanging – but as dynamic and fluid. In any case, even 'tradition' itself can be invented or reinvented for particular ends.[64] Instead of the individual being formed by culture, culture is more often seen as a tool to be used for creating and defining an identity, which is believed to be self-determined.

This new perspective refuses to see people as determined by their culture but sees them as the shapers of it. Stuart Hall, who pioneered cultural studies at the University of Birmingham, is Jamaican born. He and other intellectuals from former colonies, insisted on the importance of their cultural identity and challenged the prevailing discourse of 'Britishness' which disregarded the contribution of the former empire to British identity.[65] From their post-colonial perspective (see Chapter 5), Hall and others criticized Europeans for seeing people of other nations as defined by a culture that Europeans themselves constructed, and which often said more about themselves than about the other. Leaders of cultural studies rejected any suggestion that they could be defined by the colonizers in this way, and insisted on the right to shape their own cultural identity that was both Jamaican and British, or Palestinian and American. They also stressed the extent to which identity is multiple or hybrid.

To take another example, an 'English Christian woman' would identify as English at the football world cup, Christian at the council of faiths meeting and female when she goes to the lavatory. Instead of being fixed by birth or determined by others, in contemporary society this person is now understood to be able to exercise choice over whether or not to submit to these categories – even the gender label. While this state of affairs may be empowering for some individuals, however, it is only so if they can defy their community with impunity. For others, if they wish to remain in their community of birth, there is no option but to submit to its labels. In most societies, ethnicity, gender and religion are not matters of lifestyle choice but are considered fixed, and going against expectations may be dangerous. Redefining identity in these circumstances involves cultural programmes to change the whole society and redefine cultural norms and attitudes.

3.7 Fresh expressions in British culture

Mission-shaped Church, the report of the Mission and Public Affairs Council of the Church of England in 2004, called for 'a new inculturation of the gospel within our society'[66] in view of the rapidly changing socio-cultural context. The unprecedented popularity of the publication showed the relevance of these issues today. Central to the report was the application of an approach to gospel and culture drawn from experience outside the West. So the report began by examining the British context and then, using the analogy of planting, considered what kind of church would be most appropriate for the contemporary British soil. In terms of the models above, this is an anthropological approach.

Before re-expressing the gospel in British culture, it is necessary to clarify what or whose culture are we talking about. Are we actually thinking not of British culture as a whole but of a particular subculture such as the middle class or Christians or men? Do we mean the dominant culture of a particular elite or the popular culture of the masses? If the latter, then which popular culture? Gordon Lynch, for example, bases his inculturation on the 'generation Xers' who inhabit a post-Christian culture.[67] The Mission and Public Affairs Council avoided these questions by beginning with social trends in the country as a whole, as identified by the Office for National Statistics. Figures for 2008[68] endorse the report's picture of an aging population, smaller households, poverty among the young and old, almost as many women as men in employment – and for longer, increased net household wealth but increased debt, longer formal education, and improved health and diet but increased obesity and alcohol-related deaths. The report also shows that our individualism, social mobility and family patterns make Britain a fragmented society. Where we form relationships these are less with family and neighbours, and increasingly in networks of like-minded people. This observation led the writers of *Mission-shaped Church* to endorse work already being done in planting churches among networks rather than necessarily in geographically defined locations.[69]

Mission-shaped Church also identified consumer culture as characteristic of contemporary post-Christendom society.[70] Although most symbols of our national life are disputed, commentators generally agree that, since the end of post-war austerity, shopping has become an icon of British life.[71] Shopping repeatedly shows up in the Social Trends survey as not only a necessary but also a popular British activity, the basis of our economy since the decline of industrial production. It is not just a matter of consumption, which is basic to life and to the global economic system, but of consumerism. Shopping has become our way of life, the basis of more and more of our relationships, and a metaphor for much of contemporary Western culture.[72] Shopping is a ritualistic behaviour which has displaced some religious activities – especially on Sunday morning when more people are now found in the massive new shopping malls, which are among the few recent additions to our landscape that rival the ancient cathedrals and are frequently compared to temples to another god. Fuelled by advertising and celebrity, and now possible through the internet as well, shopping occupies our thoughts and affects our relationships as we mentally cost our life choices and select (or dream of selecting) our bodies, our education, our partners and our babies.[73]

The political journalist Andrew Marr holds the culture of consumerism responsible for the fragmentation of British life. It has 'shouldered aside other ways of understanding the world' such as 'real political visions', 'organized religion' and 'a pulsating sense of national identity'.[74] The authors of *Mission-shaped Church* also condemn 'consumerism' as a form of idolatry, which creates a self-indulgent society and excludes the poor, but nevertheless they argued that to reach out in consumer society the church must 'reshape itself around worshippers as consumers'.[75] This was a major reason for encouraging 'fresh expressions of church'. The readiness here, and in the case of network churches, to let cultural forms determine the form of church, without considering whether these cultural forms exhibit the Spirit of Christ, tends to be a weakness of the anthropological approach, as we saw above. Mission-shaped church may degenerate into simply multiplying churches,[76] exacerbating social fragmentation, without challenging individualism and helping to create a unified spirit and vision.

Statistics do reveal a great deal about the way we live our lives but there are other ways that will also help to discover more about British culture. As cross-cultural missionaries know, one of the best ways of discovering core values in any culture is to observe how children are brought up and socialized or 'enculturated'. Of course this varies across different communities in Britain but the government-defined priorities are revealed in a statement of values on which education is based which is included in the National Curriculum for England.[77]. This begins from the development of the self and moves outward in ever-increasing circles to consider relationships, society and the environment, reflecting the emphasis of Western culture since the Enlightenment on the autonomous, thinking human self. This was the foundation of the transcendent model above and it has contributed to the achievement of the West in refusing to be bound by tradition but redefining itself as modern. However, the danger in it is that, beginning from the self, relationships and society appear as secondary, 'fundamental to the development and fulfilment of ourselves' but not of our essence. Those who are not 'self' are equally autonomous 'others', and the corollary of this is respect: others are to be respected in their own right for who they are. However, their lives are not integral or necessary to ours, which we regard as self-sufficient, and this militates against the creation of a mutually supportive society.

Consumer culture and individualism are not the only reasons British society is fragmented. One of the most striking characteristics of contemporary Britain is the increasing diversity of its peoples.[78] The regional diversity of the UK has increased, especially with devolution and European funding for regional development. Immigration patterns have diversified, leading to a huge range of ethnic groups who have arrived in this country for a wide variety of reasons and have varying levels of attachment to it. This means that different groups experience the country very differently. National statistics disguise large differences in well-being in different sectors of society and suggest a shared culture, whereas in fact different groups speak different languages, eat different food and may have little in common with each other. The article also pointed out that social inequality continues to rise in general. Some groups are particularly disadvantaged in British society; these include some ethnic minorities, people with disabilities and children eligible for free school meals. All this suggests that 'fresh expressions of church' are needed – but not so much to satisfy the desires of the consumer as to serve the basic needs of diverse communities. To achieve this aim, churches should be even more diverse than is suggested in *Mission-shaped Church*, which pays little attention to ethnic minorities or the poor.

The churches have generally supported the policy of multiculturalism emphasized in the National Curriculum and pursued by government, which officially celebrates the presence of many different social groups and encourages them to maintain their own customs and cultures. Such celebration of plural society has been in keeping with the dominant theology of religions (see Chapter 6), and the wider British people have been remarkably receptive of aspects of the cultures of recent migrant communities – such as their cuisines. However, it may be that multiculturalism, combined with consumerism and the tendency to develop the self rather than society, has actually been an excuse for communal separation and cultural relativism. Especially since the 7/7 bombings in London in 2005, the extent to which some communities feel alienated from the rest of the country has become clear and a retreat from multiculturalism has been reflected in an emphasis on inclusion in educational and other institutions. London's successful bid to host the Olympics in 2012, for example, majored on inclusivity.[79] 'Fresh expressions' which aim to reach particular sections of society, and faith schools, may be contributing to the problem rather than helping to cross cultural boundaries.[80] The Archbishop of York, John Sentamu, has criticized multiculturalism for allowing minority communities to express themselves but stifling the majority community, particularly in effectively preventing them celebrating and sharing their Christian heritage; and the Bishop of Rochester, Michael Nazir-Ali, has argued that naïve multicultural policies actively encouraged the spread of fundamentalist Islam.[81] The Spirit of Christ, who urges us to love and interact with our neighbours, rather than merely respect them from a distance, is powerful in challenging our self-sufficient and relativist attitudes. At the same time, the Holy Spirit does not naïvely affirm cultures but discerns, transforms and challenges all of them. This is a time for inculturation: a true dialogue of the church with the many different cultures of this country.

Now faced with the challenges of global terrorism, climate change and economic troubles there is a recognized need for a more cohesive society which can work together for practical ends. What is more, we realize that our buy-and-throw-away mode of living is unsustainable. People are now looking for hope, leadership and a sense of common purpose rather than just the immediate thrill of shopping. British culture will always require 'fresh expressions' – that is not the issue. Fresh expressions are necessary if the gospel is to remain meaningful in changing and diverse cultural contexts. But as well as 'mission-shaped church', we are in need of 'Spirit-shaped mission'.[82] Spirit-shaped mission participates in the mission of God, which is worked out in human life, not only in the church but in all aspects of human cultures, influencing them according to the vision of the kingdom life, which Jesus taught and demonstrated. Mission is not only about changing the church but also about changing society. Without being dictated to by social pressure, churches and fresh expressions can serve diverse communities and at the same time exhibit the unity in the one Spirit showing – and spreading – just the kind of vision, commitment and solidarity which is currently lacking in Britain.

Notes

1 Samuel Rayan, *Come Holy Spirit* (Delhi: Media House, 1998), p. 13.

2 Kate Fox, *Watching the English: The Hidden Rules of English Behaviour* (London: Hodder, 2004), pp. 400–16.

3 Aylward Shorter, *Evangelization and Culture* (London: Geoffrey Chapman, 1994), p. 30.

4 William R. Burrows, 'A Seventh Paradigm? Catholics and Radical Inculturation', in Willem Saayman and Klippies Kritzinger (eds), *Mission in Bold Humility: David Bosch's Work Considered* (Maryknoll, NY: Orbis Books, 1996), pp. 121–38.

5 Cf. David J. Bosch, *Transforming Mission: Paradigm Shifts in Theology of Mission* (Maryknoll, NY: Orbis Books, 1991), pp. 448–9.

6 Roland Allen, *Missionary Methods: St Paul's or Ours?* (Grand Rapids, MI: Wm B. Eerdmans, 1962 [1912]), pp. 143–4.

7 H. R. Niebuhr, *Christ and Culture* (New York: Harper and Row, 1951).

8 See Timothy J. Gorringe, *Furthering Humanity: A Theology of Culture* (Aldershot: Ashgate, 2004), pp. 12–16.

9 Stephen B. Bevans, *Models of Contextual Theology* (Maryknoll, NY: Orbis Books, 1992).

10 Gorringe, *Furthering Humanity*, p. 16.

11 Timothy J. Gorringe, *Discerning Spirit: A Theology of Revelation* (London: SCM Press, 1990), p. 16; cf. Michael Welker, *God the Spirit*, trans. John F. Hoffmeyer (Minneapolis, MN: Fortress Press, 1994), pp. 283–96.

12 Timothy J. Gorringe, *Redeeming Time: Atonement through Education* (London: Darton, Longman and Todd, 1986), p. 88; Gorringe, *Discerning Spirit*, pp. 38, 59–70.

13 Gorringe, *Furthering Humanity*, p. 102.

14 Lesslie Newbigin, *The Gospel in a Pluralist Society* (London: SPCK, 1989), pp. 188–9.

15 Lamin Sanneh, *Translating the Message: The Missionary Impact on Culture* (Maryknoll, NY: Orbis Books, 1989), pp. 211–38.

16 Andrew F. Walls, *The Missionary Movement in Christian History: Studies in the Transmission of Faith* (Maryknoll, NY: Orbis Books, 1996), pp. 26–42.

17 Shorter, *Evangelization and Culture*, p. 30.

18 Charles H. Kraft, *Christianity in Culture: A Study in Dynamic Biblical Theologizing in Cross-Cultural Perspective* (Maryknoll, NY: Orbis Books, 1979).

19 Rob Lacey, *The Word on the Street* (Grand Rapids, MI: Zondervan, 2005).

20 Walls, *Missionary Movement in Christian History*, pp. 3–15, 7–9; Cf. Aram I, 'The Incarnation of the Gospel in Cultures: A Missionary Event', in James A. Scherer and Stephen B. Bevans (eds), *New Directions in Mission and Evangelization 3: Faith and Culture* (Maryknoll, NY: Orbis Books, 1999), pp. 29–41.

21 Charles H. Kraft, *Communication Theory for Christian Witness* (Maryknoll, NY: Orbis Books, 1991); David J. Hesselgrave, *Communicating Christ Cross-culturally* (Grand Rapids, MI: Zondervan, 1991).

22 Kwame Bediako, *Theology and Identity: The Impact of Culture upon Christian Thought in the Second Century and Modern Africa* (Oxford: Regnum Books, 1992).

23 For an introduction to cultural anthropology, see John Monaghan

and Peter Just, *Social and Cultural Anthropology: A Very Short Introduction* (Oxford: Oxford University Press, 2000); William A. Haviland et al., *Cultural Anthropology: The Human Challenge*, 12th edn (Belmont, CA: Wadsworth/Thomson Learning, 2008).

24 For example, Paul G. Hiebert, *Anthropological Insights for Missionaries* (Grand Rapids, MI: Baker Book House, 1985); Charles H. Kraft, *Anthropology for Christian Witness* (Maryknoll, NY: Orbis Books, 1996); Alan R. Tippett, *Introduction to Missiology* (Pasadena, CA: William Carey Library, 1987); Louis J. Luzbetak, *The Church and Cultures: New Perspectives in Missiological Anthropology* (Maryknoll, NY: Orbis Books, 1988).

25 Lausanne Committee for World Evangelization, *The Lausanne Covenant* (1974), section 10, 'Evangelism and Culture' – available at <www.lausanne.org>.

26 Lausanne Committee for World Evangelization, *The Willowbank Report: Consultation on Gospel and Culture*, Lausanne Occasional Paper 2 (1978) – available at <www.lausanne.org>.

27 Vincent J. Donovan, *Christianity Rediscovered: An Epistle from the Masai*, 3rd edn (London: SCM Press, 2001).

28 Rudolf Bultmann, *New Testament and Mythology, and Other Writings*, trans. Schubert M. Ogden (London: SCM Press, 1985).

29 For an erudite and helpful discussion of European uses of the word 'culture', see Gorringe, *Furthering Humanity*, pp. 1–9.

30 Timothy Yates, *Christian Mission in the Twentieth Century* (Cambridge: Cambridge University Press, 1994), pp. 34–56; Doris L. Bergen, *Twisted Cross: The German Christian Movement in the Third Reich* (London: University of Carolina Press, 1996), p. xi; Cornelia Füllkrug-Weitzel, 'A German Perspective', in Christopher Duraisingh (ed.), *Called to One Hope: The Gospel in Diverse Cultures: Report of the Conference of the CWME, Salvador, Brazil, 1996* (Geneva: WCC Publications, 1998), pp. 111–20. For the role of German mission agencies, see Werner Ustorf, *Sailing on the Next Tide: Missions, Missiology, and the Third Reich* (Oxford: Peter Lang, 2000).

31 Samuel P. Huntington, *The Clash of Civilizations and the Remaking of the World Order* (London: The Free Press, 2002 [1996]).

32 Noam Chomsky, *Hegemony or Survival? America's Quest for Global Dominance* (London: Penguin, 2004).

33 Shoki Coe, 'Contextualizing Theology', in Gerald H. Anderson and Thomas F. Stransky (eds), *Mission Trends 3: Third World Theologies* (New York: Paulist Press/Grand Rapids, MI: Wm B. Eerdmans, 1976), pp. 19–24.

34 Vinay Samuel and Christopher Sugden (eds), *Mission as Transformation: A Theology of the Whole Gospel* (Oxford: Regnum Books, 1999); David Emmanuel Singh and Bernard Farr (eds), *Christianity and*

Cultures: Shaping Christian Thinking in Context (Oxford: Regnum Books, 2008).

35 Paul F. Knitter, *One Earth Many Religions: Multifaith Dialogue and Global Responsibility* (Maryknoll, NY: Orbis Books, 1995), pp. 163–6; Bosch, *Transforming Mission*, p. 421.

36 Lausanne Committee for World Evangelization, *Willowbank Report*, Section 6B.

37 Willem Saayman, 'A South African Perspective on *Transforming Mission*', in Saayman and Kritzinger, *Mission in Bold Humility*, pp. 40–52, see pp. 50–1.

38 Dean S. Gilliland (ed.), *The Word among Us: Contextualizing Theology for Mission Today* (Dallas, TX: Word Publishers, 1989), pp. 12–13.

39 Robert Schreiter, *Constructing Local Theologies* (Maryknoll, NY: Orbis Books, 1985); Clifford Geertz, *The Interpretation of Cultures: Selected Essays* (London: Hutchinson, 1975).

40 Aylward Shorter, 'Inculturation: Win or Lose the Future', in Scherer and Bevans, *New Directions in Mission and Evangelization 3*, pp. 54–67, at pp. 57, 55; see also Shorter, *Evangelization and Culture*, pp. 30–2.

41 John Paul II, *Redemptoris Missio* ('On the permanent validity of the Church's Missionary Mandate') (1990), paras. 52–4 – available at <www.vatican.va>.

42 Shorter, *Evangelization and Culture*, p. 30.

43 Shorter, *Evangelization and Culture*, p. 32.

44 By the Congregation for Divine Worship and the Discipline of the Sacraments. Their latest guidelines, *Liturgiam authenticam* (2001), are available at <www.vatican.va>.

45 Peter C. Phan, 'Liturgical Inculturation', in Keith Pecklers (ed.), *Liturgy in a Postmodern World* (London: Continuum, 2003), pp. 55–91; see p. 65.

46 Shorter, 'Inculturation: Win or Lose the Future', *Evangelization and Culture*, pp. 36–8, 32.

47 Robert J. Schreiter, 'Inculturation of Faith or Identification with Culture?', in Scherer and Bevans, *New Directions in Mission and Evangelization 3*, pp. 68–75, 75.

48 Schreiter, *Constructing Local Theologies*, pp. 144–58; Shorter, *Evangelization and Culture*, p. 33.

49 Chung, Hyun Kyung, 'Come, Holy Spirit – Renew the Whole Creation', in Michael Kinnamon (ed.), *Signs of the Spirit: Official Report of the Seventh Assembly of the World Council of Churches, Canberra, 1991* (Geneva: WCC Publications, 1991), pp. 37–47.

50 For details see Kirsteen Kim, 'Spirit and "Spirits" at the Canberra Assembly of the World Council of Churches, 1991', *Missiology: An*

International Review 32/3 (July 2004), pp. 349–65; or Kirsteen Kim, *The Holy Spirit in the World: A Global Conversation* (Maryknoll, NY: ISPCK, 2007), pp. viii–xiv.

51 See presentations in Duraisingh, *Called to One Hope*, by Wali Fejo, Australia; Robinson Cavalcanti, Brazil; Prathia Hall Wynn, USA; Metropolitan Kirill of Smolensk and Kaliningrad; Musimbi R. A. Kanyoro, Kenya.

52 CWME Salvador conference, 'Reports from the Sections', in Duraisingh, *Called to One Hope*, pp. 29–76, see pp. 56–7, 68–9.

53 Musimbi R. A. Kanyoro, 'Called to One Hope: The Gospel in Diverse Cultures', in Duraisingh, *Called to One Hope*, pp. 96–110, at p. 96.

54 In this respect, a useful resource is Gerald A. Arbuckle, *Earthing the Gospel: An Inculturation Handbook for the Pastoral Worker* (Maryknoll, NY: Orbis Books, 1990).

55 CWME Salvador conference, 'Reports from the Sections', see pp. 30–4, 56–7, 65.

56 Christopher Duraisingh, 'Salvador: A Signpost of the New in Mission', in Duraisingh, *Called to One Hope*, pp. 190–212, at p. 202.

57 Compare Agneta Schreurs, *Psychotherapy and Spirituality: Integrating the Spiritual Dimension into Therapeutic Practice* (London: Jessica Kingsley Publishers, 2002).

58 See, for example, Abhishiktananda 1976, *Hindu–Christian Meeting Point – Within the Cave of the Heart*, rvsd edn (Delhi: ISPCK, 1976; first published in French in 1965 and in English (trans. Sarah Grant) in 1969). See also Kirsteen Kim, *Mission in the Spirit: The Holy Spirit in Indian Christian Theologies* (Delhi: ISPCK, 2003), pp. 78–137.

59 For example, Samuel Rayan, 'Review of S. Samartha, *The Hindu Response to the Unbound Christ*', *International Review of Mission* 66/262 (April 1977), pp. 186–9; Duncan B. Forrester, 'Review of S. J. Samartha, *The Hindu Response to the Unbound Christ*', *Scottish Journal of Theology* 30/4 (1977), pp. 394–6; Georges M. Soares-Prabhu, 'From Alienation to Inculturation: Some Reflections on Doing Theology in India Today', in T. K. John (ed.), *Bread and Breath: Essays in Honour of Samuel Ryan* (Anand, Gujarat: Gujarat Sahitya Prakash, 1991), pp. 55–99, at pp. 87–99.

60 Stanley J, Samartha *One Christ – Many Religions: Towards a Revised Christology* (Maryknoll, NY: Orbis Books, 1991), pp. 107–8; Vandana, 'The Christian Ashram Movement Today', in Vandana (ed.), *Christian Ashrams: A Movement with a Future?* (Delhi: ISPCK, 1993), pp. 75–85; see also Vandana, *Shabda, Shakti Sangam* (Bangalore: NBCLC, 1995).

61 For an introduction to cultural studies, see: Ziauddin Sardar and Borin Van Loon, *Introducing Cultural Studies* (Duxford: Icon Books,

1997); Mark Gibson, *Culture and Power: A History of Cultural Studies* (Oxford: Berg, 2007); Chris Barker, *Cultural Studies: Theory and Practice* (London: Sage Publications, 2000); Anthony Easthope and Kate McGowan (eds), *A Critical and Cultural Theory Reader*, 2nd edn (Maidenhead: Open University Press, 2004).

62 Schreiter, 'Inculturation of Faith or Identification with Culture?', p. 71.

63 Barker, *Cultural Studies*, pp. 166, 95.

64 Anthony Giddens, *Runaway World: How Globalization Is Reshaping Our Lives*, 2nd edn (London: Profile Books, 2002), pp. 36–50.

65 Sardar and Van Loon, *Introducing Cultural Studies*, p. 40.

66 Graham Cray (ed.), *Mission-shaped Church: Church Planting and Fresh Expressions of Church in a Changing Context* (London: Church House Publishing, 2004), p. xii – available at <www.cofe.anglican.org>.

67 Gordon Lynch, *Understanding Theology and Popular Culture* (Oxford: Blackwell, 2005); *After Religion: 'Generation X' and the Search for Meaning* (London: Darton, Longman and Todd, 2002).

68 For the 2008 figures, see <www.statistics.gov.uk>.

69 Cray, *Mission-shaped Church*, pp. 4–7.

70 Cray, *Mission-shaped Church*, pp. 9–11.

71 Andrew Marr, *A History of Modern Britain* (London: Pan Books, 2008), p. ix.

72 Zygmunt Bauman, *Consuming Life* (Cambridge: Polity, 2007), p. 26; Pete Ward, 'Liquid Church', in Howard Mellor and Timothy Yates, *Mission and Spirituality: Creative Ways of Being Church* (Sheffield: Cliff College Publishing, 2002), pp. 83–92, at p. 88; cf. Zygmunt Bauman, *Liquid Modernity* (Cambridge: Cambridge University Press, 2000).

73 See Bauman, *Consuming Life.*

74 Marr, *History of Modern Britain*, p. ix.

75 Pete Ward, *Liquid Church* (Carlisle: Paternoster Press, 2002); Bauman, *Liquid Modernity.*

76 John Hull, *Mission-shaped Church: A Theological Response* (London: SCM Press, 2006).

77 National Forum for Values in Education and the Community (May 1997) – available at <http://curriculum.qca.org.uk/> under primary education.

78 See the accompanying article to the 2008 social trends survey by the National Statistician at <www.statistics.gov.uk>.

79 See London Olympics website, <www.london2012.com>.

80 Compare Johann Hari, 'Rowan Williams has shown us one thing – why multiculturalism must be abandoned', *The Independent* (11 February 2008).

81 Ruth Gledhill, 'Multiculturalism has betrayed the English, Archbishop says', *The Times* (22 November 2005); Michael Nazir-Ali, 'Multiculturalism is to blame for perverting young Muslims', *Telegraph* (15 August 2006).

82 Andrew Lord, *Spirit-shaped Mission: A Holistic Charismatic Missiology* (Milton Keynes: Paternoster, 2005).

4

MOVEMENTS OF THE SPIRIT

The Multidirectional Spread Of Christianity

> For many centuries the Church of the East included greater numbers over vastly greater distances than the churches of Rome or Byzantium.[1]
> John C. England

In 1281, King Edward I of England attended mass in Bordeaux, France, but the rite was a little different from what he was used to. The celebrant used a liturgy that was Syriac in language and ritual, and the priest himself, called Sauma, was of Ongut race from a small monastery near Beijing. The cardinals in Rome had been very surprised to hear from Sauma that many Mongols were Christians and that they claimed to have received the Christian message directly from the Apostle Thomas, not via Rome. But when they heard him celebrate the Eucharist, they concluded that 'the language is different, but the rite is one' and allowed him to minister in Europe.[2]

World Christianity is not a phenomenon that has emerged in the twentieth century, as the above example shows. Even in the first millennium the gospel was carried and churches established across the known world. The false perception that Christianity, which began in West Asia, is a European religion came only after, for various reasons, the churches in North Africa and then Asia declined in numbers and became cut off from the rest of 'Christendom', as the bloc of Christian nations was known. To correct the Euro-centricism of much Christian history, in this chapter we will begin by surveying the spread of Christianity from Jerusalem to the East, North, West and South. This will set the second millennium, in which European

Christianity has dominated, within a wider world historical perspective.[3] As we consider the spread of the Christian faith in different directions, therefore, we will also be able to identify distinct theologies of mission. Because, from its beginning, Christianity existed within different cultures, it has never been uniform, so we should not expect to find the same theology and practice of mission in all times and all places. In fact, since the publication of David Bosch's *Transforming Mission* (1991),[4] theology of mission has been taught in terms of shifting paradigms, or ways of thinking, within the different cultural contexts in which Christianity has taken root.

4.1 The evangelization of the Greco-Roman Empire: apostles and martyrs

The story of the spread of Christianity, in whichever direction, begins with Pentecost. The book of Acts opens with the apostles waiting in Jerusalem, as Jesus had told them to do, expecting the 'power from on high' which would make them witnesses of the gospel in Jerusalem, in Judea and Samaria, and on to the ends of the earth (Acts 1.8). As 120 disciples – men and women – gathered in the upper room, they heard a sound like a rushing wind and tongues of flame appeared on their heads. They were empowered to go out and preach to those from across the Greco-Roman world, who were gathered in Jerusalem for the festival, in such a way that they all understood the message. Thousands joined them and partook in the fellowship in which they shared their possessions and broke bread together. At Pentecost the church was born, and it was already a church with a mission. It was also, from its inception, a worldwide church; the list of the nations represented in Acts 2.9–11 represents the early centres of the Christian faith.[5] The transformation of the disciples from frightened huddle to bold witnesses was due to the outpouring of the Holy Spirit. As the story of the Acts of the Apostles continues, we see the disciples testifying not only in Jerusalem but also in Judea (chaps 3—7), in Samaria (8.5–8), and beyond (chaps 9—28). The most famous of the early missionaries was Paul, who travelled across the Mediterranean Sea, establishing churches in provincial centres and other influential cities. He was supported by a network of other missionaries and co-workers, both men and women (Rom. 16.1–16).

Christianity began as a Jewish sect, but it was overwhelmingly Gentiles who responded to the message. The theology of the New Testament attempts to explain how the Messiah of the Jews is also the Saviour of the world, and how the death and resurrection of Jesus Christ opened the way for Gentiles to become equally members of the kingdom of God. As a Pharisee and also a citizen of the empire, Paul was well placed to facilitate the Hellenization of the Christian faith – a process which accelerated after the end of the first century when Jews and Christians distanced themselves from one another. Initially Christians met in homes, and only gradually developed institutional forms.[6] It was not until the conversion of Emperor Constantine – sometime between AD 312 and 315 – that Christianity became recognized as an official religion of the empire, and being a Christian became a sign of respectability. In the book of Acts, and in the first two centuries, the Christian missionary was regarded as a witness or a martyr. The two words are the same in Greek because bearing witness to Christ was risky; it could sometimes result in persecution and even death.

Reading the pages of the New Testament and other early literature shows that the first Christians were not afraid to witness in public on occasion, but that the gospel was more often shared among the household, through other friendships and networks, and through Christian literature. Before it was Christianized from above by the promotion of Christianity as the religion of state, the Greco-Roman Empire was evangelized from below as the good news was passed among ordinary people in their daily lives in a movement among the masses. It had a particular appeal to women, slaves and other disadvantaged groups.[7] Three motives for mission of the early Christians can be identified in the New Testament: gratitude for the salvation they had received; a sense of responsibility to share the message with others; and a concern for their neighbours.[8] The Apostle Paul summed up his motives of gratitude and responsibility in Romans 1.5 and 15.16, and Galatians 2.20, in the words 'grace and apostleship'. Although the apostles are often thought of as the 'pillars of the church' (Gal. 2.9), the word means 'messenger' and so designates someone who has awareness that they are sent, just as Jesus himself was sent into the world (John 20.21).

4.2 The Byzantine mission: priests and witnesses

The Greco-Roman Empire was one of the largest ever known and included many different peoples and cultures. In particular, it straddled a faultline running across the Mediterranean world from north to south between Latin-speaking peoples to the west and Greek-speakers to the east. This was a political problem for the empire, and it also led to tensions in the church. The church was organized into five patriarchates of Rome, Constantinople, Antioch, Alexandria and Jerusalem. A prototype ecumenical council is recorded in the New Testament as taking place in Jerusalem about AD 50 (Acts 15). Following this pattern, patriarchs and bishops from different regions met together to make decisions affecting the whole church at Nicaea in 325, at Constantinople in 381, at Ephesus in 431 and at Chalcedon in 451. By the fifth century the hugely diverse church, which stretched from the British Isles in the west to Persia in the east, was no longer able to agree decisions ecumenically. The first to separate were the churches of Asia that today are described as 'Oriental Orthodox', who found themselves unable to accept the Greek philosophical formulation of the doctrine of the two natures of Christ which was foreign to their languages and cultures.[9]

As the centre of empire the great metropolis of Rome had Christian migrant congregations from all parts of the empire; they communicated with one another in Greek, the lingua franca of empire rather than in the language of the local elite, Latin. They all practised their own local variations of the faith, including a different date for Easter. This state of affairs was problematic for Christian fellowship, and it was also threatening to Christian legitimacy and inhibited engagement with the political authorities. When Victor, a North African and Latin-speaker, was appointed Bishop of Rome in AD 189, he insisted in unifying the church calendar – even at the expense of excommunicating some who wished to maintain their own tradition, and laid the Latin foundations of the Church of Rome. Over the next few centuries, the patriarchate of Rome, which was the only one of the five to lie in the western part of the empire with its Latin culture, gradually separated itself from the other four. Rome became the centre of the Western or Roman Catholic Church, and Constantinople became the centre of the Eastern Orthodox family of churches. After the fall of the Greco-Roman Empire, the cultural and religious divisions persisted in the Holy Roman Empire in the west (800-1806) and the Byzantine Empire (527–1453) in the east. The Eastern and Oriental Orthodox churches kept much closer fellowship with one another than they did with Rome but are not in full communion with one another.

The Orthodox church spread within Byzantium, and to the four patriarchates were eventually added the archbishoprics of Cyprus and Sinai, the national churches of Russia, Greece, Armenia, Romania, Georgia, Bulgaria and others which exist today. Unlike the Roman Catholic Church, Orthodox believers did not constitute a single institutional church but several churches based on ethno-linguistic groups, which each adapted their liturgy and practices to some extent to their setting while remaining in communion with one another. The spread of the Orthodox faith to the Slavic peoples north of Byzantium began when the Greek church sent the monks Constantine (or Cyril) and Methodius (of Thessalonike) to Moravia in 863, where they reduced the Slavic language to writing first (creating the Cyrillic script) and then translated the Scriptures. Eventually in the early eleventh century, Vladimir, ruler of the Russians, sent a delegation to Constantinople to find out more about the Christian faith and, when their report impressed him, he converted to Christianity. Vladimir began the Christianization of Russia, which was accomplished not only by baptizing people but also by reorganizing the social structure to produce a more just society. Later Russian expansion, especially under Peter the Great from 1700, led to Russian Christianity spreading eastwards across the Ural Mountains into Central Asia, China and Siberia, and from there across the Aleutian Islands to Alaska (which belonged to Russia until sold to the United States in 1867) and down the west coast of North America.

The Western Crusaders who went to the Holy Land to reclaim the pilgrimage sites from Arab control were partly inspired by belief in Prester John, who controlled a large Christian empire in the East. However, when they did encounter other Christians who practised their faith significantly differently – in the shape of the Byzantine Christians – they attacked them. In 1204 the great Christian city of Constantinople or Byzantium was sacked not by Muslims but by Crusaders. The city did eventually fall to the (Muslim) Turks in 1453, after which Moscow became known as the 'new Constantinople' or the 'third Rome' because it became the leading centre of Orthodoxy. However, the Communist Revolution in Russia in 1917 put an end to the dominance of the church there and in other places in Eastern Europe. After many years of suffering under atheistic communism, in Russia and many of the newly independent countries of Eastern Europe and Central Asia, the Orthodox churches have experienced revival since the fall of the Berlin Wall in 1989 and the collapse of Communist regimes.[10] Being national churches, the Orthodox churches are often associated with nationalist movements and they tend to see themselves as the only legitimate form of Christianity in their territory. They have also expressed concern that over the centuries they have been victims of aggressive evangelism by the Roman Catholic Church and other Western churches, which many in formerly Orthodox lands have chosen to join. As a result Orthodox leaders encouraged the World Council of Churches to condemn proselytism as a 'corruption of Christian witness' in which 'cajolery, bribery, undue pressure or intimidation is used – subtly or openly

– to bring about seeming conversion'.[11] Although there are examples of Orthodox missions of conversion, the theology of mission mediated to the West emphasizes a centripetal model, in which Christians glorify Christ and live the new life in Christ in such a way that others will be attracted to come and experience this 'heaven on earth'.[12]

Eastern Orthodox theology is developed from the Nicene Creed and is distinct from Western theology in several respects, which affect Orthodox understanding of mission. In Orthodox thought, the church's primary role is, by the power of the Holy Spirit, to bear witness to Jesus Christ so glorifying God the Father (Acts 1.8; John 17.1). So the Orthodox image of a missionary is a saint rather than preacher (1 Thess. 1.15), and the Orthodox missionary enterprise (at its best) is manifesting the kingdom rather than annexing new territory (John 1.39). The primary locus of Christian witness is not the individual Christian missionary but the church in celebration of the liturgy. The Eucharist is a missionary event in which the people and things of the world are gathered up to God in prayer and the Holy Spirit is called down (invoked) to sanctify the earth through the offerings presented. As Romanian theologian Ion Bria has explained, the word 'liturgy' – *laos* (people) plus *ergon* (work) – is literally both the work of the people (on behalf of the world) and the celebration of work for the people (for the sake of the world). What goes on in church is representative of the mission of the people in their whole lives, so that mission can also be described as 'the liturgy after the liturgy' (Acts 2.42–7).[13] In other words, mission is worship – the offering of our lives, and worship is mission – the service of the people (Rom. 12.1).

In this model, mission is directed both outward and inward. It is both centripetal and centrifugal. It is not only going out into the world but also gathering the world in the church. This is why mission and unity are inseparable in the Orthodox theology. The Roman Catholic and Orthodox churches mutually excommunicated each other in 1054 but the initiative for the unity between East and West came from the Orthodox churches, who approached Protestants at the end of the nineteenth century. It was the Patriarch of Constantinople who first proposed a 'league of churches' as a precursor to what became the World Council of Churches.[14] The Orthodox theologians who have interpreted Orthodoxy to the West since the late nineteenth century have taken very seriously the prayer of Jesus that Christians should be one and believe that this unity is what testifies to God, the Three-in-One (John 17.20–3). They do not urge unity simply as a pragmatic measure to enhance missionary effectiveness but see mission as a movement for unity, because the result of Christian mission is the reconciliation of God, humanity and the whole universe: all will be gathered into one under Christ as head (Col. 1.20; Eph. 2.14–22).[15]

4.3 The spread of the Oriental Orthodox churches: merchants and sages

The spread of Christianity to the East did not stop at the borders of the Greco-Roman Empire. At Pentecost there were Jews from Parthia, Media, Elam and Mesopotamia, all beyond the eastern reaches of the empire. Later, the gospel was carried by merchants along the trade routes to Persia, India and China, and chains of monasteries were established as monks followed the trail. Trade and cultural influence was also in the other direction. The New Testament records that, at the birth of Jesus, 'wise men' or *magi* – from a Persian word for sage or astrologer – came from the east to worship him. The Christian Syrians and the Persians were non-Greeks and used the Syriac translation of the Bible, the *Peshitta*. Rejecting the Chalcedonian formulation, which stated that the Lord Jesus Christ was 'to be acknowledged in two natures, without confusion, without change, without division, or without separation', the Syrian or West Syrian Church emphasized the union of the two natures in Christ, the so-called 'monophysite' ('one nature') view. This tradition spread to Armenia, which became the first nation to declare itself Christian in 294, to Ethiopia, and to Egypt where the Coptic Church was formed.[16] The Persian Church, also known as Assyrian, East Syrian, or 'The Church of the East', adopted the so-called 'dyophysite' view attributed to Nestorius, which made more of the distinction between the divine and human natures of Christ. The Persian city states of Edessa, Oshroene and Arbela, and Adiabene were Christian by the end of the second century. Persecution by the Zoroastrian rulers led to a Persian Christian diaspora and the spread of Persian Christianity eastwards to Central Asia, China, Tibet and possibly Korea and Japan, and southwards to India (including what is now Pakistan), Ceylon, Burma, Siam (modern Thailand), Annam (North Vietnam), Malaya (Malaysia and Singapore), Java and Sumatra (in modern Indonesia).[17] Already the Council at Nicea in 325 included a representative of Persia and India.

The spread of Persian Christianity to China in the seventh to ninth centuries is a particularly fascinating story. In 1625 workmen near the city of Xian in north-west China were surprised to unearth a toppled monument, originally three metres high, covered in Chinese characters. These tell of Persian Christianity's arrival in China, give an outline of Christian doctrine, and describe the fortunes of a church that had existed in that region nearly a thousand years before. According to the monument, the 'Religion of Light' (Christianity) was brought by A-lo-pen, a Persian bishop, who arrived in Xian, then the capital of China, in 635. The tablet praises the wisdom of the emperor, who permitted the propagation of this 'Way' and allowed the establishment of a monastery. 'Way' (*dao*) is a Chinese word for a religion and also a Christian one (Acts 9.2). God, or *Alaha* – the Syriac word, is described as 'Three-One' (Trinity), inspirer of all wise men, or sages, who created the world and humankind, though humans were tempted by Satan and 'lost their way'. The inscription recounts the incarnation of the Second Person of the Trinity as a sage, born of a virgin in Syria, and includes a reference to the wise men from Persia. The divine and human nature of Jesus is mentioned but the two natures are separated, following Nestorius. The monument tells how Jesus Christ fulfilled the 'old law spoken by the sages' and established a new religion of the Holy Spirit (or

Holy Wind) of 'good works' and 'right faith'. It also relates the death, resurrection and ascension of Christ. This part of the text ends with descriptions of other aspects of Christian belief and practice: the New Testament, baptism, Christian worship and the Eucharist. In the final section we learn that Christianity had flourished in China until 698, when Buddhists caused controversy and later violence against Christians. However in 742 their fortunes had been restored by the emperor and at the time the monument was erected the Christians hoped to continue to influence China in the 'right way'.[18]

Having conducted detailed study of early Christianity in Asia, John C. England concludes that 'for many centuries the Church of the East included greater numbers over vastly greater distances than the churches of Rome or Byzantium'.[19] He also notes that the faith was spread not by imperial domination but by the witness of Christian believers, who travelled as holy men, or saints, or as merchants, and by the life of minority Christian communities, some of them displaced from their homelands. There are no Christian communities in China now that are directly descended from the Persian mission. Many reasons have been suggested for this; these include the suggestion that the faith was too inculturated and not distinctively Christian, or that Christianity was mainly practised by immigrant communities who later assimilated, voluntarily or by force, or were forced elsewhere.[20] However, it is possible that a residual ancient Christianity survived and was taken up into later Catholic missions in China.

Unlike the churches of Europe, the Oriental churches have experienced minority status for all of their history, and in recent centuries Eastern Orthodox Christians in many places have also faced discrimination and sometimes persecution. Both Eastern and Oriental Orthodox Christians were effectively cut off from the other Christian nations by the rise of the Arabs in the Eastern Mediterranean from the end of the seventh century, because they controlled the trade routes. Christians were expelled from Arabia. Elsewhere they were encouraged to convert to Islam but otherwise allowed to practise their faith as long as they surrendered their arms, paid a poll tax, refrained from criticizing Mohammad and the Qur'an, and made no public display of their religion. Muslims who converted to Christianity risked being killed. This system of *dhimmi* protected Christian (and Jewish) minorities but at the same time marginalized them. Gradually, however, over the next few centuries the pressures on Christians increased, and the majority of Christians under Islamic rule converted or were absorbed by marriage.[21] The rulers of the extensive Mongol empire (1227–1405) became Muslim from 1295, and also tended to discriminate against non-Muslim citizens. Nevertheless substantial Christian communities remain in Muslim lands to this day – the churches being the main way in which the different identities and heritages of the various peoples were preserved.

4.4 The Christianization of Western Europe: saints and seers

From Jerusalem after Pentecost the word also spread to the West. The Apostle Paul claimed to have preached the gospel from Jerusalem as far west as Illyricum and had plans to go on to Spain – the end of the known world at that time (Rom. 15.19, 28). The Western Roman Empire also included much of North Africa, and it was there where the most famous theologian of the Western church – Augustine of Hippo – was born, but in this section we will concentrate on the growth of the church in Europe, returning to Africa later. Paul did not get as far as Spain or Africa, but it seems he and St Peter did reach Rome, which became the most important Christian centre, especially after the destruction of the temple in Jerusalem in AD 70. The city of Rome, like any imperial capital, was a microcosm of the empire and within it were migrant churches from across the whole world. It was the need to defend Christianity against persecution and also the desire to influence Roman society for the better that encouraged the diverse churches in the city to come together and appoint a single bishop, Victor – also North African – in AD 189. The patriarch of Rome, who came to be known as the Pope, was regarded as the first among equals during the ecumenical period.

After the Christian faith was established as the religion of imperial Rome, following the conversion of Emperor Constantine, people flocked to the churches for baptism and church leaders became increasingly taken up with teaching and pastoral care of the local people. However, it was in the political interests of its rulers to evangelize the Barbarian tribes who were causing trouble along the empire's borders, and so the church co-operated with the state to turn its enemies into Christian brothers. The evangelization of Northern Europe could be described as from the top down, in contrast to the growth of early Mediterranean Christianity from the bottom up. Whereas, before Constantine, Christians had been oppressed by soldiers, now they could be portrayed as soldiers in the service of Christ. The missionary approach, backed by force, was to the rulers and chiefs of the tribal peoples, and their assent led to the conversion of whole people groups or nations.

The peoples to be evangelized included the Franks, a Germanic group along the Rhine who later spread into Gaul (which became France) and to Spain, whose king Clovis was baptized a Catholic around 500. This began the long alliance between the ruler of the Franks and the Roman pontiff, which came to be called 'the Holy Roman Empire' and reached its height under the Emperor Charlemagne. Other peoples were the Angles, Saxons and other groups of the northern German plains. These were reached through their relatives who had migrated to the British Isles. The peoples of these islands were the object of a mission sent from Rome by Pope Gregory the Great in 596 led by Augustine of Canterbury, and also by another missionary movement from Ireland into western Scotland, and from there to northern England. Ireland had already been brought to Christian faith in the fifth century by Patrick, who followed a Celtic rather than Roman pattern of belief and worship. The Irish mission to Britain was initiated by Columba (521–97), who established a base on the island of Iona. When the two missions from North and South encountered each other, it was found unthinkable that British Christianity should follow more than one set of practices, and at the Synod of Whitby (663–4) it was decided that Britain would come under the authority of Rome. After this, England became a base for wider missionary activity by missionary monks: Wilfrid (634–709) led the evangelization of the Saxons in England; Willibrord (658–739) was sent to the Frisians; and Boniface (680-754) was the apostle of Germany.[22] The rest of Northern Europe was evangelized gradually. The Finns and other peoples of the Baltic were the last to turn to Christianity, but by about 1400 virtually all the people of Europe professed Christianity.

As with subsequent missions to tribal people in many different parts of the world, the performance of signs and wonders was effective in proving the superiority of the Christian faith in encounter with their traditional gods. Boniface used a 'power encounter' method when he demonstrated the power of the Christian God over the old ones by chopping down the sacred oak of Thor, God of thunder, and using the wood to make a church. As a result he baptized many Germans, although later he died a martyr's death. This is an approach that seems to be advocated in the closing words of Mark's Gospel, which records signs which 'will accompany those who believe', including exorcism, new tongues, freedom from harm and healing (Mark 16.15–18), and recalls the challenge of Elijah to the prophets of Baal (1 Kings 18.20–40).

4.5 Medieval Roman Catholic missions: monks and soldiers

The ongoing Christianization of the European people was carried out through the monasteries.[23] The monasteries were centres of education and learning; they introduced new technological developments, especially in agriculture; they provided healthcare, gave alms and other help to the poor, and offered hospitality to pilgrims and other travellers. Though their later power and wealth somewhat obscured their religious purposes, generally the life of the monks was an example to the local population and the monasteries were the centres of a rural mission movement, which followed a centripetal model of witness that drew people in. In contrast, later religious orders, known as friars, who developed to evangelize the cities of the medieval period, went out (centrifugal) from the religious community to preach and meet the needs of people. Friars, who included the Dominicans and Franciscans, were mendicants who followed the instructions of Jesus when he sent out the disciples carrying no purse, and expecting to receive their living from those to whom they ministered (Mark 6.7–13 and parallels).

In the medieval period outgoing European Christian activity also took a violent form. The Crusades were a combination of holy war and pilgrimage intended to recover the Holy Lands from those regarded as 'infidels'. The ordinary men, women and even children who set off for the Holy Land were persuaded that it was acceptable to kill Muslims for the love of God. The result was a series of chaotic and ill-disciplined forays into the eastern Mediterranean which greatly increased the trail of bitterness in Christian–Muslim relations that lasts to the present day. It was not only the Muslims in the Holy Land who suffered: the Crusaders also did permanent damage to East–West church relations, especially after they sacked Constantinople; and the anti-Semitism of the time resulted in violence and rape against the Jewish population. There were, however, Christian leaders who believed there must be an alternative way of winning back the sacred sites. St Francis of Assisi (1182–1226) was one such, and he made three attempts to preach the gospel to the sultan of Egypt, believing that, if he only heard the gospel of Jesus Christ, he would believe. This was erroneous, as it turned out, but Francis continues to be revered for his peacemaking activities.[24]

The military model of mission that Francis opposed was continued, though in a metaphorical sense, by the next major initiative within Roman Catholicism. St Ignatius of Loyola (*c.*1491–1556) had been a soldier but, while recovering from injuries, was convicted of his sins and determined in future to be a 'soldier of Christ'. His famous programme of spiritual exercises, still in use today, was intended to discipline the Christian for service under Christ's banner. He founded the Society of Jesus, better known as the Jesuits, to meet the needs of the church in a period where the Catholic nations of Spain and Portugal were establishing colonies and trading posts across the world. The Jesuit order offered a centrally organized, highly trained 'force' of men who could be sent to different parts of the world for the advancement of the Christian faith. In keeping with Ignatius's high standards, the Jesuits specialized in scholarship and education. Famous Jesuit missionaries included Francis Xavier (1506–52), who served in India and Japan, Matteo Ricci (1552–1610), who went to China (see below), and Robert de Nobili (1577–1656), who worked among Brahmins in India.[25]

Many Jesuits, along with members of other orders, were sent to the Americas. The rapidly expanding merchant powers of Spain and Portugal were frequently frustrated by the Arab stranglehold on trade with Asia, or the 'Indies', through the eastern end of the Mediterranean. When Christopher Columbus, sailing west, became the first European to visit the Americas in 1492, although believing he was in the 'West Indies', he rejoiced for 'the expansion of Christendom' by which he meant both the 'great increase of larger realms and dominions' and also the spreading of 'the Holy Christian religion'.[26] For the 'Indians' of Latin America, however, a combination of brutal treatment, exposure to new diseases against which they had no resistance and despair led to perhaps 20 or 25 million deaths.[27] While the conquistadores set about extracting the wealth of the territory by conquest and exploitation of the people, the church was mandated by the Spanish rulers Ferdinand and Isabella to Christianize them. The missionaries baptized the people and then settled them in working villages, which greatly infringed their freedom, but offered some protection against slavery by the colonists (under the *encomienda* system) and suffering at the ruthless hands of the traders.[28] Though they may have mitigated its excesses, the missionaries were complicit in the programme of colonization of the Americas. Most did not challenge the injustices perpetrated upon the indigenous population, but one who did was Bartholomé de las Casas (1474–1566). After several years in the Americas, he concluded that the treatment of the Indians was wrong and tyrannical, and returned to Europe to persuade the Pope to recognize the rights of the native Americans.[29]

The situation for the people of Latin America was made worse by the rivalry between the colonial powers of Spain and Portugal. It was so intense that the Pope had to settle the dispute by the system of 'patronage', which divided the whole world into Spanish and Portuguese spheres. Brazil and everything to the east (including Africa, India and much of Indo-China) came under Portuguese jurisdiction. Spain retained the rest of the Americas, and the Pacific as far as the Philippines. The pattern of conquest and Christianization in the Americas could hardly be repeated in Asia, which was generally more densely populated and whose societies were often more sophisticated and stable than those of contemporary Europe. Only the Philippines was evangelized by the *encomienda* method by the Spanish from across the Pacific. When the Jesuit missionary Matteo Ricci entered in China in 1583, he was highly impressed by the level of learning and cultural development. He brought examples of Western technology and expounded Western philosophy, in order to gain a hearing at the imperial court, and when he had the opportunity to communicate the gospel he expressed it in Chinese terms. Ricci's approach was not shared by other Christian missionaries in China, however, particularly the Dominicans, who complained to Rome about Ricci's 'Chinese rites'. The controversy about the relationship between Christian faith and local culture was not resolved in the Roman Catholic Church until the mid-twentieth century. The Roman Catholic Church in China which was supported by the three 'pillars', the scholars Paul Hsu, Michael Yang and Leon Li, who also introduced Western science and philosophy to the nation, was weakened by the controversy and fell out of imperial favour when the rites were banned. Christians suffered greatly but the church was not destroyed and is the origin of the thriving Roman Catholic Christianity in China today.[30]

David Bosch has described the Roman Catholic mission paradigm as 'direct and indirect missionary war'. He explains that Christians believed the apostles in the first century had been obedient to the command of Christ to preach the gospel to the ends of the earth. Therefore, peoples who were not Christians were either heretics, who had fallen away from the truth of the gospel they had once heard, or infidels, or who wilfully refused to believe. The strong medieval belief in the punishment of hell for such people justified force, and even (in the case of the Inquisition) torture to get people to repent. One of the biblical verses used to support such an approach was Luke 14.23, where Jesus tells the disciples to go to the people in the highways and byways and 'compel them to come in'. William Burrows has countered that, alongside this more aggressive mode, on the ground in missionary work the more sympathetic approach of Ricci prevailed. Missionaries were prepared, like the Apostle Paul, to become 'all things to all men' (1 Cor. 9.22) and practised 'radical inculturation', re-expressing the gospel in terms the local people could understand, to win people for Christ.[31]

4.6 Protestant missions: preachers and teachers

Among the many ways in which the Reformation can be viewed is as a contextualization of the gospel for Northern Europe. The Western church split into several parts after the Protestant Reformation, which began in 1517, when Martin Luther pinned his theses for the reform of the church to the door of Wittenberg Castle Church in Germany. No longer did the princes of the North wish to be dominated by Rome, and they had the support of many of the people in wishing to define a more local identity in the form of national churches, which used the vernacular language. The Reformation was a stage in Northern Europe's journey from being an agrarian backwater to developing its own art, culture and institutions as it became more urban and industrial. Eventually its power was to eclipse that of Spain and Portugal, and successive North European powers would take over from them.

The Protestant Reformers, Luther, John Calvin and Huldrych Zwingli were concerned with the reform of the church and its pastoral responsibilities to the people of Europe. They inherited a territorial understanding of religions and gradually a pattern emerged where each of the emerging nations of Northern Europe had its own established church: Lutheran or Reformed in different German lands, Anglican in England and Wales, Presbyterian in Scotland, Reformed in the Netherlands, Lutheran in the Scandinavian countries and so on. There were some more radical Reformation movements, like the Anabaptists, who incurred the wrath of state rulers by disregarding the authority of their churches.[32] But so long as their flock remained in Europe, mainstream Protestants had no vision for worldwide mission. Furthermore, unlike the Roman Catholic Church, initially in Protestantism there was no mobile mission 'force' like the missionary orders, who could be sent to work overseas. However, Protestant views changed as Britain and other countries became colonial powers. Revd Thomas Bray (1658–1730) was an Anglican clergyman who, aware of the need to support the church in the overseas colonies, founded the Society for the Propagation of Christian Knowledge (SPCK) in 1698 to provide education and books and then, in 1701, the Society for the Propagation of the Gospel in Foreign Parts (SPG) to provide clergy assistance to the Anglican Church in the American colonies and elsewhere. What Bray did was to create a new structure which would allow missionary activity by Protestants overseas: the voluntary society.[33] By raising funds in this way, Bray was able to finance the support of missionary priests in the colonies.

John Wesley, whose later ministry to revive the Church of England led to the formation of the Methodist Church, went as an SPG missionary to Georgia, one of the American colonies. He went as a single man, and complications of love and other reasons led to a sense of failure in his mission. Wesley had practised an Anglo-Catholic spirituality from his Oxford days until his heart was 'strangely warmed' by loud prayer and emotional singing of the Moravians, whom he encountered on board ship and later in Aldersgate in London. They were a radical group who claimed a personal religious experience in the continental Pietist tradition which led them to imitate the first apostles in going to all nations to spread the gospel. Inspired by them, Wesley then took on his mission of reviving the church by preaching all over the country, especially to the unchurched of the industrial areas. The response to Wesley's preaching was known as the Evangelical Revival (1735–45), from which Methodism was born and which also led to widespread social transformation. Wesley's famous dictum, 'the world is my parish', was not primarily a statement of a world mission but an insistence that he did not regard himself as excluded from ministry when parish church pulpits were barred to him.[34] Nevertheless, it indicated a wideness of vision that refused to set limits on the work of God.

A further stage in the development of the modern missionary movement was signalled by William Carey (1761–1834), who founded the Baptist Missionary Society (BMS) in 1792. Carey was a cobbler in Northamptonshire but was remarkably well informed about international affairs as a result of the globalization brought about by the British colonization. Carey drew attention to the command of Jesus Christ to preach the gospel to all nations (Matt. 28.18–20; Mark 16.15–18), which Bray had also used to justify the SPG. Most of his fellow Baptists, in common with many Christians of the time, felt that this command was to the first apostles, who had fulfilled it. Furthermore, they took the line that humans were predestined to heaven or hell, and that the conversion of the heathen was God's sovereign act and not of human agency. In his famous pamphlet of 1792, Carey argued that what he called the 'Great Commission' was a continuing obligation on all Christians today, and furthermore, through the voluntary society and the infrastructure of British trade connections, God had provided the means to accomplish it. Carey was himself sent out by the

BMS to India. As a nonconformist he was not welcomed in the British colonies but established a mission compound at Serampore, which was Danish. There, together with William Ward and Joshua Marshman, he translated and printed the Bible in several different languages, engaged in dialogue with Indian leaders, and undertook educational, healthcare and agricultural projects. Carey's famous maxim was 'Expect great things from God; attempt great things for God', and he became the archetype of the entrepreneurial 'modern missionary'.[35]

Successive Evangelical revivals each tended to spawn new movements supporting different interests. These ranged from the abolition of slavery to the reform of prisons, the provision of Sunday schools and overseas missions. Evangelicals like William Wilberforce were leading social reformers in the early nineteenth century but later Evangelicals withdrew from social involvement. Partly due to events in the USA (see Chapter 7), they ceased to believe there was hope for the world, and instead insisted that the Christian mission was primarily to save souls for a life after death. At the revival which began in 1857, which popularized the hymnody of Ira Sankey, the evangelist D. L. Moody preached that mission was like pulling drowning people out of the water and into a lifeboat. His 'premillennialist' view was supported by Matthew 24.14, which he interpreted to mean that proclaiming the gospel in all the earth would hasten the inevitable end, when Christ would save those who believed in him from the destruction.[36] James Hudson Taylor was influenced by Moody and had a great concern for 'China's millions', all those people in China who, Taylor believed, needed only to hear the gospel and acknowledge Jesus Christ as Lord to avoid a lost eternity. He argued the urgency of preaching the gospel in inland China, because this was not being reached by most missions, which were based in the so-called 'treaty ports' on the coast. Though he used his knowledge of medicines to win a hearing, for him this was a means to an end, which was the conversion of souls. The China Inland Mission (CIM) was founded in 1865. It was non-denominational in the sense that it was not part of any denomination and the churches it founded were local independent congregations. So as not to compete with denominational missions, Taylor laid down that missionaries should live 'by faith alone'; that is, they should not solicit funds but take their needs to God in prayer and ask him to meet them. He was convinced that 'God's work done in God's way will never lack God's supplies'.[37] Many more such 'faith missions' with specialist ministries were founded in the late nineteenth century.[38]

Taylor married twice and regarded both his first wife Maria and his second Jenny as partners with him in missionary activity. Not being constrained by denominational structures, he also encouraged the ministry of single women. This was in marked contrast to William Carey who had persisted in his plan to go to India despite his wife Dorothy's protestations. Carey and his supporters saw Dorothy's inability to cope and eventual mental illness as another cross he had to bear, rather than as a sign that wives also needed a sense of call and training for missionary life.[39] As well as using channels such as the CIM, women also joined together in this period to form their own mission societies to support missionary activities and send their single sisters to the 'mission fields', especially for work to improve the lives of women. Famous women missionaries of the period include Amy Carmichael (1867–1951), who rescued temple prostitutes in South India, and Charlotte 'Lottie' Moon (1840–1912), who was an evangelist in China.[40] R. Pierce Beaver has argued that this women's missionary movement was the first feminist movement, predating the movement for women's suffrage by several decades.[41] Many women found a freedom in ministry overseas which was denied to them at home. Such was women's commitment to foreign mission that by 1900 the ratio of women to men in the field was 2:1; roughly half the women were there as wives (who might also be engaged in mission activities) and the others were single. On the 'mission field' countless 'bible women' supported the missionary effort as evangelists and local organizers and at home women were eager fund-raisers.[42]

The modern Protestant mission paradigm was based on the obligation to fulfil the 'Great Commission' (Matt. 28.18–20) by going to all nations to make disciples; this was generally understood as converting the natives to Christianity, or as 'civilizing' them. Often these amounted to the same thing and in the colonial period most agencies were involved in education, healthcare and other ways of meeting the practical needs of the people as well as in preaching. But with the rise of the Faith Missions, with their emphasis on the urgent need of individual conversion, a divergence gradually appeared between those who stressed the 'Social Gospel' and others who concentrated on proclamation of the message. The split was most marked in the United States, which after World War Two became the largest missionary sending country.

Colonial missionaries generally operated from a mission compound, often in a rural setting, which (like the monasteries of the medieval period) included a church, a school, a hospital and other facilities. Because they found it difficult to co-operate with one another, agreement was reached between the mainstream Protestant churches to divide up the countries where they were working into different spheres of influence, under a system referred to as 'comity' (which bore similarities to the Roman Catholic 'patronage'). By the high imperial period, it was clear that Europeans felt a special responsibility – sometimes referred to as 'the white man's burden', because of their presumed superiority to other races, to meet the needs of the 'heathen', who were understood to be calling them to 'come over and help us' (Acts 16.9).[43] Evangelical missionaries were joined by Roman Catholic missions revived in France[44] and the Anglo-Catholic missionaries of the Oxford movement.[45] Christian missionaries of all kinds usually failed to distinguish themselves and their motives from those of the colonists and imperialists. Missionaries and their work almost always enjoyed the protection of the imperial power, whose interests they were perceived to be supporting, and local churches were dominated by foreign missionaries. Missionaries were feted at home but scant recognition was given to local people who did the basic work of evangelism.

4.7 The evangelization of Africa and black Christianity: slaves and prophets

At this point we need to backtrack chronologically and look at the spread of Christianity at Pentecost in the third direction – to the South, and particularly to Africa, which was represented by Jewish believers from Egypt and Cyrene at that event. There is a long connection in the Old Testament between Israel and Africa. According to the story of the exodus the people of Israel lived in Egypt, having fled there from famine in the time of Joseph, until they were liberated by Moses (Gen. 42—50; Ex. 1—15). Egypt again became a place of refuge for Jesus' parents soon after he was born (Matt. 2.13–23). There are several references in the New Testament to Christians from the African continent. Simon of Cyrene, who carried Jesus' cross (Mark 15.21), and his sons Rufus and Alexander were from among the Greek-speaking Jewish communities of North Africa. From their home town came some who preached to the Gentiles in Antioch (Acts 11.20). The teachers there included Lucius from Cyrene and 'Simeon who was called Niger [black]' (Acts 13.1). Apollos, whose rival missionary work caused problems for the Apostle Paul, was an Alexandrian Jew (Acts 18.24; cf. 1 Cor. 3). But the most striking hint in the New Testament that Christianity was to take root in Africa comes in the way that the narrative of the Acts of the Apostles, which moves from Jerusalem westwards to Rome, is interrupted by the story of Philip's encounter with an Ethiopian courtier, who took baptism (Acts 8.26–40).

The church in Carthage, a cosmopolitan city of North Africa and home of the theologian Tertullian (*c.* 160–220) and later Augustine of Hippo, was first recorded when several local believers were killed in 180. These included two women, Perpetua and her slave Felicitas, whose fearless testimony raised the profile of Christianity in the region. The North African churches were administered by the patriarchate of Rome, but many of its zealous Christians, who suffered particularly under persecution by the emperor Diocletian, split from the emerging

Catholic Church in the Donatist schism of the fourth and fifth centuries for fear of compromising their faith. The Donatists claimed the doctrine of Cyprian, Bishop of Carthage, that 'there is no salvation outside the church'. In the five centuries following its conquest by Arab Muslim armies, Christianity all but disappeared from North Africa. Several theories have been advanced to explain this: because it lacked indigenous roots, because of political and economic incentives to convert, or because most Christians fled north to Spain.[46]

Further east along the coast, the Christian community in Alexandria was established very early, and almost certainly among the very large Jewish community in the city. Mark the Evangelist is said to have been the first to preach the gospel in the city. Christianity spread rapidly among the Egyptian masses, the Copts, who translated the Scriptures in the first two centuries and made the gospel their own. The teaching of Athanasius, Bishop of Alexandria (*c.* 293–373), became the basis of the Nicene Creed. The Coptic Church did not adopt the declaration of Chalcedon (451), however, preferring to express its national identity through a 'monophysite' theology. In the deserts of Egypt and Arabia lived Christian ascetics, whose extreme devotion soon attracted Christian leaders from around the world. The rulebook for ascetic community life written by the Egyptian Pachomius (292–346) became the basis for Christian monasticism, both East and West. Christians were in a majority in Egypt until the tenth century, but were gradually marginalized by Arab rule and successive waves of Arab immigration. Today Copts number only 6 per cent of the population but they are the largest Christian population in the Middle East and underwent a renewal in the late twentieth century. However, in the face of increased discrimination, Coptic Christians have joined the exodus of Christians from the Middle East which has accelerated in recent years.[47]

The existence of Christianity in Ethiopia was reported by Clement of Alexandria in the second century, reputedly begun by the Apostle Matthew. Firm historical evidence dates from the mid-fourth century when the king of Axum – a kingdom independent of either Rome or Persia – became a Christian according to the Catholic-Orthodox tradition through the agency of a Syrian missionary, Frumentius. The Church in Ethiopia, nominally under the Coptic Bishop of Alexandria, developed its own distinctive style of worship in its own language and unique traditions of music and dance. Many practices preserve aspects of the teaching of the Old Testament, in which Ethiopia (Cush) is called to 'stretch out its hands to God' (Ps. 68.31), such as dietary and purity rules, its claim to hold the original Ark of the Covenant and its emphasis on Solomon's liaison with the Queen of Sheba (1 Kings 10) – Sheba is believed to be in Ethiopia. The church was closely bound up with a feudal society that successfully fended off attempted Arab invasions and Western attempts at colonization, but in the Communist Revolution of 1974 it was deprived of its wealth and lands. About half the Ethiopian population remains Christian today – mostly Orthodox. Ethiopia has become an inspiration for African nationalism and a justification for modern independent black African churches.[48]

The Christian message probably only reached Africa south of the Sahara in the fifteenth century as the Portuguese began to establish trading posts, which also dealt in slaves, from the Cape Verde islands down the west coast, around the Cape and up the east coast en route to India. Only in Angola and Mozambique was there significant indigenous response to Portuguese efforts at evangelization. This was repeatedly undermined by the slave trade but supported by black priests from the Cape Verde islands.[49] Today, independent from the Portuguese, these countries are major centres of African Catholicism. The British gradually took over most of the other Portuguese interests in Africa and continued the slave trade. After three-and-a-half centuries, during which between 9 and 15 million Africans were imported to the Americas (and some to Europe), the result was the creation of the 'black Atlantic', a diaspora of people of African descent spread through the Americas and Europe with a particular concentration in the Caribbean islands.[50] In Africa black civilizations were weakened and people groups were set against each other by slave-trading. Across the American continent black people were constantly humiliated and ill-treated and, even after the ending of slavery and overt segregation, most continue to face discrimination.

The evangelization of the 'black Atlantic' took place by several different means. Western churches and mission agencies evangelized slaves in the Americas and taught them in churches which the agencies organized – although slave owners sometimes objected to this because of the recognition it implied for the slaves' human rights and lost Sunday labour. European evangelizing activities in Africa in the nineteenth century were inseparable from efforts to end slavery.[51] In 1787 and in 1822 British and American agencies founded Sierra Leone and Liberia, respectively, as homelands for freed slaves. With a similar end in view to bring 'Christianity and commerce' to central Africa, David Livingstone, who began as a missionary of the London Missionary Society based in modern South Africa, opened up the African interior to trade and mission work in the 1860s, while Roman Catholic missions worked among freed slaves in East Africa.[52] Although foreign missionaries were relatively numerous and active from the later nineteenth century, that the Christian message took root in Africa to such a great extent is largely due to the efforts of Africans themselves. Freed slaves spread the gospel to other Africans, such as George Lisle, a freed slave from the US state of Virginia, who founded the Baptist church in Jamaica in 1783. Soon black missionaries were being sent from the Caribbean to Africa. At least 115 black US Americans are known to have served as missionaries in Africa in the last quarter of the nineteenth century, supported from the limited resources of churches of recently freed slaves.[53] The most famous nineteenth-century African missionary is Samuel Ajayi Crowther (*c.* 1807–91), a Yoruba who, in his efforts to translate the Christian Scriptures, laid the foundations of Yoruba literature and ethnic identity. Ordained as the first African bishop of the Anglican Church he led two decades of missionary work until he was undermined by Western missionaries.[54] In East Africa, black evangelists, many of them employed by Western missions, crossed cultural boundaries and spread the gospel at great personal risk just as Western missionaries did. Their stories and those of others from across the continent are only now being gathered as a testimony.[55] The good news was also carried by lay Christians who were part of the great migrations across the continent as Africa has encountered the modern world.[56]

4.8 Mission from everywhere to everywhere

Of the 20 native Christians listed as present at the Edinburgh 1910 conference, only one was African, and this is indicative of the fact that Africans were least well regarded among the other races at that time and so missionary control was stronger in African churches than elsewhere. Africans reacted to this by a series of independence movements and the formation of new churches led by African prophet-leaders (see Chapter 8). Nowadays the African Independent, or African Initiated, Churches (AICs) are commonly treated as part of one movement of global Pentecostalism. Pentecostalism is seen to have a number of roots but one of the strongest is in black Christianity.[57] Many of the characteristics of Pentecostal-style worship are found in black spirituality more generally – both in sub-Saharan Africa and in the African diasporas. Walter Hollenweger, formerly at the University of Birmingham, identified the beginnings of Pentecostalism in a revival which took place in Azusa Street in Los Angeles in 1906. The revival was led by William Seymour, an African American, but attracted people of many different races in what was a very cosmopolitan city. The congregation drew on the deep roots of black spirituality as well as on the traditions of the Holiness movement, which grew out of John Wesley's ministry. Hollenweger's argument for the priority of Azusa Street was not because it was historically the first movement to be described as Pentecostal or because it gave birth to all the others (although it was an extremely influential event worldwide) but because he saw it as the prototype of what he saw as central to Pentecostalism: the breaking down of social barriers.[58] Azusa Street resulted in a number of new denominations, of which the largest is the black-majority Church of God in Christ. The revival in Los Angeles also broke barriers in another respect. Free from the constraints of traditional church life, women played a prominent role in worship, including Jennie Moore who became Seymour's wife.

The historical origins of Pentecostalism are very complex. It seems that there were many revivals of a similar kind in different parts of the world in the early twentieth century: Wales in 1904–5, Pune and the Khasi Hills in India in 1905, Korea in 1907, Oslo and Sunderland in 1907, Valparaiso (Chile) in 1909, Lagos (Nigeria) in 1918, and many others. Some of these were connected with Azusa Street but Pentecostals in other parts of the world dispute claims that Pentecostalism originated in North America and argue that it is a worldwide, polycentric indigenous movement.[59] Pentecostal-type spirituality crossed into the older Christian churches in the charismatic movement which began in the 1960s within the Roman Catholic Church in the USA. Charismatic Christianity also developed as a non-denominational movement, in which Christians meet in fellowships or house churches such as Vineyard and New Wine. Neo-Pentecostalism is the result of the preaching of televangelists and others who have a message of blessing and prosperity for those who believe. Charismatic leaders have built up 'mega-churches' in different cities of the world, which not only have huge congregations locally but are also multiplying globally. Examples include Yoido Full Gospel Church in Seoul and the Redeemed Christian Church of God in Lagos.

Pentecostalism is the fastest growing form of Christianity today. It may be regarded as a 'globalization from below', or even an Africanization of Christianity, which may determine the shape of Christianity in the twenty-first century.[60] Allan Anderson, Professor of Global Pentecostalism at the University of Birmingham, defines Pentecostalism not as a denomination or a system of beliefs but as a particular form of worship, which is understood as an experience of the Holy Spirit. He lists four universal characteristics of Pentecostal-type worship:

first, Pentecostals emphasize the immediate presence of God at the worship service; second, they expect some sign of miraculous or powerful intervention from God during it; third, they encourage congregational participation, especially praise and prayer; fourth, there is one preacher, who leads the worship and calls for response. Speaking in tongues, which is emphasized by some groups as the definitive sign of baptism in the Spirit or fullness of the Spirit, is not understood this way by all. Other widespread features include: an oral, rather than written liturgy; spontaneity, applause and laughter; dancing and singing as part of worship; practice of simultaneous loud praying; the exercise of 'gifts of the Spirit' (1 Cor. 12–14; Rom. 12.3–8); evidence of 'signs and wonders', including healing; personal testimony to what God has done and a general emphasis on experiencing the Spirit of God; frequent use of interjections such as 'amen' and 'hallelujah'; and the interpretation of dreams and utterances in 'tongues'.[61]

Many different reasons have been suggested for the growth of Pentecostal-charismatic Christianity. Harvey Cox speculated that it represented the resurgence in a Christian form of a 'primal' religiosity common to all people in the fluid and millennialist conditions of the late twentieth century.[62] Sociologist David Martin has argued that the movement is peculiarly suited to the conditions of late modernity, in which it provides the poor, dispossessed and migrants with a place to feel at home and with social benefits (see Chapter 8).[63] Some researchers focus on the strategies put in place by church leaders to promote growth, such as cell groups.[64] Material inducement is another factor. Many are critical of theologies of blessing which lead people to expect material prosperity and healing as a result of believing in Jesus Christ, although others insist that material well-being cannot be separated from the gospel message.[65] Anderson points to the inherently missionary nature of Pentecostalism, which means that each new revival spawns efforts at evangelism.[66] And leading Pentecostal theologian Amos Yong shows that the Pentecostal narrative itself is oriented toward reaching out across barriers.[67] Ultimately, for most Pentecostals and charismatics, their growth is inexplicable except as an outpouring of the blessing of the Holy Spirit.

It is not possible to mention all the different movements of the Spirit which led to the growth of Christianity worldwide or all the countries of the world where Christianity has taken hold. We have omitted, for example, to say anything about the growth of churches in Australia and New Zealand among white settlers, indigenous people and more recent migrants, or to discuss the spread of the gospel across the Pacific, often by the islanders themselves. But, we should note that, much to the surprise of commentators who regarded Christianity as a superficial colonial import, the most striking Christian growth took place in colonized countries after independence.[68] A 'Christian missionary' is often assumed to be white but we have already mentioned black missionaries and evangelists. As we go on we shall see that the gospel was spread around the world in the colonial period primarily by the efforts of the colonized people themselves. Now the non-biological growth of the church is largely the result of local mission activity in all continents. Internationally also mission personnel are changing as agencies internationalize. Roman Catholic missionary orders often have personnel in and from many different countries of the world and new orders have been founded in what were once considered 'mission fields'. Shortages of clergy in Western countries have led to the importing of priests from parts of the world where Christianity is growing rapidly. Although often not recognized as cross-cultural missionaries, their work demands similar skills. Furthermore, alongside organized mission activities, there are many unorganized ways in which the gospel is carried around the world: for example, by trafficking and migration movements within and between regions.

In Britain, it is sometimes said, we are undergoing 'reverse mission' as Christians from former colonized countries in Africa, Asia and the Americas look at the decline of the historic churches in the West and conclude that the 'great commission' to preach the gospel to the whole creation now falls on their shoulders.[69] Interest in the phenomenon in Northern Europe has centred on African migrants, particularly West Africans, who found their own churches and also reach out to local people.[70] The largest single congregation in the UK, Kingsway International Christian Church, is Nigerian-led, as is Europe's largest church in Ukraine. But the movement from West Africa is only one of a number of 'reverse missions' in Europe. Brazilians are active in Spain and Portugal, for example, and Francophone Africans in France. Most major European cities now have Christian churches among some of their newer communities, which also include Chinese, Korean and Tamil (from South India). The pastors of these churches may often be regarded as missionaries, and members of the congregation may also see themselves in this way. The most organized and intentional transnational mission activity is from South Korea, which is the second largest missionary sending country in the world, after the USA.

In one sense history has come full circle. Like ancient Rome, our cities now have many different ethnic congregations, and worldwide we have many diverse forms of Christianity, and different understandings of mission. When mission is 'from everywhere to everywhere',[71] whether and how we can recognize and accommodate one another is perhaps our greatest challenge today.

Notes

1 John C. England, *The Hidden History of Christianity in Asia: The Churches of the East before 1500* (Delhi: ISPCK, 1996), p. 2.

2 Samuel Hugh Moffett, *A History of Christianity in Asia, Volume I: Beginnings to 1500* (Maryknoll, NY: Orbis Books, 2001), pp. 433–4.

3 Much of the historical material in this chapter can be found in recent world histories of Christianity, the most outstanding of which is: Dale T. Irvin and Scott W. Sunquist, *History of the World Christian Movement. Vol I: Earliest Christianity to 1453* (Maryknoll, NY: Orbis Books, 2001). See also: Timothy Yates, *The Expansion of Christianity* (Oxford: Lion Publishing, 2004); Frederick W. Norris, *Christianity: A Short Global History* (Oxford: Oneworld, 2002); John McManners (ed.), *The Oxford History of Christianity*, 2nd edn (Oxford: Oxford University Press, 2002); Adrian Hastings (ed.), *A World History of*

Christianity (London: Cassell, 1999); Paul R. Spickard and Kevin M. Cragg, *A Global History of Christians: How Everyday Believers Experienced Their World* (Grand Rapids, MI: Baker Academic, 1994).

4 David J. Bosch, *Transforming Mission: Paradigm Shifts in Theology of Mission* (Maryknoll, NY: Orbis Books, 1991).

5 Amos Yong, *The Spirit Poured Out on All Flesh: Pentecostalism and the Possibility of Global Theology* (Grand Rapids, MI: Baker Academic, 2005), pp. 171–6.

6 Elisabeth Schüssler Fiorenza, *In Memory of Her: A Feminist Theological Reconstruction of Christian Origins* (London: SCM Press, 1983), pp. 160–204.

7 Irvin and Sunquist, *History of the World Christian Movement. Vol I*, pp. 25–44.

8 Bosch, *Transforming Mission*, pp. 133–5.

9 Irvin and Sunquist, *History of the World Christian Movement. Vol I*, pp. 191–4.

10 Darrell Jackson, 'Pax Europa: Crux Europa', in Timothy Yates (ed.), *Mission and the Next Christendom* (Sheffield: Cliff College, 2005), pp. 85–106.

11 World Council of Churches, 'Christian Witness, Proselytism and Religious Liberty in the Setting of the World Council of Churches', *Ecumenical Review* 9/1 (October 1956), pp. 48–56. Cf. World Council of Churches, 'Towards Common Witness: A Call to Adopt Responsible Relationships in Mission and to Renounce Proselytism' (1997), in Jacques Matthey (ed.), *'You Are the Light of the World': Statements on Mission by the World Council of Churches 1980–2005* (Geneva: WCC Publications, 2005), pp. 42–58 – available at <www.oikoumene.org>.

12 Ion Bria (ed.), *Go Forth in Peace: Orthodox Perspectives on Mission* (Geneva: WCC Publications, 1986), pp. 10–12.

13 Ion Bria, *The Liturgy after the Liturgy: Mission and Witness from an Orthodox Perspective* (Geneva: WCC Publications, 1996).

14 Nicolas Zernov, 'The Eastern Churches and the Ecumenical Movement in the twentieth century', in Ruth Rouse and Stephen Charles Neill (eds), *A History of the Ecumenical Movement, Vol. 1, 1517–1948*, 4th edn (Geneva: WCC Publications, 1993), pp. 645–76, at p. 654.

15 Bria, *Go Forth in Peace*, pp. 69–72.

16 Today the St Thomas Christians of India are mostly Syrian but the church was probably founded by a Persian merchant, Thomas of Cana, although legend has it that Thomas the disciple of Jesus first spread the gospel there. See Irvin and Sunquist, *History of the World Christian Movement, Vol I*, pp. 93–5.

17 Irvin and Sunquist, *History of the World Christian Movement,*

Vol I, pp. 57–65, 195–208, 271–88; Moffett, *History of Christianity in Asia, Volume I.*

18 England, *Hidden History of Christianity in Asia*; Moffett, *History of Christianity in Asia, Volume I*, pp. 287–323.

19 England, *Hidden History of Christianity in Asia*, p. 2.

20 Irvin and Sunquist, *History of the World Christian Movement, Vol I*, pp. 320–2; Moffett, *History of Christianity in Asia, Volume I*, pp. 287–323.

21 For further discussion of the experience of Christians in Muslim lands, see Rollin Armour, *Islam, Christianity, and the West: A Troubled History* (Maryknoll, NY: Orbis Books, 2002); Colin Chapman, *Whose Promised Land? The Continuing Crisis over Israel and Palestine* (Oxford: Lion, 2002).

22 Irvin and Sunquist, *History of the World Christian Movement. Vol I*, pp. 327–41; Henry Mayr-Harting, 'The West: The Age of Conversion (700–1050)', in McManners, *Oxford History of Christianity*, pp. 101–29, at pp. 101–10.

23 Bosch, *Transforming Mission*, pp. 230–6; Stephen B. Bevans and Roger P. Schroeder, *Constants in Context: A Theology of Mission for Today* (Maryknoll, NY: Orbis Books, 2004), pp. 119–29.

24 Armour, *Islam, Christianity, and the West*, pp. 61–79; Bevans and Schroeder, *Constants in Context*, pp. 142–4.

25 Bevans and Schroeder, *Constants in Context*, pp. 183–91.

26 Christopher Columbus, *The Log of Christopher Columbus*, trans. Robert H. Fuson (Southampton: Ashford Press Publishing, 1987), pp. 195, 105.

27 Gustavo Gutiérrez, *Las Casas: In Search of the Poor of Jesus Christ*, trans. Robert R. Barr (Maryknoll, NY: Orbis Books, 1993 [1992]), pp. 461–4.

28 Enrique Dussel, *A History of the Church in Latin America*, trans. Alan Neely (Grand Rapids, MI: Wm B. Eerdmans, 1981), pp. 49–61.

29 Gutiérrez, *Las Casas*.

30 Ka-Lun Leung, 'China', in Scott W. Sunquist (ed.), *A Dictionary of Asian Christianity* (Grand Rapids, MI: Wm B. Eerdmans, 2001), pp. 139–46.

31 William R. Burrows, 'A Seventh Paradigm? Catholics and Radical Inculturation', in Willem Saayman and Klippies Kritzinger (eds), *Mission in Bold Humility: David Bosch's Work Considered* (Maryknoll, NY: Orbis Books, 1996), pp. 121–38.

32 Andrew F. Walls, *The Cross-cultural Process in Christian History: Studies in the Transmission and Appropriation of Faith* (Maryknoll, NY: Orbis Books, 2002), p. 37.

33 Daniel O'Connor (ed.), *Three Centuries of Mission: The United Society for the Propagation of the Gospel, 1701–2000* (London: Con-

tinuum, 2002); cf. Andrew F. Walls, *The Missionary Movement in Christian History: Studies in the Transmission of Faith* (Maryknoll, NY: Orbis Books, 1996), pp. 241–54.

34 Henry D. Rack, *Reasonable Enthusiast: John Wesley and the Rise of Methodism*, 3rd edn (London: Epworth Press, 2002), p. 189.

35 William Carey, *An Enquiry into the Obligation of Christians to Use Means for the Conversion of the Heathens* (Leicester: Ann Ireland, 1792); Brian Stanley, *The History of the Baptist Missionary Society, 1792–1992* (Edinburgh: T&T Clark, 1992); Walls, *Missionary Movement in Christian History*, pp. 243–7.

36 George M. Marsden, *Fundamentalism and American Culture*, 2nd edn (Oxford: Oxford University Press, 2006), pp. 37–8; Peter Williams, *America's Religions: Traditions and Cultures* (New York: Macmillan, 1990), p. 254.

37 Howard Taylor, *Biography of James Hudson Taylor* (London: CIM/OMF, 1965), p. 171.

38 James Hudson Taylor, *China's Spiritual Need and Claims* (London, 1865); Alfred Broomhall, *Hudson Taylor and China's Open Century*, 7 vols (London: Hodder and Stoughton, 1982–9); Klaus Fiedler, *The Story of Faith Missions* (Oxford: Regnum, 1994).

39 Ruth A. Tucker, *From Jerusalem to Irian Jaya: A Biographical History of Christian Missions* (Grand Rapids, MI: Zondervan, 1983), pp. 114–21, 173–88.

40 Tucker, *From Jerusalem to Irian Jaya*, pp. 234–42.

41 R. Pierce Beaver, *American Protestant Women in World Mission* (Grand Rapids, MI: Wm B. Eerdmans, 1980).

42 See Tucker, *From Jerusalem to Irian Jaya*, pp. 9–10, 61–2; Ruth A. Tucker and Walter Liefeld, *Daughters of the Church: Women and Ministry from New Testament Times to the Present* (Grand Rapids, MI: Zondervan, 1987), pp. 239–58; see also Dana Lee Robert, *American Women in Mission* 2nd edn (Macon, GA: Mercer University Press, 1997); Cathy Rae Ross, *Women with a Mission: Rediscovering Missionary Wives in Early New Zealand* (Auckland, NZ: Penguin, 2006); Rhonda Semple, *Missionary Women: Gender, Professionalism, and the Victorian Idea of Christian Mission* (Rochester, NY: Boydell Press, 2003).

43 Bosch, *Transforming Mission*, pp. 289–91.

44 Bevans and Schroeder, *Constants in Context*, pp. 221–6.

45 For example, in the Pacific: Sara Sohmer, 'Anglican Tradition and Mission: Sources for Mission Methodology in the Nineteenth Century Pacific', in O'Connor, *Three Centuries of Mission*, pp. 301–13, at pp. 309–13.

46 Elizabeth Isichei, *A History of Christianity in Africa, from Antiquity to the Present* (Grand Rapids, MI: Wm B. Eerdmans, 1995),

p. 44; Kevin Ward, 'Africa', in Hastings, *World History of Christianity*, pp. 192–237, at pp. 193–4.

47 Anthony O'Mahony, 'The Politics of Religious Renewal: Coptic Christianity in Egypt', in Anthony O'Mahony (ed.), *Eastern Christianity: Studies in Modern History, Religion and Politics* (London: Melisende, 2004), pp. 66–111.

48 Isichei, *History of Christianity in Africa*, pp. 32–3; Christine Chaillot, *The Ethiopian Orthodox Tewahedo Church Tradition: A Brief Introduction to Its Life and Spirituality* (Paris: Inter-Orthodox Dialogue, 2002); Joachim Persoon, 'Between Ancient Axum and Revolutionary Moscow: The Ethiopian Church in the Twentieth Century', in O'Mahony, *Eastern Christianity*, pp. 160-214; Walls, *Cross-cultural Process in Christian History*, pp. 90–1.

49 Isichei, *History of Christianity in Africa*, pp. 52–67.

50 Paul Gilroy, *The Black Atlantic: Modernity and Double Consciousness* (London: Verso, 1993).

51 Walls, *Cross-cultural Process in Christian History*, pp. 94–5.

52 Ward, 'Africa', pp. 213–6; Lamin Sanneh, 'The CMS and the African transformation: Samuel Ajayi Crowther and the Opening of Nigeria', in Kevin Ward and Brian Stanley (eds), *The Church Mission Society and World Christianity, 1799–1999* (Grand Rapids, MI: Wm B. Eerdmans, 2000), pp. 173–97.

53 Isichei, *History of Christianity in Africa*, pp. 166–7.

54 Sanneh, 'CMS and the African Transformation', pp. 193–4; Ward, 'Africa', pp. 208–9; Walls, *Cross-cultural Process in Christian History*, pp. 163–4.

55 For example, Louise Pirouet, *Black Evangelists: The Spread of Christianity in Uganda, 1891–1914* (London: Collings, 1978); *Dictionary of African Christian Biography* website, <www.dacb.org>.

56 Walls, *Missionary Movement in Christian History*, p. 87; Emma Wild-Wood, *Migration and Christian Identity in Congo (DRC)* (Leiden: Brill, 2008).

57 Walter J. Hollenweger, *Pentecostalism: Origins and Developments Worldwide* (Peabody, MA: Hendrickson Publishers, 1997), pp. 17–141.

58 Hollenweger, *Pentecostalism*, pp. 18–24.

59 See Allan Anderson, *An Introduction to Pentecostalism* (Cambridge: Cambridge University Press, 2004), pp. 166–83; Juan Sepúlveda, 'Indigenous Pentecostalism and the Chilean Experience', in Allan H. Anderson and Walter J. Hollenweger (eds), *Pentecostals after a Century: Global Perspectives on a Movement in Transition* (Sheffield: Sheffield Academic Press, 1999), pp. 111–34; Everett A. Wilson, 'They Crossed the Red Sea, Didn't They? Critical History and Pentecostal Beginnings', in Murray W. Dempster, Byron D. Klaus and Douglas Petersen (eds),

The Globalization of Pentecostalism: A Religion Made to Travel (Oxford: Regnum, 1999), pp. 85–115.

60 Harvey Cox, *Fire From Heaven: The Rise of Pentecostal Spirituality and the Reshaping of Religion in the Twenty-first Century* (London: Cassell, 1996); David Martin, *Pentecostalism: The World Their Parish* (Oxford: Blackwell, 2002), pp. 5–6.

61 Anderson, *Introduction to Pentecostalism*, p. 9.

62 Cox, *Fire from Heaven.*

63 Martin, *Pentecostalism*, pp. 79–80.

64 For example, Joel Comiskey, 'Rev. Cho's Cell Groups and Dynamics of Church Growth', in Myung Sung-Hoon and Hong Young-Gi (eds), *Charis and Charisma: David Yonggi Cho and the Growth of Yoido Full Gospel Church* (Oxford: Regnum Books, 2003), pp. 143–57.

65 Martin, *Pentecostalism*, p. 161; Cox, *Fire from Heaven*, p. 226; Juan Sepúlveda, 'Pentecostalism and Liberation Theology: Two Manifestations of the Work of the Holy Spirit for the Renewal of the Church', in Harold D. Hunter and Peter D. Hocken (eds), *All Together in One Place: Theological Papers from the Brighton Conference on World Evangelization* (Sheffield: Sheffield Academic Press, 1990), pp. 51–64.

66 Allan Anderson, *Spreading Fires: The Missionary Nature of Early Pentecostalism* (London: SCM Press, 2007).

67 Yong, *Spirit Poured Out on All Flesh.*

68 Dana Robert, 'Shifting Southward: Global Christianity since 1945', *International Bulletin of Missionary Research* 24/2 (2000), pp. 50–8.

69 Rebecca Catto, 'Non-Western Christian Missionaries in England: Has Mission Been Reversed?', *British and Irish Association for Mission Studies Bulletin* 30 (March 2008), pp. 2–9.

70 A. Adogame and C. Weissköppel (eds), *Religion in the Context of African Migration* (Bayreuth: Bayreuth University, 2005); Gerrie ter Haar, *Halfway to Paradise: African Christians in Europe* (Cardiff: Cardiff Academic Press, 1998); Afe Adogame, Roswith Gerloff and Klaus Hock (eds), *Christianity in Africa and the African Diaspora: The Appropriation of a Scattered Heritage* (London: Continuum, 2008).

71 Michael Nazir-Ali, *From Everywhere to Everywhere: A World View of Christian Mission* (London: Collins, 1991).

5

EMPOWERMENT OF THE SPIRIT

Struggles for Justice, Freedom and Well-being

Western bishop: 'How does your church reach the poor?'
Latin American church leader: 'We don't reach the poor; we *are* the poor'.[1]

Following the tradition of the Hebrew Scriptures and the example of Jesus Christ, the church has always claimed to have a concern for the poor. But often the church as an institution is rich and preoccupied with many issues. Liberation theology was born in Latin America in the late 1960s when theologians and bishops of the Roman Catholic Church recognized that it is composed mainly of poor people. Rereading the Scriptures they discovered that Jesus Christ had a special concern for the poor and oppressed. Since then a new way of doing theology from the perspective of the poor has influenced Christians of all traditions all over the world. In this chapter we shall look at the context in which these developments first took place – 1960s and 1970s Latin America. We shall consider how the way we do theology can be influenced by our situation in life by also looking at post-colonial, feminist and political theologies.

The key bible verse for liberation theologies is Luke 4.18 where Jesus, invited to preach his first sermon in his home synagogue in Nazareth, announces 'good news to the poor'. This phrase is often quoted without making a connection with the words which precede it. The full sentence is: '*The Spirit of the Lord is upon me*, because he has anointed me to bring good news to the poor.' In his Gospel, Luke particularly draws attention to the way that Jesus as Messiah (anointed one) was empowered by the Holy Spirit. And the particular concern that Jesus shows toward the poor in Luke's Gospel is shown to be as a result of the Spirit, who animates Jesus from his conception onwards (Luke 1.35, 80; 3.22; 4.1–2, 14, 18; 23.46). Jesus is quoting from the prophet Isaiah who amplifies the meaning of the good news as freedom from oppression, heartbreak, captivity and imprisonment (Luke 4.19; Isa. 62.1–2). Jesus' proclamation of 'the year of the Lord's favour' is a reference to the law of jubilee in ancient Israel (Lev. 25) according to which, every 50 years, debts would be cancelled and the land returned to its original owners. The discovery of Latin American liberation theologians was that the freedom of the Spirit is not just 'spiritual' in an other-worldly sense, but it can be political and material as well.

5.1 The movement for liberation in Latin America

In Chapter 4 we mentioned how southern and central America was Christianized by force by conquerors, mostly from Spain and Portugal, who were enticed by the tremendous wealth of this continent. The great empires of the Incas and Aztecs soon collapsed, and the indigenous population was enslaved and greatly reduced by atrocity and disease. Not only were they physically abused but they also came to despair as their culture and religion were also subjected to violence.[2] Replacement labour was imported from Africa, as part of the slave trade. Millions more Europeans migrated to Latin America in the late nineteenth and early twentieth centuries, and more recently there have been influxes from many Asian (especially East Asian) countries. The different racial groups have intermarried to a great extent, though in many places the indigenous people are still marginalized. European culture and religion derived from sixteenth-century Spain and Portugal has been the most dominant and much of social life is ordered according to a 'pigmentocracy', with people of African descent on the lowest rung of the social ladder.[3]

The countries of Latin America (numbering about 20) had been relatively prosperous at the end of World War Two but for a number of reasons their economies declined markedly in the following decades. Some suspected that North America's growing wealth was at the expense of her poorer neighbours – a view known as 'dependency theory'. But there were internal reasons as well. Most countries had gained their independence from the colonial powers – Spain and Portugal – in the 1820s. They had not established democracies, however, and were subject to unjust government and military dictatorships. There were gross economic inequalities, with a small elite holding most of the land, but movements for greater equality were seen as communist and heavily suppressed, sometimes with North American help. What is more, the hierarchy of the Roman Catholic Church had remained close to governments and therefore complicit in the injustices. But in Medellín, Columbia, in 1968, the old order was overturned. Roman Catholic bishops meeting in conference took a decisive step on behalf of the people when they called for social liberation as part of evangelization. Despite opposition from the hierarchy, at the bishops' conference in Pueblo in 1979 this was reaffirmed and described as 'the preferential option for the poor'. The church in Latin America broke with the static model of Christendom and shifted to a missionary stance.[4]

A number of different developments led to this decisive step and to the emergence of a distinctively new way of theologizing from Latin America. Being a predominantly Roman Catholic continent, the conclusions of the Second Vatican Council, 1962–5, are important in understanding what happened. The most significant innovation of the Council was a redefinition of the church: no longer was it understood as a hierarchy of priests and bishops, but it was now described primarily as the people of God. In this understanding, the church was now orientated toward the lay people or ordinary church members, who in Latin America were overwhelmingly poor. A second result of

Vatican Two was the endorsement of inculturation (see Chapter 3) and therefore the possibility of reshaping Christian faith according to local contexts. An important consequence of both of these decisions was that ordinary Catholics were enabled to read and interpret the Bible for themselves. Because of the perennial shortage of priests they were encouraged to do this in small groups – base ecclesial communities – led by lay people with priestly supervision.[5]

Vatican Two was applicable across the Roman Catholic world but in Latin America base communities took a new turn when, with the support of Archbishop Hélder Câmara, some priests and lay people in poor communities in Recife in north-east Brazil experimented in their base communities with the educational method of Paulo Freire.[6] Freire used a method of 'conscientization' in which people were encouraged to question their social situation and raise awareness of the ideologies used to legitimate it. The groups began to combine bible study with analysis of their social context based on the theories of Karl Marx. This led them to question the economic and political status quo, and the ways in which this was justified by both church and state. For example, they asked why the church emphasized that the people should be obedient to its teaching, and yet failed to stress that Jesus challenged the religious authorities of his own day for abusing the trust placed in them and neglecting the poor. A political reading of Jesus' messiahship, informed by Luke 4.18–19 and Jesus' work for the poor, inspired many with a messianic vision for bringing the kingdom of God on earth through education and radical social change. Most liberation theologians espoused some form of socialism but were not members of the communist party.

Their experience of solidarity with poor people in base communities and seeing the Bible from their perspective led some priests to develop a new way of doing theology. This became known as 'theology of liberation' but it was also 'the liberation of theology' from being 'the erudite theology of textbooks' to 'a theology arising out of the urgent problems of real life'[7] in the tradition of the biblical prophets. Beginning from practical experience and refusing to 'spiritualize' the text, liberation theologians revealed the extent to which the Bible was concerned with social, economic and political affairs. For example, Gustavo Gutiérrez showed that the rescue of Israel from oppression in Egypt, often interpreted only as a metaphor for spiritual liberation, was also a political act. The context was the oppression of Israel by the Egyptian rulers, who suffered 'repression (Ex. 1.10–11), alienated work (5.6–14), humiliations (1.13–14), enforced birth control policy (1.15–22)' and brutality (3.7–10). Attentive to the cry of the poor, Yahweh awakened a liberator, Moses, to rescue them. Their eventual liberation was the result of a long and hard struggle with the ruling powers, which Moses also used as a process of education for the people about the true cause of their suffering and the divine intention for human society.[8]

Similarly, Gutiérrez saw Jesus Christ as a political figure. He was not politically neutral but sided with the poor in what he preached. 'The meek shall inherit the earth' (Matt. 5.5), for example, has radical political implications. So Gutiérrez argued that to know Christ is to do justice and to hope to see it done in history. Furthermore, he reasoned on the basis of documents of Vatican Two that the church should signify the salvation it announces; in other words, it should be a place of liberation. The Eucharist should be a demonstration of human charity, the word preached should challenge injustice, and the church should be committed to serving the poor.[9] In this way liberation theology provided a biblical basis for reflective Christian action on behalf of the poor – what it called 'praxis'. And it justified theologically the instinctive Christian efforts to challenge structural injustices and the ideologies used to support them, and to call for a redistribution of wealth from the rich to the poor.[10] Evangelization and social action were seen to be part of one-and-the-same mission in the way of Jesus Christ.

The social criticism of liberation theology was directed at the Roman Catholic hierarchy, who had supported military regimes in Latin America, at the regimes themselves, and at the model of development within the global market system, which seemed to be benefiting North rather than South America. The Roman Catholic hierarchy condemned aspects of liberation theology, explicitly because of its use of Marxist socio-economics and socialist solutions.[11] The unexpressed reason for criticism was probably that the hierarchy was uncomfortable with the rapid growth of the base communities and their 'reinvention of the church'.[12] Pope John Paul II, who had been linked with the struggle against Communism in Poland, was naturally worried by the Marxist connections but equally mindful of the need for solidarity with the poor. Under his leadership the 'option for the poor', but not the liberation theology method, was incorporated into Catholic social teaching.[13] Because of their work on behalf of the poor and action to reduce the power of the land-owning elite, Catholic priests, nuns and church workers suffered violent attack and persecution in the militarized societies of 1970s and 1980s Latin America, and there were many martyrs. The most prominent of these was Archbishop, Óscar Romero, an advocate of the poor, who was gunned down while celebrating Mass in his cathedral in El Salvador in 1980.

The danger facing activist movements is that the end justifies the means. Liberation theology has been accused of violence in aiming to bring about social revolution and some were tempted. The film *The Mission* (1986); starring Robert de Niro and Jeremy Irons, to which the US American Jesuit and political activist Daniel Berrigan was a consultant, well illustrated the dilemmas faced by priests wishing to protect the poor. But theologians rejected violent methods as incompatible with the liberating ministry of Jesus Christ. Soon it was recognized that liberation theology was a spirituality as well as a method, a spirituality of costly identification and solidarity with the suffering and belief in the possibility of social transformation.[14]

5.2 Liberation theologies worldwide

The method of liberation theology is defined as 'critical reflection on Christian praxis in the light of the Word'.[15] It differs from traditional methods of theologizing in several ways. First, it is different from liberal theology in its approach to the biblical text, which is not historical or literary criticism, but takes the biblical text at face value and uses it, as long as it has a liberating message. At the same time, liberation theology applies 'the hermeneutics of suspicion' which questions the text and interpretation of church leaders.[16] It asks questions like 'Whose side is the writer or interpreter on?', 'Whose interests are being served here?' in order to recognize the bias of vested interest and reinterpret the message as good news to the poor. So, for example, why in the eighteenth century was Paul's injunction to Onesimus to receive his runaway slave back 'no longer as a slave but more than a slave, a beloved brother . . . both in the flesh and in the Lord' (Philemon 16) ignored while Paul's advice to slaves to 'obey your earthly masters' (Eph. 6.5) was preached from so many pulpits?

Liberation theology also differs from most Western theologies in that it emphasizes right practice (orthopraxis) before right doctrine or belief (orthodoxy). Its intention is not only to interpret the text but also to change society, and its concern is not with academics but with social transformation. Praxis is not merely practice but action informed by reflection. Liberation theology suggested a new pattern of doing theology that combined action with theological reflection. It began with identifying with the poor, listening to them, rereading the Bible in the light of their experience, raising questions of theology and other structures of authority, and joining with people's movements to bring about change from the grassroots. This involvement in turn led to further reinterpretation of the Bible. This 'hermeneutical circle' method[17] led to the development of faith-based methods of participation for local development.

Like any theology, liberation theology too has its weaknesses and dangers. For example, it reads the whole of Scripture through one particular lens: that of liberation. It is therefore selective and in danger of reducing the gospel only to what applies to its own context. But redemption is more than liberation, human life is more than politics, and theology is not social theory.[18] Furthermore, liberation theology may become idealistic or utopian and overly confident in human ability to realize what God alone can bring about. It is also questionable to what extent liberation theology represents the perspective of the poor, as it claims (see below). Nevertheless many Christians around the world have appreciated its perspective. Liberation theology soon spread from Latin America to North America, Asia, Africa and the West. In Asia liberation theology took several forms, which include *Minjung* theology in Korea, which championed human and civil rights in a time of military dictatorship (see Chapter 9), and Dalit theology in India, which is done by the former outcastes themselves to assert their dignity and rights (see Chapter 6). In each of these cases it was recognized that the socio-economic analysis which predominated in Latin America needed to be combined with issues of culture and identity in addressing the causes of oppression and articulating the meaning of liberation. Liberation theology is often said to include black theology and feminist theology, which will both be treated below.

Latin American liberation theology was mediated to British Christians through several key figures. Andrew Kirk, a former missionary in Latin America and Dean of the School of Mission and World Christianity in Selly Oak, Birmingham, drew on the biblical reflections of the liberation theologians. The Evangelical constituency he addressed was shy of political involvement at the time, seeing it as a distraction from the central task of evangelization. By showing that bringing good news to the poor was part of the biblical mandate, Kirk encouraged Evangelical support for social action and advocacy and laid the seeds of Evangelical participation in Jubilee 2000 and Make Poverty History (2005) and other initiatives. Liberation perspectives are central to Kirk's developed theology of mission.[19] Christopher Rowland, Professor of Biblical Exegesis at Oxford University, is a political theologian inspired by the work of William Blake and in dialogue with movements in Latin America. He regards Blake as an early liberation theologian who interpreted the prophecies of the book of Revelation in a very concrete way. His hymn 'Jerusalem' encourages social action to turn industrial England of 'dark, satanic mills' into the new Jerusalem envisaged in Revelation.[20]

5.3 Post-colonial theologies

Liberation theology represents a dialogue with Marxism and therefore engages particularly with the economic structures that disadvantage poor people and nations, particularly colonized peoples. However, colonialism is not just an economic system; it also includes what post-colonial writers call 'colonization of the mind', which persists even among those who are politically and economically liberated. Post-colonial theory deals with the cultural legacy of colonial rule and the ongoing effects of the cultural or hegemonic power exercised by the West – especially now the USA – over non-Western countries. Criticism of European cultures by those who had been colonized has been voiced most strongly in post-colonial literature, for example, by Nigerian novelist Chinua Achebe and Indian Trinidadian writer V. S. Naipaul, who expose imperial attitudes.[21] Being concerned with the cultural and psychological dimensions of the oppression of colonialism it is closely related to 'cultural studies' (Chapter 3). In his ground-breaking book, *Orientalism* (1978), which laid foundations for post-colonial theory, Palestinian academic Edward Said critically examined Western study of the East or Orient and literary portrayal of non-Western cultures – especially Muslim cultures. Drawing on the work of both Gramsci and the French philosopher Michel Foucault, he showed how this was ideologically loaded in the interests of Western power over the Orient. As such, Orientalism constructed views of 'the East' rather than objectively describing it, and portrayed the Orient as inferior to what was conceived as 'the West'.[22] Post-colonial theory shows how colonial and neo-colonial experience continue to shape relations between the West and its former colonies.[23]

Post-colonial theory also recognizes that colonial oppression is not restricted to the foreign power's oppression of the colonized but it includes an internal system of oppression as well.

Colonial power is exercised through a social elite who oppress those they perceive to be 'beneath' them. Indian post-colonial or 'subaltern' studies, for example, aims to uncover the underside of colonial history in the experience of outcastes (dalits) and tribal people (*adivasis*) in Indian society.[24] In this way post-colonial theory undermines the simple portrayal of the world as divided into victims and victimizers, as liberation theology tended to do. The post-colonial view is of complexity, plurality and ambiguity in relationships and identity. It relates questions of culture to nationalism, globalization, migration and the hybrid cultural identities of those who live in diaspora groups. Also unlike Marxist and liberation theory, post-colonialism does not prescribe a universal solution or have a goal of liberation in view. It raises questions rather than answers them.[25] In this section we will consider two ways in which post-colonial theory has impacted Christian thought: in biblical studies and in discussion of Christian identity.

Like postmodernism (see Chapter 7), post-colonial theory uses a literary method to deconstruct 'texts', which are not necessarily written but include visual representations, film and other media. The post-colonial interpreter is interested in a text not for what its author intended but for what it reveals of colonial perceptions and power relationships, and for how it plays alongside other texts.[26] In view of its interest in literature, it is not surprising that post-colonial theory first impacted Christian theology in the area of biblical studies. R. S. Sugirtharajah, originally from Sri Lanka and Professor of Biblical Hermeneutics at the University of Birmingham, has pioneered this area.[27] The first impact of post-colonial theory on biblical studies is in raising awareness of the imperial context of the New Testament and much of the rest of the Bible. The colonization of Palestine by the Romans explains many features of the Gospel narratives: the discussions of tax and tax collecting, for example, which were particularly controversial because they were not paid to the Palestinian government but to the occupying power. Another aspect of the colonial context is the prevalence of day-labourers, who could be hired in the marketplace. The effect of colonization is to deprive people of their land and make them dependent on a wider economic system. It was the context of colonization which made the people of Israel look to Jesus as a political figure, and the reason for the political charges against him.[28]

Second, whereas liberation theologians took the liberative message of biblical authors at face value, post-colonial scholars have turned the 'hermeneutic of suspicion' on the Bible and its expositors. For example, the partiality of biblical authors and the violent tendencies of liberation theology were exposed by Native American theologians; one of whom was Robert Allen Warrior, who pointed out that his people, as victims of settlers, identified with the Canaanites rather than the people of Israel who conquered them.[29] In another case, Indian liberation theologian Samuel Rayan investigated the positions taken by biblical commentaries before and after the colonial period with regard to Jesus' answer to the question about taxes. At the height of the colonial period, all the biblical commentaries interpreted Jesus' answer, 'Give to Caesar what is Caesar's and to God what is God's', as an injunction to be good subjects and pay taxes. Only towards the end of the period and after it was this interpretation questioned. Rayan himself understands that Jesus is alluding to Psalm 24.1, where it is written 'The earth is the Lord's'. Therefore, what his reply meant was 'Give to Caesar only what is Caesar's' in the knowledge that everything belongs to God. In this way Jesus was questioning or even denying the emperor's right to levy taxes from the occupied people.[30] Such observations raise serious questions about the discipline of biblical studies which has tended to be seen as objective and scientific, without cultural bias.[31]

Third, post-colonialism encourages a variety of readings and interpretations of biblical texts without insisting on a right interpretation. The story of Jesus' encounter with the woman at the well, for example, is read differently by three women from different contexts. Mukti Barton from Bangladesh stresses the namelessness of the woman in the story as evidence of patriarchy and unwillingness by the biblical authors to recognize women in mission, whereas Vandana from India draws attention to the woman as a channel of Jesus' universal offer of spiritual life, regardless of religious difference, and Teresa Okure from Nigeria emphasizes that all – women as well as men – are equal participants in God's mission.[32] Fourth, Sugirtharajah and other post-colonial theologians recognize that the Bible is read in a multi-religious world and that religious scriptures need not separate different communities but may be shared. They take into account readings of the Bible from people of other religions and also read biblical texts alongside other scriptures in a comparative and inter-cultural way.[33] Post-colonial studies muddies the waters of biblical scholarship by stressing the uncertainty and ambiguity about the meaning of texts and the freedom of the interpreter.[34]

5.4 Black theologies

A second area of theology to which post-colonial studies contributes is Christian identity. Post-colonial theory questions the identities given to oppressed people and recognizes that migration, urbanization and other social forces result in hybrid identities – Black American, British Muslim and so on. These are not fixed but have to be negotiated between contrasting realities. Christianity too is hybrid. The identity of Jesus is divine-human; many different identities (Jew, Gentile etc.) meet in the church, and Christians are encouraged to cross cultural boundaries.[35] In Britain theologians from the Caribbean especially have been leaders in developing post-colonial black theologies. The Caribbean is extremely diverse and its identity is not easy to define. Linguistically, different countries use English (e.g. Jamaica, Trinidad), French (e.g. Haiti, Dominica), Spanish (e.g. Cuba, Puerto Rico) or Dutch (Guyana), as well as mixed tongues and local languages. Nearly 90 per cent of the people of the Caribbean are of African descent; most of their ancestors were imported as slaves to work on plantations. However, the balance of population may vary greatly in specific countries and also includes significant Amerindian, Indian,

Chinese, European and other populations. Each country of the Caribbean represents a different mixing of peoples and circumstances. What they have in common is a history of slavery, colonization and forced migrations, and this is the basis of their shared identity and theological reflection.[36] People from the Caribbean who migrated to Britain have added another layer to their already complex identity.

In the Caribbean and other slave-owning areas, the Bible was used by the colonizers to justify the oppression of blacks. The myth that Africans were the descendents of Ham, who was apparently cursed by his father Noah to be the 'lowest of slaves' (Gen. 9.18–29; 10.6), allowed for a biblical justification to be made for the practice of slavery, and led to the development of the myth that 'negroes' were suitable for slavery because they were savage and barbarous.[37] As part of the decolonization process of Caribbean peoples, the Bible was subjected to a rereading by the newly emancipated. Not only Christians but also people of all faiths participated in this process.[38] Rereading the Bible is an important part of the indigenous Rastafari religious movement, made familiar across the world in the songs of Bob Marley. Rastafaris believe that the Bible was changed in interests of whites but, by interpreting it to mean that Ethiopian emperor Haile Selassi is the black messiah, Rastafaris have made it 'an instrument for black dignity, pride, and hope in the God of the future'.[39] This is an 'emancipation from below' to complement the political 'emancipation from above' which freed slaves but kept populations still bound into the cultural, racial and economic systems established by the former slave-owning powers.[40]

Black theology could be said to have started with Olaudah Equiano and other freed slaves who worked for the abolition of the slave trade.[41] A century and a half later, Martin Luther King Jr, a Baptist minister, preached a biblically founded social gospel as he led the non-violent civil rights movement in the USA.[42] Black liberation theology was initiated by US American James H. Cone, in the context of the civil rights movement in the United States in the 1960s and 70s, which campaigned to end the segregation of black people. It emerged from a combination of the spirituality of the slaves and the biblical stories of the God who liberates with the ideologies of the civil rights movement led by Martin Luther King and of the black power movements led by Malcolm X.[43] Cone argued that King's Jesus was not black enough and took from the black power ideology of Malcolm X the need to affirm black identity and the right to self-determination. He insisted that Christianity offered political liberation and was forthright in his criticism of the dominant white Christianity which endorsed segregation.[44] A second generation of black theologians in the 1980s and 1990s developed black theology by dialoguing with Third World theologians, particularly with political theologians of South Africa who had been inspired by Cone's work.[45]

In South Africa, liberation theology contributed to the development of theologies of black consciousness and black power in dialogue with movements in the USA.[46] These were part of the campaign to end the system of apartheid which separated the races and discriminated particularly against the black majority population, and which was endorsed by the leading denomination, the Dutch Reformed Church. These resulted in the famous Kairos document of 1985. This statement, drafted by Pentecostal leader Frank Chicane and Catholic theologian Albert Nolan, and supported by a very wide grouping of mainly black church leaders, challenged the white churches to take a decision to oppose apartheid. It is seen as a turning point in the political struggle which led to the ending of apartheid and a new South African constitution in the early 1990s.[47]

The recent development of black theology in Britain, centres on Birmingham and cultural studies, and owes much to Robert Beckford, Anthony Reddie, Michael Jagessar and others with Caribbean roots. Some Asian theologians such as Mukti Barton and David Joy also identify with them in so far as black theology is understood as post-colonial rather than being racially defined. Robert Beckford's focus has been on empowering black people and black Pentecostal churches, for example by showing that 'Jesus is Dread'. Beckford explains how Rastafarians inverted the traditional English word 'dread' to mean 'mental decolonization, freedom, power and upliftment', symbolized by dreadlock hair. By portraying Jesus Christ as Dread, Beckford challenges black Christians to be themselves and identify with the black quest for freedom.[48] Reddie and Jagessar address not black culture but the dominant British culture in seeking to release biblical texts and theological notions from bondage to white culture, and challenging leading white theologians to take into account the perceptions of Blacks and Asians.[49] Michael Jagessar compares the practice of black theology to Anancy, the spider trickster of many Caribbean legends. He envisages the creature with its eight hairy legs spread in an ungainly way across every continent, combining multiple worlds and confusing the neat categories of traditional theology. Awkward to deal with, poking fun and weaving stories, Anancy stirs the imagination, relishes ambiguities and defies boundaries, always questioning identities, cultural mores and religious dogma.[50] In this way Anancy is the personification of all post-colonial theologizing which does not always offer answers but unsettles any comfortable status quo.

5.5 Feminist theologies

The liberating mission for which Jesus Christ was anointed by the Holy Spirit covered many different categories of person: the poor, the captives, the blind, the oppressed. Feminist theology recognizes that women are included in this description and take this as the starting point from which to understand the Scriptures and do theology. In contemporary Britain it is not always apparent that women need liberating. Women are now prominent in the media and public life, achieve higher grades at school and often command high salaries. Although there are continuing concerns such as disparity in pay scales and earnings over a lifetime and violence against women, few women today see the need for a consciously feminist agenda. Gender studies continues to highlight women's experience but it does not have a programme of liberation like feminism. When approached in global perspective, however, the lower social status of women and its detrimental effects is obvious.

Latin America, for example, is known for its 'macho' culture. *Machismo* is an exaggerated masculinity; the assertion of masculine power and control over women (and other men). It is associated with a cult of virility and the repudiation of anything feminine. At the same time the feminine is exaggerated as women are idealized as the polar opposite of the macho male. The origins of this may lie in the indigenous male response to Spanish domination, in the Spanish culture of male honour, or in pre-Columban Aztec culture[51] but, whatever the reason, it is experienced as oppressive by many women. Maria's story is not untypical. She grew up in a poor home and her parents had little education. Her father thought that women and girls were not full human beings. Whereas her brothers were given considerable freedom, she was often locked up and beaten. After only four years he stopped her going to school because he said educating a girl was 'like casting pearls before swine'. Thinking she could escape from her father by getting married, Maria married the first man who proposed to her. But her life became even worse because he bullied and enslaved her. She had a succession of children and because of their poverty she also had to labour in the fields. Though he never hit her, her husband beat the children, which Maria found far harder to endure. When she sought advice from her mother, she simply told Maria that 'women are born to suffer' and that they have to obey their husbands. It was through a women's group at the church that Maria began to find a way out of her hopeless situation. Together they began to realize their worth as women and to understand the system of patriarchy that oppressed them. It was with the help of the group that Maria realized that her husband's illiteracy had given him a great inferiority complex, and she was able to persuade him to do a literacy course. Being able to read and write increased his self-respect; he calmed down, stopped hitting the children and began to treat Maria better. Together he and Maria were helped to see how many of their difficulties arose from poverty and they became involved in campaigning for their land rights and those of other poor people.[52]

In this overwhelmingly Catholic context, Maria is a common name. The most famous biblical Maria, or Mary, is Mary the mother of Jesus, and in Latin America she stands as the ideal of womanhood, both virgin and mother. In traditional Roman Catholic teaching, Mary is the pre-eminent example of faith. At the annunciation – the announcement by the angel to Mary that she was going to bear a child – Mary is seen as a symbol of obedience and submission. In contrast to Eve, through whom sin entered the world, Mary submits to God's will and makes remission of sin possible. Traditional Catholic theology has special doctrines about Mary not shared by Protestantism: her conception was 'immaculate' (that is, without the sin); she did not die but was 'assumed' into heaven, where she is 'Heavenly Queen'. She is the 'Mediatrix' who intercedes with Christ for the people (cf. John 2.1–11), the 'Compassionate One', Mother of Christ and Mother of the Church. Mary is described as the icon, or image, of the church, the Bride, who represents the church (Rev. 21.2), 'Our Lady', 'Madonna', symbol of purity and virtue. And so Catholics pray the prayer that begins 'Hail Mary' which venerates her as 'Mother of God'.[53]

In Latin America, there are several cults of the Virgin, which seem to combine Catholic theology with indigenous beliefs. The most famous is the Virgin of Guadalupe in Mexico. The cult originated in a vision of 'a lady from heaven' by a native American, Cuauhtlatoatzin, baptized Juan Diego, on the hill near what is now Mexico City where the shrine of Tonantzín – the Aztec fertility goddess – once stood. Diego understood he had seen the Virgin Mary but he saw Mary from within his own world, with darker skin and speaking in his native tongue. She promised to hear the laments of the nations and 'cure all their miseries, misfortunes, and sorrows'.[54] The vision was followed by mass conversions of Indians to Christianity and the church was compelled to recognize this indigenous version of Christian faith. In 1999, Pope John Paul II declared Our Lady of Guadalupe the patron saint of all the Americas and the Virgin's feast day, 12 December, is a date of major celebration.[55] However, many commentators are concerned that the popular portrayals of Mary in indigenous Catholicism encourage traditional views and practices which are oppressive toward women. No real woman can live up to the ideal of womanhood represented in Mary, and this paradox reflects the way women in the continent are both idolized and suppressed at the same time. Feminist theologians in Latin America, like liberation theologians in general, advocate a liberative praxis: in this case the liberation of women from the oppressive system of patriarchy.

In this Roman Catholic context, women theologians have re-read the story of Mary in the conviction that God made women, as well as men, in his image, and this means that Christians should struggle against male domination. Looking again at the opening chapters of Luke's Gospel (Luke 1.26–55; 2.1–7), they see Mary as a poor woman, and a symbol of the poor, who is empowered to play a part in the liberation of all humanity. At the annunciation, far from being passive, Mary questions God, and her willingness to accede to God's will is not a capitulation but the active participation of one who knew her own mind. The meeting between Mary and her cousin Elizabeth can be interpreted as an example of solidarity between women that enables them to strengthen one another. Mary's song, the Magnificat, tells of liberation from all forms of oppression, which expresses confidence that God is just and on the side of the poor and hungry. If this message of good news for the poor was what Jesus learnt on his mother's knee, then Mary is not a symbol of meekness and passivity but becomes a symbol of strength and source of compassion on all.[56]

Christian feminist theology sometimes recognizes a difference between feminist theology in the global North and in the South. While this polarization of the world is not always helpful, there are noticeable differences between the feminist identity of middle-class white women and those who speak for the women of African, Asian and Latino descent.[57] There are three main ways in which this shows: first, Northern feminism since its 'second wave' beginning in the late 1960s has been developed in societies in which women can live independently of male support, and without children if they so choose, whereas for 'Southern' feminists this is not so. The 'Northern' feminist theologians of the 1970s and 1980s were most concerned to rethink church in such a way that women could have freedom and be included within it.[58] Northern feminist theology has encouraged women's autonomy and self-defined identity. However, in the more traditional gender relationships in the South, women were more likely to be inextricably linked to men and to have dependants. As the above example from Latin America illustrates, Southern feminist theology more characteristically recognizes patriarchy as a social system which is detrimental not only to women but also to the family and the society. Therefore women's liberation is not primarily emancipation from male control but the freedom of all from patriarchal society by the development of women's gifts – particularly through education, which is seen to bring benefits to men, children and the whole society. One of the first 'Southern' feminist theologians, the Indonesian Marianne Katoppo, argued that 'woman's liberation is also man's'.[59] Second, Southern feminist theologians emerged in the context of international development issues, liberation theology and later post-colonial theology, and so were more likely to connect women's liberation with the wider economic and social change agenda, including liberation from colonialism and cultural systems of oppression.[60] Third, Asian and African cultures make a close connection between woman and the earth, and construe the Spirit of life as feminine. So Asian feminists in these continents particularly have been leaders of eco-feminist movements opposing the exploitation of the earth and advocating its healing.[61] From women's perspective, therefore, the liberation of women is central to all other liberation, and a new way of seeing the world is called for in which domination and violence of one over another is rejected.

In traditional societies, women's roles are confined to domestic life; it is through the roles of daughter, wife and mother that they must exercise their mission. For some the most important task of mission is the struggle against *machismo* or patriarchy. Some have criticized mission itself – at least as practised in the initial evangelization of the Americas – as macho. It was aggressive, violent and an assertion of power over the land. As in many conflicts, rape of the land also involved rape of the local women.[62] Reflecting on the mission of Mary (Maria), it is possible to envisage an alternative way of doing mission that is not destructive but life-giving. According to John's Gospel, Jesus likened the mission of the disciples to childbirth, as he bade them farewell (John 16.20–2). Childbirth involves suffering and labour but results in joy at the new creation that results.

5.6 Spiritual conflict

As a result of liberation theology, the Roman Catholic Church in Latin America opted for the poor but, as is often pointed out, many of the poor themselves opted for Pentecostalism. In Chapter 4, we drew attention to the rise of Pentecostalism worldwide. The figures and definitions are contested but Pentecostal-charismatic Christians form the fastest growing category of Christians today, and also one of the largest. In 1960 the number of Pentecostals in Latin America was negligible but by 2004 Pentecostals numbered at least 10 per cent of the Christian population, and this figure rises to 25 per cent in Guatemala and Chile.[63] This is not a new movement; the first Pentecostal-style revivals in Latin America were in 1909 in Chile and in 1911 in Brazil but they have grown rapidly since. Their rise has worried the Roman Catholic Church, which has seen its membership drop. One of the ways in which the church has responded is by encouraging the charismatic movement within the Roman Catholic Church. As a result there are probably more people who participate in Pentecostal-style worship within the Catholic Church than outside. Like the base communities of liberation theology, the charismatic movement also encourages meeting in small groups for prayer, bible study and mutual support. Some parishes have both base communities and charismatic fellowships, and the same people may be members of both, but more often a priest encourages one or other expression of spirituality.[64] It is interesting to compare these two different movements.

Both liberation theology and the Pentecostal-charismatic movement in Latin America are concerned with the problem of poverty but they offer two very different solutions to it. Liberation theology locates the problem in unjust structures in society such as hierarchy and capitalism. Pentecostals and charismatics tend to identify supernatural forces of evil – Satan and evil spirits – as the cause of poverty and suffering. Liberation theologians aim to bring about structural change in church and society but Pentecostal-charismatic Christianity is concerned with solving personal spiritual problems so that people can enjoy health and wealth. The methods used are also different. Liberationists address poverty through education and through communal solidarity in political action based on a reading of the Bible as having social and political implications. In the charismatic groups of poor people, the main methods are corporate prayer, bible exposition and worship, which are believed to bring about miraculous intervention from God and result in personal transformation. But the net result may be similar in both cases. The base communities' struggle to change social structures also results in personal transformation and spiritual growth – as in the case of Maria above. At the same time, joining a Pentecostal-charismatic fellowship is generally linked to upward social mobility (see Chapter 8) – although studies demonstrating this have generally looked at Pentecostal churches independent of the Catholic Church.

Both liberation theology and charismatic spirituality empower individuals and groups, and both deal with the powerful forces that affect people's lives, but they understand those forces differently. Liberation theology identifies forces of evil as lying in social and economic structures, of which the poor and marginalized are victims. Pentecostal-charismatic Christianity sees the forces of evil which hold people back from realizing God's blessing as supernatural powers to be encountered through prayer. In their recognition of evil forces at work in the world and their confidence to confront them both movements share some common biblical and theological foundations.

The Synoptic Gospels recount many instances of Jesus confronting demonic powers which were understood to possess individuals and exorcizing them, casting them out. His disciples and the apostles, did the same. John's Gospel is the only one not to include any records of exorcism but nevertheless includes a theology of power by setting the mission of Jesus Christ within the context of a cosmic struggle between light and darkness. The ministry of exorcism has inspired both Pentecostal-charismatics and also liberation theologians to see themselves as engaged in spiritual conflict. Pentecostal-charismatic approaches derive from the experience of three North American missionaries, Paul Hiebert, Alan Tippett and Charles Kraft, who became lecturers at Fuller Theological Seminary in the 1970s and 1980s. They had all witnessed exorcism and deliverance on the 'mission field' in India, the Pacific and West Africa (respectively) and recognized it as part of the biblical ministry of Jesus. Being trained in cultural anthropology, instead of dismissing it as earlier generations of missionaries had done, they argued missionaries should practise such a ministry of confrontational prayer as a missionary method, which they called 'power encounter'.[65] Charismatic church leader John Wimber, also based in Los Angeles, popularized this method as 'power evangelism'.[66] Peter Wagner, one of the leaders of the 'third wave' of the charismatic movement, took this further and identified not only supernatural demonic powers which oppressed individuals but also 'territorial spirits' possessing differing locations which needed to be confronted in prayer with the power of God. This became known as 'spiritual warfare'[67] and Wagner taught it as part of his strategy for church growth at Fuller. 'Power encounter' or 'spiritual warfare' has been strongly criticized within the Evangelical movement and outside it because of its naïve use of the Bible and antagonistic method[68] but the sense of being involved in spiritual conflict is common in Pentecostal-charismatic Christianity.

A similar language of 'spiritual conflict' is also used by liberation theologians. Walter Wink, Professor of New Testament Interpretation at Auburn Theological Seminary in New York, made a study of the biblical terminology of spirits, demons and angels and applied it to dealing with social and political powers and systems. In a series of books, Wink argued that Jesus' way of dealing with evil spirits was to 'name' and 'unmask' and then 'engage' them. Transferring this method of exorcism into modern society, Wink called on Christians to identify evil in societal structures, expose institutional evil and then take action to transform or 'redeem' 'fallen' corporate culture or spirituality. Wink emphasizes that the struggle against the powers is by non-violent resistance such as practised by Mahatma Gandhi and Martin Luther King.[69] Peter Wagner and other advocates of 'power encounter' and 'spiritual warfare' used the biblical studies of Wink to build the biblical foundation for their method; and Wink expressed appreciation of some of the insights of Wagner and others into 'spiritual warfare', especially their emphasis on prayer as a weapon in the struggle.[70]

Theologically, liberation theology and Pentecostal-charismatic spirituality both understand themselves as movements of the Holy Spirit. Although it is not always explicit, the emphasis on the liberating power of God gives a pneumatological framework to liberation theology. José Comblin is a Belgian (Catholic) missionary and liberation theologian who has lived and worked in Brazil since 1958, making his home among the very poor. He shows that the work of the Spirit in the New Testament produces transformative action in the world, freedom that comes from liberation of self, bold speech, supportive community built from the bottom up, and an aspiration to a higher life.[71] The outpouring of the Holy Spirit on the disciples at Pentecost, he points out, led directly to such personal and community transformation (Acts 2.40–7).

Pentecostals also experience the liberating power of the Spirit of God, although they may see this more in personal terms and the results in terms of spiritual gifts, healing and material well-being. They look back to the same occasion of Pentecost but they may be more impressed by the quotation by the Apostle Peter from the book of Joel on that occasion about the pouring out of the Spirit in the form of prophecy, visions, signs and wonders (Acts 2.16–21). Latin American Pentecostal theologian Juan Sepúlveda has compared Pentecostal churches with base communities and identifies four areas of commonality between them: both grew up among the poorest of society; in both the participants gain a direct experience of God's love; both encourage common people to read the Bible; and both understand the church as a community. Therefore, he concludes that Pentecostalism and liberation theology may be regarded as 'two manifestations of the work of the Holy Spirit for the renewal of the Church'.[72]

5.7 Political theology

In the West liberation theologies have been included under the wider heading of 'political theology', which covers any theology which engages in 'the analysis and criticism of political arrangements'.[73] In this sense 'political theology' can include the Old Testament prophets and classical theologians like Augustine, Thomas Aquinas and John Calvin, and twentieth-century figures engaging with Nazism like Karl Barth and Dietrich Bonhoeffer. But the recent popularization of the term derives from the work of German theologians Johann Baptist Metz, a Roman Catholic, and Jürgen Moltmann, Protestant, beginning in the 1960s.[74] They shared a common interest in Christian–Marxist dialogue in the context of the Cold War, a common concern to challenge the silence of churches about German crimes against humanity – especially the Jewish people, and an 'openness to the future' as the sphere of God's activity. Metz and Moltmann developed a theology of Christian participation in history's movement toward the future, mindful of the realities both of suffering and hope, as symbolized by the biblical testimony to both the cross and the resurrection.

Metz and Moltmann were engaged in dialogue with the Latin Americans like Gutiérrez, Juan Luis Segundo and Leonardo Boff, and Moltmann has compared and contrasted his political theology with liberation theology.[75] Political theology grew up in the 1960s in the context of East–West conflict in Europe. Liberation theology arose in Latin America in the same decade but in the context of the North–South divide between rich and poor nations. Both engaged in Christian–Marxist dialogue but whereas political theology mainly criticized the indifference of privatized religion, liberation theologians argued against the injustice of economic development models and the churches which supported them. Political theology took its biblical starting point from the Sermon on the Mount. It aimed to bring hope and free the victims of atrocities. Liberation theology began with the 'Nazareth manifesto'. It urged a revolutionary approach to liberate the poor.

Political theology of any kind is done in a changing world. Among the huge changes in global politics since World War Two, the greatest has been the end of the Cold War. This was the most important factor in the demise of both communism and right-wing dictatorships. But, under the influence of liberation theology, the Roman Catholic and other churches played an important role in the rise of democracy in the new countries of Eastern Europe and in former dictatorships, especially in Latin America, by giving the new popular democracy religious legitimacy. The church acted as a brake on extremists and a mediator between factions, for example, in both El Salvador and Guatemala by sponsoring 'national dalogue' to widen participation and strengthen democracy. In the Andean nations of Bolivia and Peru the church became an advocate of the rights of the Indians, and in Brazil and Chile it supported the main opposition. In many cases it was the only body with enough support to break the deadlock between opposing forces.[76]

The liberation theological interpretation of the gospel as good news to the poor was based on the Bible and the documents of Vatican Two and is now widely accepted. It has helped change the Roman Catholic Church from a supporter of right-wing regimes to perhaps the world's most powerful advocate of democracy and human rights. But the failure of communism to build a long-term viable economic and political system is problematic for liberation theologies in so far as they utilized Marxist social analysis and put forward a political and economic alternative in socialism. Since 1990, political theologies have taken one of two new directions. The first is to continue to challenge the state, but without recourse to other political theories, 'simply by responding to the dynamics of its own proper themes', such as Christ, salvation, the church, the Trinity, the kingdom.[77] Second, in the absence of any alternative to capitalist liberal democracy in the world at the moment, proponents of what is called 'public theology' argue that the church should find ways of contributing to improve the existing systems.[78] The rise of democratic participation has led to the growth of 'civil society', that is, of voluntary civic and social organizations and institutions as distinct from structures of the state and the activities of business. The church, which is such an organization, can engage in public debate and support public life through this sector without necessarily siding with a political position – although Christians may take sides on particular issues. In contemporary Latin America, the Roman Catholic Church is learning to operate in a different political culture, and one in which it is no longer looked to as the chief moral authority. It has to share the public space with Evangelical and Pentecostal churches which, unlike in some parts of the world, are very active politically, as well as with other religions.[79]

Both Pentecostal theology and Roman Catholic theology since Vatican Two are concerned with empowerment of the people of God, and this cannot but impinge on political power at some point in struggles for justice, freedom and well-being. The power of God, which is the Holy Spirit, can be seen at work in the changes brought about through liberation, postcolonial, black and feminist theologies. But the way in which the Holy Spirit works is different from political processes because the Holy Spirit is the Spirit of love (Rom. 5.5; 1 Cor. 13).[80] The Spirit confers a higher spiritual power of love and at the same time constrains the way Christians and the Christian community operate in the political and public spheres. The achievement of justice, freedom and well-being for selfish gain or without loving intent is dishonouring to the servant God of Jesus Christ, and ultimately as ineffective as 'a noisy gong or a clanging symbol' (1 Cor. 13.1).

Notes

1 A probably apocryphal story heard in a lecture by Dr John Corrie at the United College of the Ascension, Selly Oak, Birmingham, *c.*2004.

2 Gustavo Gutiérrez, *Las Casas: In Search of the Poor of Jesus Christ*, trans. Robert R. Barr (Maryknoll, NY: Orbis Books, 1993 [1992]), pp. 461–4; Virgil Elizondo, *Guadalupe, Mother of a New Creation* (Maryknoll, NY: Orbis Books, 1997), p. xiv; see also José Oscar Beozzo, 'Humiliated and Exploited Natives', in Leonardo Boff and Virgil Elizondo (eds), *1492–1992: The Voice of the Victims* (London: SCM Press, 1990), pp. 78–89.

3 Howard J. Wiarda, *The Soul of Latin America: The Cultural and Political Tradition* (New Haven: Yale Divinity Press, 2001), p. 100.

4 Adrian Hastings, 'Latin America', in Adrian Hastings (ed.), *A World History of Christianity* (London: Cassell, 1999), pp. 328–68, at p. 360; for documents, see A. T. Hennelly, *Liberation Theology: A Documentary History* (Maryknoll, NY: Orbis Books, 1990), pp. 89–119; for details, see Enrique Dussel, *A History of the Church in Latin America*, trans. Alan Neely (Grand Rapids, MI: Wm B. Eerdmans, 1981), pp. 141–7, 255.

5 Hastings, 'Latin America', p. 361.

6 Paulo Freire, *Pedagogy of the Oppressed*, trans. Myra Bergman Ramos (New York: Seabury Press, 1970 [1968]).

7 Juan Luis Segundo, *The Liberation of Theology*, trans. John Drury (Maryknoll, NY: Orbis Books, 1976 [1975]), pp. 4–5.

8 Gustavo Gutiérrez, *A Theology of Liberation*, trans. Caridad Inda and John Eagleson (Maryknoll, NY: Orbis Books, 1973 [1971]), p. 88.

9 Gutiérrez, *Theology of Liberation*, pp. 81–173.

10 Hennelly, *Liberation Theology*, pp. xv–xvi.

11 Hennelly, *Liberation Theology*, pp. 121–4.

12 Leonardo Boff, *Ecclesiogenesis: The Base Communities Reinvent the Church*, trans. Robert R. Barr (London: Collins, 1986); Hastings, 'Latin America', pp. 360–2.

13 John Paul II, *Sollicitudo rei socialis* ('On Social Concern') (1987), para. 42; John Paul II, *Centesimus Annus* ('On the Hundredth Anniversary') (1991), para. 11 – both available at <www.vatican.va>; Donal Dorr, *Option for the Poor: A Hundred Years of Vatican Social Teaching*, rvsd edn (Maryknoll, NY: Orbis Books, 1992), pp. 233–51.

14 Gustavo Gutiérrez, *We Drink from Our Own Wells: The Spiritual Journey of a People* (Maryknoll, NY: Orbis Books, 1984).

15 Gutiérrez, *Theology of Liberation*, p. 11.

16 José Miguez Bonino, *Doing Theology in a Revolutionary Situation* (Philadelphia, PA: Fortress Press, 1975), p. 91.

17 Segundo, *Liberation of Theology.*

18 Rebecca S. Chopp, 'Latin American Liberation Theology', in David F. Ford (ed.), *The Modern Theologians: An Introduction to Christian Theology of the Twentieth Century* (Oxford: Blackwell, 1997), pp. 409–25, at p. 419.

19 J. Andrew Kirk, *Loosing the Chains: Religion as Opium and Liberation* (London: Hodder & Stoughton, 1992); *What Is Mission? Theological Explorations* (London: Darton, Longman and Todd, 1999).

20 Christopher Rowland, *The Open Heaven: A Study of Apocalyptic in Judaism and Early Christianity* (London: SPCK, 1985).

21 Chinua Achebe, *Things Fall Apart* (London: Heinemann, 1958); V. S. Naipaul, *In a Free State* (Harmondsworth: Deutsch, 1971).

22 Edward Said, *Orientalism: Western Conceptions of the Orient*, 3rd edn (London: Penguin, 1995).

23 See Leela Gandhi, *Postcolonial Theory: A Critical Introduction* (Edinburgh: Edinburgh University Press, 1998).

24 Satianathan Clarke, 'Subalterns, Identity Politics and Christian Theology in India', in Sebastian C. H. Kim (ed.), *Christian Theology in Asia* (Cambridge: Cambridge University Press, 2008) pp. 271–90.

25 See R. S. Sugirtharajah, *The Bible and the Third World: Precolonial, Colonial and Postcolonial Encounters* (Cambridge: Cambridge University Press, 2001), pp. 259–71.

26 For example, Gayatri Chakravorty Spivak, *A Critique of Postcolonial Reason: Towards a History of the Vanishing Present* (Cambridge, MA: Harvard University Press, 1999).

27 R. S. Sugirtharajah, *The Bible and Empire: Postcolonial Explorations* (Cambridge: Cambridge University Press, 2005); *Postcolonial Reconfigurations: An Alternative Way of Reading the Bible and Doing Theology* (London: SCM Press, 2003); *Postcolonial Criticism and Biblical Interpretation* (Oxford: Oxford University Press, 2002); *Bible and the Third World*; *Asian Biblical Hermeneutics and Post Colonialism: Contesting the Interpretations* (Maryknoll, NY: Orbis Books, 1998).

28 Sebastian Kappen (ed.), *Jesus Today* (Madras: AICUF, 1985).

29 Robert Allen Warrior, 'Canaanites, Cowboys, and Indians', in R. S. Sugirtharajah (ed.), *Vernacular Hermeneutics* (Sheffield: Sheffield Academic Press, 1999), pp. 277–85.

30 Samuel Rayan, 'Caesar Versus God', in Kappen, *Jesus Today*, pp. 88–97.

31 R. S. Sugirtharajah, (ed.), *Postcolonial Bible* (Sheffield: Sheffield

Academic Press, 1998); *Postcolonial Biblical Reader* (Oxford: Blackwell Publishing, 2006); *A Postcolonial Commentary on the New Testament Writings* (London: Continuum, 2007).

32 Mukti Barton, *Scripture as Empowerment for Liberation and Justice: The Experience of Christian and Muslim Women in Bangladesh* (Bristol: University of Bristol, 1999), pp. 107–18; Vandana, *Waters of Fire* (Bangalore: Asia Trading Corporation, 1989), pp. 76–92; Teresa Okure, *The Johannine Approach to Mission: A Contextual Study of John 4.1–42* (Tübingen: J. C. B. Mohr, 1988). For further examples see, R. S. Sugirtharajah (ed.), *Voices from the Margin: Interpreting the Bible from the Third World*, rvsd edn (Maryknoll, NY: Orbis Books, 1995).

33 See the following articles in Sugirtharajah, *Voices from the Margin*: George M. Soares-Prabhu, 'Two Mission Commands: An Interpretation of Matt 28:16–20 in the Light of a Buddhist Text', pp. 319–38; Archie C. C. Lee, 'The Chinese Creation Myth of Nu Kua and the Biblical Narrative in Gen 1—11', pp. 368–80; S. Gandaran and Israel Selvanayagam, 'The Communion of Saints: Christian and Tamil Śaiva Perspectives', pp. 381–93.

34 Cf. Sugirtharajah, *Postcolonial Reconfigurations*, p. 8.

35 Catherine Keller, Michael Nausner and Mayra Riviera (eds), *Postcolonial Theologies: Divinity and Empire* (St Louis, MS: Chalice Press, 2004), p. 13.

36 Gerald Boodoo, 'Christologies, Caribbean', in Virginia Fabella and R. S. Sugirtharajah (eds), *Dictionary of Third World Theologies* (Maryknoll, NY: Orbis Books, 2000), pp. 52–3; Lewin L. Williams, *Caribbean Theology* (Frankfurt: Peter Lang, 1994), pp. 62–5.

37 Laënnec Hurbon, 'The Slave Trade and Black Slavery in America', in Boff and Elizondo, *1492–1992*, pp. 90-100.

38 Hemchand Gossai and Nathaniel Samuel Murrell (eds), *Religion, Culture, and Tradition in the Caribbean* (London: Macmillan, 2000).

39 Nathaniel Samuel Murrell, 'Blackman's Bible and Garveyite Ethiopianist Epic with Commentary', in Gossai and Murrell, *Religion, Culture, and Tradition in the Caribbean*, pp. 271–306, see p. 304.

40 Kortright Davis, *Emancipation Still Comin': Explorations in Caribbean Emancipatory Theology* (Maryknoll, NY: Orbis Books, 1990), pp. 135–9.

41 Shelly Eversley (ed.), *The Interesting Narrative of the Life of Olaudah Equiano or, Gustavus Vassa, the African, Written by Himself* (New York: The Modern Library, 2004).

42 Vincent Harding, *Martin Luther King: The Inconvenient Hero* (Maryknoll, NY: Orbis Books, 1996), p. 55.

43 Dwight N. Hopkins, *Introducing Black Theology of Liberation* (Maryknoll, NY: Orbis Books, 1999), pp. 15–48.

44 James H. Cone, *A Black Theology of Liberation* 3rd edn (Maryknoll, NY: Orbis Books, 1990 [1970]), pp. 37–8, 63–4.

45 Hopkins, *Introducing Black Theology of Liberation*.

46 For example, Manas Buthelezi, 'Salvation as Wholeness', in John Parratt (ed.), *A Reader in African Christian Theology*, 2nd edn (London: SPCK, 1997; article first published in 1972), pp. 85–90; Allan Aubrey Boesak, *Farewell to Innocence: A Socio-ethical Study on Black Theology and Power* (Maryknoll, NY: Orbis Books, 1977).

47 John W. de Gruchy, *The Church Struggle in South Africa*, 3rd edn (London: SCM Press, 2004). For the Kairos document, see Norman E. Thomas (ed.), *Classic Texts in Mission and World Christianity* (Maryknoll, NY: Orbis Books, 1995), pp. 197–8.

48 Robert Beckford, *Jesus Is Dread: Black Theology and Black Culture in Britain* (London: Darton, Longman and Todd, 1998), at p. 144.

49 Michael N. Jagessar and Anthony C. Reddie (eds), *Postcolonial Black British Theology: New Textures and Themes* (Peterborough: Epworth, 2007), pp. xi–xxvii.

50 Michael N. Jagessar, 'Spinning Theology: Trickster, Texts and Theology', in Jagessar and Reddie, *Postcolonial Black British Theology*, pp. 124–45.

51 Sylvia Chant with Nikki Craske, *Gender in Latin America* (London: Latin America Bureau, 2003).

52 Caipora Women's Group, *Women in Brazil* (London: Latin America Bureau, 1993), pp. 21–3.

53 *Catechism of the Catholic Church*, part 1, section 2, chapter 3, article 9, paragraph 6 – available at <www.vatican.va>; Marina Warner, *Alone of All Her Sex: The Myth and Cult of the Virgin Mary* (London: Picador, 1985).

54 Elizondo, *Guadalupe*, p. 8.

55 See John Paul II, *Redemptoris Mater* ('On the Blessed Virgin Mary') (1987) – available at <www.vatican.va>.

56 Marianne Katoppo, *Compassionate and Free: An Asian Woman's Theology* (Geneva: WCC Publications, 1979), pp. 16–24; Vandana, *And the Mother of Jesus was There: Mary in the Light of Indian Spirituality* (Garhwal, UP: Jeevan Dhara Ashram Society, 1991).

57 The following introduce Asian, African and Latin American feminist theology (respectively): Kwok, Pui-Lan, *Introducing Asian Feminist Theology* (Sheffield: Sheffield Academic Press, 2000); Mercy Amba Oduyoye, *Introducing African Women's Theology* (Sheffield: Sheffield Academic Press, 2001); Ada María Isasi-Díaz, *Mujerista Theology: A Theology for the Twenty-first Century* (Maryknoll, NY: Orbis Books, 1996).

58 Rosemary Radford Ruether, 'The Emergence of Christian Feminist

Theology', in Susan Frank Parsons (ed.), *The Cambridge Companion to Feminist Theology* (Cambridge: Cambridge University Press, 2002), pp. 3–22, see pp. 7–8; Elaine Graham, 'Feminist Theology, Northern', in Peter Scott and William T. Cavanaugh (eds), *The Blackwell Companion to Political Theology* (Oxford: Blackwell, 2004), pp. 210–26, at p. 210.

59 John Parratt, *Reinventing Christianity: African Theology Today* (Grand Rapids, MI: Wm B. Eerdmans, 1995), p. 51; Katoppo, *Compassionate and Free*, pp. 9–24.

60 Kwok, Pui-lan, 'Feminist Theology, Southern', in Scott and Cavanaugh, *Blackwell Companion to Political Theology*, pp. 194–209, at p. 194; Kwok, Pui-lan, 'Feminist Theology as Intercultural Discourse', in Parsons, *Cambridge Companion to Feminist Theology*, pp. 23–39.

61 Chung, Hyun Kyung, 'Ecology, Feminism and African and Asian Spirituality: Towards a Spirituality of Eco-feminism', in David G. Hallman (ed.), *Ecotheology: Voices from South and North* (Geneva: WCC Publications, 1994), pp. 175–8; Mercy Amba Oduyoye, *Beads and Strands: Reflections of an African Woman on Christianity in Africa* (Oxford: Regnum, 2002), pp. 57–63.

62 Mary Daly, *Beyond God the Father: Toward a Philosophy of Women's Liberation* (London: The Women's Press, 1973), pp. 114–22.

63 Allan Anderson, *An Introduction to Pentecostalism* (Cambridge: Cambridge University Press, 2004), pp. 10–13, 63, 68, 76.

64 Anthony Gill, 'The Struggle to be Soul Provider: Catholic Responses to Protestant Growth in Latin America', in Christian Smith and Joshua Pokopy (eds), *Latin American Religion in Motion* (New York: Routledge, 1999), pp. 17–42; Marjo de Theije, 'CEBs and Catholic Charismatics in Brazil', in Smith and Pokopy, *Latin American Religion in Motion*, pp. 111–24.

65 Charles H. Kraft, 'Allegiance, Truth and Power Encounters in Christian Witness', in Jan A. B. Jongeneel, *Pentecost, Mission and Ecumenism: Essays on Intercultural Theology* (Frankfurt am Main: Peter Lang, 1992), pp. 215–30.

66 John Wimber, *Power Evangelism* (New York: Harper and Row, 1985).

67 Peter C. Wagner, 'Territorial Spirits and World Missions', *Evangelical Missions Quarterly* 25/3 (1989), pp. 278–88.

68 Chuck Lowe, *Territorial Spirits and World Evangelization? A Biblical, Historical and Missiological Critique of 'Strategic Level Spiritual Warfare'* (Sevenoaks, UK: Mentor, 1998); Martyn Percy, *Words, Wonders and Power: Understanding Contemporary Christian Fundamentalism and Revivalism* (London: SPCK, 1996).

69 Walter Wink, *Naming the Powers: The Language of Power in the New Testament* (Minneapolis, MN: Fortress Press, 1984); *Unmasking*

the Powers: The Invisible Forces That Determine Human Existence (Minneapolis, MN: Fortress Press, 1986); *Engaging the Powers: Discernment and Resistance in a World of Domination* (Minneapolis, MN: Fortress Press, 1992); *The Powers That Be: Theology for a New Millennium* (New York and London: Doubleday, 1998).

70 Wink, *Engaging the Powers*, pp. ii, 313–14.

71 José Comblin, *The Holy Spirit and Liberation* (Maryknoll, NY: Orbis Books, 1989), pp. xii, 20.

72 Juan Sepúlveda, 'Pentecostalism and Liberation Theology: Two Manifestations of the Work of the Holy Spirit for the Renewal of the Church', in Harold D. Hunter and Peter D. Hocken (eds), *All Together in One Place: Theological Papers from the Brighton Conference on World Evangelization* (Sheffield: Sheffield Academic Press, 1990), pp. 51–64. Compare the case of Afro-Caribbean religion: Mark Lewis Taylor, 'Spirit', in Scott and Cavanaugh, *Blackwell Companion to Political Theology*, pp. 377–92.

73 Scott and Cavanaugh, *Blackwell Companion to Political Theology*, p. 2.

74 See the following chapters in Scott and Cavanaugh, *Blackwell Companion to Political Theology*: Nicholas Adams, 'Jürgen Moltmann', pp. 227–40; J. Matthew Ashley, 'Johann Baptist Metz', pp. 241–55.

75 Jürgen Moltmann, *God for a Secular Society* (London: SCM Press, 1999), pp. 47–51.

76 Jeffrey Klaiber, *The Church, Dictatorships, and Democracy in Latin America* (Maryknoll, NY: Orbis Books, 1998).

77 Oliver O'Donovan, *The Desire of Nations: Rediscovering the Roots of Political Theology* (Cambridge: Cambridge University Press, 1996).

78 William F. Storrar and Andrew R. Morton, *Public Theology for the 21st Century* (Edinburgh: T&T Clark, 2004); see *International Journal of Public Theology* (Leiden: Brill).

79 Edward L. Cleary and Hannah W. Stewart-Gambino (eds), *Power, Politics and Pentecostals in Latin America* (Boulder, CO: Westview, 1998); Paul Freston, *Evangelicals and Politics in Asia, Africa and Latin America* (Cambridge: Cambridge University Press, 2001); Sarah Brooks, 'Catholic Activism in the1990s: New Strategies for the Neoliberal Age', in Smith and Pokopy, *Latin American Religion in Motion*, pp. 67–89.

80 Steven J. Land, *Pentecostal Spirituality: A Passion for the Kingdom* (Sheffield: Sheffield Academic Press, 1993), pp. 131–6.

6

SPIRIT-UALITY

Christian Witness in a Multi-faith Context

> For an East Asian Christian, 'other living faiths exist inside as well as outside'.[1]
> Jong Chun Park

All the major world religions – including Christianity – originate from the one continent we call Asia, and so it is not surprising to find that the experience of Christians in Asia lies behind most Christian reflection on interfaith relations. The early twentieth-century Indian theologian Pandipeddi Chenchiah, a lawyer and convert from Hinduism, recognized that 'No man can serve two masters' but nevertheless believed that 'every man can love two parents, father and mother'. So, as a child of both Hinduism and Christianity he argued that 'instead of using Christ and Christian experience as a searchlight to discover the defects of Hinduism, we use Hinduism and Hindu experience to the elucidation of the meaning and purpose of Christ'. Chenchiah maintained that, as a convert, he was doubly emancipated from the traditions of Hinduism and Christianity and, at the same time, though committed to Christ, he was indebted to both. The convert, he wrote, 'discovers the supreme value of Christ, not in spite of Hinduism but because Hinduism has taught him to discern spiritual greatness'. And his position as a convert, he believed, enabled him to discover the distinctive core of Christianity.[2]

The gospel writers evince some discomfort about the fact that Jesus submitted himself to baptism at the hands of his cousin John. However, in this period before Christianity became separate from Judaism, the embarrassment was because John's baptism was 'for the forgiveness of sins', whereas Jesus is perceived to be the sinless one, and not at all because baptism was a Jewish religious practice.[3] Sri Lankan Jesuit Aloysius Pieris argues that, as Jesus committed himself to ministry by submitting to the religious practice of his time, baptism in 'the Jordon of Asian religions' is not problematic but necessary for one who is going to minister in that context.[4] It was during or after his baptism in the waters of the Jordan that the Holy Spirit descended on Jesus in the form of a dove, confirming him in the knowledge that he was God's beloved Son (Mark 1.10 and parallels). The Holy Spirit did not indwell Jesus Christ *in spite of* his Jewishness and Hebrew heritage but *through* it, transforming it into something new. Christianity, argued Chenchiah, is not so much a new religion as a new creation, brought about by the inbreaking into the universe of a fresh Spirit in Jesus Christ. A Christian is someone reborn of the Holy Spirit, the cosmic power released into the world through the incarnation of Jesus Christ. As such he urged Christians not to be afraid of the other religions of India but to experience the transforming power of God in and through the 'confluence of spiritual rivers' there.[5]

In this chapter we will discuss Christian witness in a world of many faiths, especially through Indian experience. We will consider theology of religions and theology of dialogue and discuss a theological approach to religions that begins from acknowledging the freedom of the Spirit of Jesus Christ from the constraints of religious boundaries.

6.1 Thinking about religions

Theology of religions in the British context has been dominated by the figure of Professor John Hick of the University of Birmingham and his 'pluralistic hypothesis'. Hick argued that each of the major religions could be regarded as merely a different perception or lens viewing the same God or Ultimate Reality, and therefore relativized the differences between religions. 'God has many names', wrote Hick and called for a 'Copernican revolution' in attitudes. In the case of Christianity this meant a shift in focus from Jesus Christ to the God (or Reality) in whom Jesus himself believed.[6] Hick's philosophy of religions arose from his own life-experience of an Evangelical conversion, ministry in what is now the United Reformed Church, and then uneasiness about what the claims he had made about Jesus Christ seemed to imply for those of other faiths. This feeling was heightened when in 1967 he moved to Birmingham to take up a chair in theology at the university and witnessed at first hand colonial attitudes to immigrants and their faiths. Hick's experience of working with local religious leaders to prevent violence against religious minorities led him to emphasize that what religions had in common was more important than their differences. In his book *God and the Universe of Faiths* (first published in 1973), Hick laid out a new universal 'map' in which the major world religions are seen to be circling the one 'Ultimate Reality' to which he believed they all pointed.[7]

In a model clearly biased toward the Hickian pluralistic perspective, Church of England clergyman Alan Race classified Christian attitudes to other religions as 'exclusivist', 'inclusivist' or 'pluralist'.[8] Exclusivists believe salvation is only available to those who explicitly confess Jesus Christ – a view usually ascribed to conservative Evangelicals and Fundamentalists. Inclusivists hold that salvation is only possible through Jesus Christ but that his work covers not only those who know him but also others, such as those 'anonymous Christians' described by the Roman Catholic theologian Karl Rahner, who seek God in their own tradition or exhibit Christ-likeness. Pluralists recognize many different saviour-figures and different paths to salvation. The most glaring weakness of the threefold model, as exposed by S. Mark Heim, is that it presupposes that all religions have the same end, which is called 'salvation', a form of self-transcendence or relating to the Ultimate. Heim points out that, in this case, so-called 'pluralistic theology' denies any 'pluralism of authentic religious consequence. The specific details of the faiths seem to become irrelevant.' He argues that salvation is not singular but plural because different religions have different ends. Instead of different paths up the same mountain, we may be dealing with different mountains, all with their own paths.[9] The pluralistic hypothesis and the shift among intellectuals toward a relativistic view of religions as equally valid, in a way parallel to cultural relativism (Chapter 3), meant that religious claims to truth became perceived as a form of aggression toward others and are no longer considered politically correct.

The change Hick called for from exclusivism to pluralism was not merely attitudinal; it was also doctrinal. In particular, according to pluralists, Christians must cease to regard the incarnation as a unique event in which God took human flesh, and understand it instead in a mythic or metaphorical way. To do otherwise, in Hick's view, would be both to condemn other faiths as non-salvific and also to disregard the results of historical criticism.[10] Christian uniqueness, claimed Hick, was a myth constructed to support the imperial expansion of the West, whereas a sober assessment would indicate that all the world religions were 'more or less on a par with each other' as mixtures of good and evil and 'none can be singled out as manifestly superior'.[11] Although Hick contributed a great deal to interfaith relations in Birmingham and elsewhere, his cavalier attitude to Christian tradition alienated many Christians. The Hickian view met a robust response led by Gavin d'Costa at the University of Bristol, who tried to show that Hick's pluralistic theology of religions was itself a myth constructed to achieve certain social goals. Hick's approach was criticized as neo-colonialist because it made global claims about all religions based on Western philosophy. He was accused of disregarding questions of truth, being disrespectful of religious difference, and not pluralistic himself because he attempted to reduce all religions to theism or monism.[12] Lesslie Newbigin pointed out that the pluralistic approach made truth claims just as much as the exclusivist one. He found Hick's proposal 'logically self-defeating' because if Reality is truly unknown by any religion, then there is nothing more to be said.[13] And Rowan Williams, finding inspiration in the Hindu–Christian approach of Raimundo Panikkar, argued that rather than being discarded as an exclusive and unfounded claim, the doctrine of the Trinity can be used to provide the foundation for a Christian theology of religions.[14]

6.2 Encountering Indian multi-faith experience

The Indian subcontinent has been the 'laboratory' of most reflection on interreligious dialogue.[15] India is the homeland of Hindu religion and culture in its many forms, and the related faiths of Jainism, Buddhism and Sikhism. Hinduism does not have a single historical point of origin but is the result of unifying philosophies which have reconciled many different spiritual pathways. It forms a complex religious culture which has been compared to a *banyan* tree: it is a family of religions held together by a number of features that overlap but none of which define it. Some of these are the ancient scriptures (the Vedas), the priesthood (*brahminism*), belief in *karma* (acquired merit or demerit) and rebirth, the caste system, and the ancient language of Sanskrit. Hinduism's diversity is linked to its inclusivity: its readiness to absorb other religious traditions into its spreading branches.[16] Vedantic Hinduism, which is dominant philosophically, is mystical thought in which the aim is to transcend the human condition by means of knowledge of Ultimate Reality or the Universal Spirit. This gnostic approach relativizes specific religious practices in view of what are believed to be higher spiritual goals. Indian commentators on Hick's work – both those who support his approach and those who challenge it – have seen parallels between Hindu philosophical approaches to religious difference and Hick's philosophy of religious pluralism.[17]

The majority of the Indian population comes within the Hindu canopy but there are also substantial Muslim and Christian minorities, Buddhists and long-established Zoroastrian (Parsi) and Jewish communities. Religious differences are closely related to the many ethnic distinctions in what is well described as a subcontinent. Therefore peace between religions is significant for the stability of the region as a whole. The leaders of the independence movement, Mohandas K. Gandhi, Jawaharlal Nehru and others who shaped the constitution of modern India, did so with acute awareness of the subcontinent's multi-religiosity. They established India as a secular state, not in the sense of 'a state which is separate from religion' but in the sense of 'a state which aids all religions impartially', and justified this on the basis of modern Hinduism.[18] The importance of peace between religions was underlined when agreement with the Muslim community could not be reached and in 1947, amid much bloodshed, colonial India was partitioned into India and Pakistan.

According to government statistics Christianity represents between 2 and 3 per cent of the population of the nation of India. It has been present on the Indian subcontinent since at least the second century when the St Thomas Orthodox Church was established. According to tradition, the Apostle Thomas came to India, landing in Malabar in AD 52; historically, the community goes back at least to the second century. The St Thomas Christians have a distinctive and continuous history in India and have preserved an ancient Syriac liturgy. The first Roman Catholics to arrive in the fifteenth century from Portugal, who established themselves at Goa, tried to bring the indigenous Christians under the authority of Rome by force of law. From the sixteenth century Catholicism grew as believers in other faiths responded to the gospel through the labour of Jesuit and other missionaries. Protestant churches in India trace their origins to the early eighteenth-century work of missionaries such as Ziegenbalg and Plütschau of the Danish-Halle Mission, East India Company chaplain Henry Martyn, and the Baptist William Carey. During the period of direct British rule in India (1857–1947), missionary-run institutions (staffed largely by local Christians) supported much of the school and health care systems of the subcontinent. Protestant Christians today belong to the united Church of South India or Church of North India, or to independent denominations. Pentecostal groups particularly are multiplying.

India's different communities are often described in terms of caste, a highly complex and continually evolving system of inherited social status.[19] The 'untouchables' refers to those deemed outside the caste system, who were treated in a subhuman way because they were traditionally regarded as polluted by birth and by occupations such as sweeping and carrying night soil. 'Dalit' is the self-designation of this group, which is not homogeneous but divided into many different communities. Meaning 'broken' or 'downtrodden', the term recognizes the continuing suffering and humiliation these people undergo daily at the hands of higher castes whom they are expected to serve. Dalits represent about 15 per cent of the Indian population and are overwhelmingly found in the rural areas, where they are usually landless and excluded from access to even the most basic amenities, such as village wells. Economic poverty is not identical with caste status but affects the low and outcastes disproportionately. The constitution of the modern state of India does not recognize caste and provides for positive discrimination on behalf of lower and outcastes in the form of welfare benefits and quotas through a system which is probably unparalleled in any other country. However, the ancient caste system continues to be supported by certain forms of Hinduism, and discrimination on grounds of birth blocks the social mobility of many, even in the thriving economy of contemporary India. Since the 1970s dalits have faced increasing violence from caste Hindus as they have actively campaigned for their human rights. In a similar position outside the caste system are tribal communities (*adivasis*) – about 5 to 7 per cent of the total population – who also receive certain social benefits.[20]

The famous dalit leader B. R. Ambedkar championed the dalit cause during the nationalist movement and in newly independent India. From his point of view, Hinduism was not tolerant, but the chief cause of dalit oppression. He did not wish to be included in it and sought an alternative. Christian missionaries hoped he would convert to Christianity, and there were many mass conversions of dalit communities to Christianity during the colonial period.[21] However, Christian churches vary in their attitude to caste. Over 2,000 years, the Syrian Orthodox community has integrated into the caste system and believes itself to be among the higher castes; Syrian churches do not include dalits and there is much resistance to attempts by some to reach out to them. To the anger of many dalits and their supporters, the Roman Catholic Church has accommodated to caste by providing separate cups for different communities at the Eucharist. Protestant churches have made strong statements against caste and draw most of their membership from dalit communities who converted en masse, but in practice local congregations tend to be caste based. Some church leaders and theologians are from dalit backgrounds but not in proportion to dalit numbers.[22]

In the end, Ambedkar and a large group of followers opted in 1956 for Buddhism. Buddhism could be regarded as an Indian religion because it originated there but it repudiates caste. Islam and Christianity, having been introduced into India from elsewhere, fall outside the Hindu system – although Muslims and Christians are always in danger of being accommodated as caste groups. On the grounds that they are free from caste, dalit converts to these religions are not eligible for the compensatory benefits enjoyed by dalits of other faiths. Contemporary dalit Christians therefore face double discrimination in Indian society. Christian social activists in India have long campaigned on their behalf. Dalit theology was initiated in the late 1980s by A. P. Nirmal as a liberation theology *of* the dalits rather than *for* them. Nirmal insisted that no one outside the dalit community could appreciate the depth of suffering of his community except Jesus Christ. Jesus, he argued, was himself a dalit. The evidence for this was that Jesus was of lowly birth and, as the dalits are born to serve the higher castes, Jesus was the servant/slave of all (Mark 10.45; John 13). He was 'despised and rejected' (Isa. 53.3) and, like the dalits who are sweepers, he cleaned the temple (Luke 19.45–8). Nirmal therefore conceived the incarnation as an identification with suffering humanity and regarded the example of Jesus Christ as affirming dalit identity and dignity. He saw the resurrection as vindication of suffering, and salvation as participation in the risen Christ's messianic movement, campaigning for dalit human and civil rights.[23]

The structure of Indian society into a hierarchy of castes which do not mix with one another has faced generations of missionaries with a dilemma: should they aim to reach the high caste leaders of the society in the hopes that their conversion will bring about change all the way down, or would it be more effective, and more Christlike, to work among the poor and bring about the conversion of the masses, hoping in this way to change the society from below? Of the great Jesuit missionaries to India, Francis Xavier took the latter approach and evangelized the Parava fishing community but Robert de Nobili, though anxious to refute Hindu religion, adopted the lifestyle of a *sannyasi* (Hindu contemplative) and studied Sanskrit in order to convert brahmins (the highest, priestly caste). British missionaries were similarly divided but generally speaking, during the colonial period, there were relatively few converts from the higher castes – although many were educated in Christian schools – and most who turned to the Christian faith were low or outcaste. Even today there is a sharp opposition between 'liberationists', who engage in social action with the poor and outcaste in base communities, and the 'ashramites', who practise a 'dialogue of contemplation' with caste Hindus, using Hindu forms of spirituality in ashrams (gathering places for ascetics). The latter may also be motivated to overcome caste but, because they take a pluralist approach to religions which venerate Hindu tradition, they find that differences between Hindus and Christians are best overcome by developing a shared spiritual approach to the Ultimate.[24] Observing this, Paul Knitter, a US American Roman Catholic theologian and an associate of Hick, has noticeably shifted his emphasis from philosophical discussion of how different religions relate to one another to more concrete questions of how religions can together address human rights and environmental justice.[25]

6.3 Catholic theology of religions

Whereas Knitter takes an experimental approach to theology of religions, Belgian Jesuit priest Jacques Dupuis (1923–2004), who spent 36 years in India, aimed to develop a Christian theology of religious pluralism that recognized Indian realities but would be acceptable within the framework of orthodox Catholic teaching. The Church's position as expressed at Vatican Two in the decree *Nostra Aetate* was influenced by Karl Rahner's theology of 'anonymous Christians'. Rahner explained that 'Christ is present and efficacious in the non-Christian believer (and therefore in the non-Christian religions) through his Spirit' – and this presence can be salvific. But the salvation of 'non-Christians' (which may be implicit rather than explicitly in the name of Jesus Christ) always depends on Christ and the Church since 'the Church is nothing else than the visible manifestation of the Spirit in the world'.[26] In other words, Christianity is absolute, and other religions cannot be its equal but are approached with reverence as possible vehicles of God's saving grace. *Nostra Aetate* recognized that other religions may 'often reflect a ray of that Truth which enlightens all men' and envisaged the religions as concentric circles with the Roman Catholic Church at the centre, Judaism as the next circle, Islam as the next, and Buddhism and Hinduism beyond that.[27]

Dupuis went further, while still confessing the indispensability of Jesus Christ and his church for salvation, to argue that religious plurality was not an awkward fact of life, or an opportunity for Christian evangelism, but a positive part of God's creative plan. Like Panikkar and many other Indian theologians, he saw the doctrine of the Trinity as the key to a theology of religions that was Christian and yet appreciative of the presence of other faiths, and in India he made a special study of the Holy Spirit. Dupuis argued that, since the Father has 'two hands' – Word and Spirit (Irenaeus), two Christologies are implied by the doctrine of the Trinity: *Logos* Christology and Spirit Christology. He agreed with Indian theologians that the presence of the Spirit before and after the incarnation means

God's revelation in Jesus Christ does not exhaust the mystery of God and that the doctrine of the Trinity allows for salvation outside the church through the Spirit (Spirit Christology). At the same time, by the doctrine of the Trinity, this salvation is necessarily linked with God's unique saving action in Jesus Christ (*Logos* Christology). Therefore, in Christian theology, salvation is brought about by Jesus Christ.[28]

Vatican officials were nervous of such developments, which seemed to undermine the status of the church and the necessity for missionary proclamation. In 1988, Cardinal Jozef Tomko, Prefect of the Catholic Church's Congregation for the Evangelization of Peoples, publicly criticized two Indian theologians for suggesting that Jesus Christ is 'revealed in other ways through other religions'.[29] Samuel Rayan mounted a robust defence of Indian Christian theology, accusing Tomko of having a 'sense of superiority and exclusiveness' and of 'political and partisan' motives associated with colonial missions 'which destroyed the credibility of the Christian name for decades to come in our land'. He argued that '[t]he suggestion that God provides for peoples' salvation only with the life and death of Jesus of Nazareth is unfair to God, too narrow for biblical perspectives, and too inept for a Spirit-led [human] history of over two million years'. In Rayan's opinion, lack of appreciation of pneumatology was the reason why the Cardinal showed a 'pre-Vatican II missiology' in keeping with the 'one-way mission' attitudes of the colonial era, instead of listening to the voices and traditions of others. Theology, he claimed, is not done by 'faith-statements and doxologies from the Scriptures' but by reflection on 'mission in the Spirit' which takes place where the Spirit is at work in human realities and relationships.[30]

The 1991 papal encyclical on mission, *Redemptoris Missio*, was understood in India to be directed against Indian theologians. It directly addressed the question of the Spirit's role in mission. It affirmed the 'pre-eminence' of the Spirit as 'the principal agent' of the church's mission *ad gentes*, recalling statements of Vatican Two about the Spirit's presence and activity 'in every time and place' and recognizing this as an element in the foundations for interreligious dialogue. But it also stressed that the Spirit is 'not an alternative to Christ' and resisted what it saw as a separation of the work of the Spirit from Christ or the church. The encyclical emphasized the 'permanent priority' of gospel proclamation. Responding to it, Indian theologian Augustine Kanjamala identified in the encyclical

> a certain opposition between the mission of Christ, which is mediated in and through the church, and the work of the Holy Spirit, which is present and operative in a less visible manner outside the church in the religions and cultures of the world

and suggested that it was the theologians of the Vatican, and not those of India, who were failing to keep the Christ and the Spirit together.[31] Dupuis's work, published in 1997, was received enthusiastically by many but criticized by the Sacred Congregation for the Doctrine of the Faith, whose head at the time was Cardinal Joseph Ratzinger, now Pope Benedict XVI. He recognized Dupuis's intention to remain faithful to the church's teaching but expressed concern that doctrinal 'ambiguities and difficulties' could lead the reader into error about the uniqueness and universality of salvation in Jesus Christ.[32]

6.4 Ecumenical theology of dialogue

When the World Council of Churches set up a unit on interfaith dialogue in 1971, they appointed an Indian as its first director. Stanley J. Samartha (1920–2001) was raised in the South Indian town of Mangalore where his father was a Methodist pastor. Samartha remembers harmonious interreligious relations, in what was a very religiously diverse district, and the 'unifying cultural force' of Hindu symbols, myths, songs and dances, philosophy and religious ritual from which he and Christians excluded themselves. Samartha grew up under the influence of the theology of religions of Hendrik Kraemer. Following Barth's negative appraisal of cultures and religions as a way of knowing God, Kraemer was concerned with proclaiming 'the Christian message in a non-Christian world'.[33]

So Samartha rejected other religions and emphasized the exclusive claims of Christ. However, through his further studies in the more cosmopolitan city of Bangalore, where he became actively involved in interfaith dialogue, and in the USA, where he studied under Paul Tillich, Samartha came to appreciate many aspects of Hinduism. As a result, he refuted what he now regarded as an 'exclusivist' approach and embraced a theology of 'pluralism'.[34]

Samartha studied the reception of Christ in India and argued against, on the one hand, Raimundo Panikkar's mystical conception of 'the unknown Christ of Hinduism' because Christianity is not 'Hinduism in disguise'. On the other hand, he criticized his Bangalore colleague M. M. Thomas's argument that Christianity was visible in India in the transformation of Hinduism from an other-worldly to a socially engaged faith. Thomas, Samartha complained, was too taken up with the role of Christianity in the socio-economic development of India to the neglect of the enduring religions of the subcontinent. He himself preferred to think of 'the unbound Christ of Hinduism' because he found that Jesus Christ had crossed the boundaries of the religions of India and was known explicitly and appreciated by many Hindus, who he said formed an 'unbaptized koinonia' beyond the Christian community.[35]

No longer regarding other religious communities as a threat to Christian faith, in Geneva Samartha drafted for the World Council of Churches *Guidelines for Dialogue*, which expressed his approach of 'commitment' (to one's own faith) with 'openness' (to the faith of others) and his insistence that dialogue takes place between people and communities not just at a theological level.[36] In the document Samartha outlined several foundations for dialogue, including a pneumatological one. Because the Holy Spirit 'blows where it wills' (John 3.8) and 'leads into all truth' (John 16.13), Samartha argued, the Spirit may speak through any and all of the partners in dialogue and partners in dialogue may together arrive at greater understanding of truth. In Samartha's theology, the Spirit is both the impulse to dialogue and the medium in which dialogue takes place. 'Dialogue', he writes, is a 'mood, spirit, and attitude'.[37] Paul Knitter later suggested, and Samartha accepted, that his theology of the Unbound Christ was best understood pneumatologically.[38] It is by and in the Spirit that there is 'traffic across the boundaries' of religions. Samartha's religious pluralism was therefore grounded not in philosophical argument like Hick but in a theology of the Holy Spirit as a unifying force, which he parallels with Hindu belief in *advaita* – non-duality or oneness – brought about by the Universal Spirit.

Eventually in 1979 *Guidelines for Dialogue* became accepted as the ecumenical approach to other faiths, but only after considerable opposition from Evangelicals within the World Council of Churches, of whom the most outspoken was Lesslie Newbigin. Newbigin, who had done long missionary service in India and was bishop of the Church of South India, also had a strong appreciation of the work of the Spirit in mission but, commenting on John 16.13, said he could not conceive that the Holy Spirit could 'lead past, or beyond, or away from Jesus'.[39] Unlike Samartha, Newbigin emphasized the uniqueness of Christ and the counter-cultural nature of the Christian gospel in India (especially in condemning caste). Newbigin defended the separateness of the Christian community on the grounds that the church was called to demonstrate the new life in Christ. Like Barth, Newbigin began his theology of religions from the cross of Jesus Christ, understood as a unique event of universal significance, to which Christians – out of loyalty to Christ – are bound to testify. He denied that his Christian faith claims were a condemnation of others or an attempt to convert them, because conversion and salvation are the work of God by the Holy Spirit. For Newbigin it was not evident that all roads lead to the top of the same mountain for 'there are roads which lead over the precipice'. Christians, he wrote, have been shown the road in Christ and owe it to others to point it out to them.[40]

Samartha criticized Evangelicals for perpetuating a colonial missiology and a separatist attitude. Since Samartha seemed to be surrendering some of the essentials of biblical Christian faith and appeared to be closer to Hindus than his fellow Christians, Evangelicals found it difficult to appreciate his approach. Indian Evangelical theologians, who represent popular Indian Christianity, and therefore more of those who find Hinduism oppressive, continue to stress the distinctiveness of the Christian faith and community and the Christian responsibility to evangelize and call for conversion, although they also search for a theology of religions which, while upholding biblical tradition, allows a greater openness to recognizing the work of God outside the boundaries of the Christian church.[41] The famous statement from the World Council of Churches mission conference at San Antonio, Texas (1989) summarizes the tension: 'We cannot point to any other way of salvation than Jesus Christ; at the same time we cannot set limits to the saving power of God.'[42]

6.5 Evangelism and dialogue

After Samartha retired to Bangalore in 1981, he observed the rise in tension between religious communities and increasing militancy of Hindus which threaten the secular nature of the Indian state.[43] Although the vast majority of Indians follow traditional religious practices of India under the broad umbrella of Hinduism, for several hundred years Hindus were ruled by Muslims and then Christians, and India now has a secular government. The *Hindutva* or 'Hindu-ness' movement aims to claim India as Hindu and unify it under a common Hindu culture. Originating in the 1920s, its nationalist inspiration, sense of grievance and belief in cultural superiority has attracted the label of fascism, although this is disputed. The movement rose to prominence in the 1980s and 1990s as a result of concern that the government was being too accommodating to the Muslim minority which, like the Christian, is allowed to live by its own system of personal and family law. Its political wing has achieved wide popular support and held power in central and state governments. It has militant wings, some of which have been implicated in violence against Muslim targets – such as the destruction in 1992 of a mosque believed to have been built on the site of the birthplace of Lord Ram, and more recently in attacks on Christians and churches.[44]

Ever since Swami Vivekananda addressed the first World's Parliament of Religions in 1893,[45] Hinduism has been portrayed in the West as a tolerant faith, and Westerners have admired the way in which for centuries different religious groups have lived together harmoniously on the Indian subcontinent. The assertive nature of *Hindutva* may come as a surprise but in his book *The Saffron Mission* C. V. Mathew, Principal of Jubilee Memorial Bible College, Chennai, argues that Hinduism is as much a missionary religion as Christianity, Islam or Buddhism – as evidenced by its early spread across South-East Asia and its current expansionist agenda.[46] *Hindutva* policy is not primarily intended to exclude minorities but insists that, as they live in India, they should include themselves under the umbrella of Hinduism. In this respect it has some commonality with movements in other religions described as 'fundamentalist'. *Hindutva* leaders also extend an invitation to dalits and tribals to identify as Hindus, and if they have converted to other religions to celebrate a 'home-coming' (*shuddhi*) to Hinduism. For many minorities this attitude is at best patronizing, and at worst hypocritical in view of casteism, and threatening.

Since religious faith in India is a matter of community-belonging and a legal matter to which personal laws apply, conversion from one community to another is not a personal but a public decision, which may have implications for family relations, employment, marriage and other areas of life. In this tense climate the statistical size of each community is an extremely sensitive political issue, and so missionary activity aimed at conversion has been the main target of Hindu complaints about Christians. Significant numbers of conversions, such as have occurred in mass movements to Christianity, upset the balance of power between communities and may be seen as disloyalty to the nation. Hindus have argued that mass movements under colonialism or foreign-financed campaigns of evangelism represent foreign interference and bring about conversion for 'ulterior motives', which are not 'spiritual' but political or economic. At Christian insistence, the right to 'propagate' religion was enshrined in the Indian constitution in 1947 but since then its meaning has been challenged. Freedom to evangelize is restricted in India and several states have passed laws to control and effectively block individuals or groups from changing their community allegiance, except by 'home-coming' to Hinduism. These acts are called 'freedom of religion acts', not in any attempt at irony but because the Hindu majority regard religious freedom as primarily the freedom to maintain the nation's ancient *dharma* (duty or religion) without interference, rather than as freedom to convert from one religion to another.[47]

Hindus, whose religion is inclusive of many diverse traditions, have found it difficult to understand Christian emphasis on conversion, which appears arrogant and exclusive. They regard their own 'welcome' to all communities to join Hinduism as legitimate in India but reject what they see as the 'proselytizing' activities of Christians. Samartha's resistance to Evangelical strategies of proclamation was partly a response to Hindu sensitivities, and he emphatically distanced his theology of dialogue from mission. However, his openness to Hindus was severely challenged by the growing politicization of Hinduism moving into the 1980s. Theology of dialogue founders when the other party/parties do not wish to dialogue. Samartha increasingly saw dialogue not as a political activity but as a form of spirituality. Without dialogue partners and with few opportunities for words, Christian witness in India is more a matter of 'Spirit-uality', living out the Spirit of Christ. As he once wrote, 'The claim that God's presence is with us is not for us to make. It is for our neighbours to recognize.'[48]

Israel Selvanayagam, now Principal of Union Theological Seminary in Bangalore where Samartha once taught, while greatly appreciating Samartha's legacy, has developed a more robust understanding of interfaith dialogue in the light of recent debates and of dialogue with Hindu nationalists. Selvanayagam writes of Christians in India that 'as converts, mostly from the

Hindu or pre-Hindu religious traditions, their existence as a religious minority cannot be justified unless they take the unique position of being evangelical and dialogical'. He urges Christians to take more seriously the evangelistic passion of the Apostle Paul and the biblical message that the Christian message is for all people, while also engaging in friendly dialogue, without which it is impossible for Christians or Hindus to know what is distinctive about Christianity. Being 'evangelical and dialogical' means, on the one hand, resisting fundamentalism and respecting other faiths and, on the other hand, sharing what is known of God in and through Jesus Christ in word and in deed. Selvanayagam insists that Christians should challenge those of other faiths with their distinctive message, but only as long as Christians are prepared themselves to be challenged by their neighbours.[49]

Selvanayagam has put forward Acts 27 as a model for interreligious relations in India,[50] and I will elaborate on his suggestion here. Acts 27 describes a fourth journey of the Apostle Paul across the Mediterranean world, but it is seldom, if ever, designated a 'missionary journey' as are the other three. And yet this journey exemplifies Paul's definition of mission in 2 Corinthians 4.5–12 because Paul is a missionary in chains. He witnesses to his Lord in weakness and in a vulnerable position in which he is not in control. He is entirely dependent on the goodwill of the Roman centurion who has been given charge of him to take him to Rome to plead his case before the emperor. Most commentators have treated Acts 27 as an interesting travelogue – the more so because of the 'we passages' which indicate the presence of Luke himself on the trip and the eyewitness detail. But why should this chapter not be expected to yield missionary themes as does the rest of the book of Acts? The reason seems to be that because Paul is not preaching and teaching, he is not perceived to be missionary. But it is precisely this that makes the passage all the more interesting because it shows how the great missionary bears witness in a situation similar to that which so many Christians experience of being constrained and without a platform from which to speak.

Furthermore, Selvanayagam recognizes that this is a parable of the Indian context because 'obviously, the passengers of this ship are interreligious' – a key point which seems to have escaped Western commentators. On the ship would have been sailors, soldiers, cooks, slaves, travellers from all over the empire – all in the same boat. The Christian group was a minority, and a minority in an uncomfortable position.

The story in Acts 27 recounts how the ship was caught in a storm; everyone is afraid; and in this situation Paul and his Christian colleagues take the initiative in a way that leads to the salvation from shipwreck of everyone on board. Selvanayagam applies five aspects of their behaviour to the multi-religious context of India in which Christians are a minority who sink or swim with the nation as a whole. First, being a minority did not hinder the Christian group from acting according to their vision for the good of all. Paul foresaw that God was going to save them and worked to that end. Second, the minority group identified with the majority in the crisis. Unlike the group of sailors who try to escape in the lifeboat and leave the rest to their fate, the Christians are committed to the salvation of all. Third, the Christian group facilitated a safe outcome by advising and encouraging the leadership – even when their suggestions were disregarded – using secular language that the majority could appreciate. Fourth, Paul did not preach Christ or make any specifically Christian claims, at least not in public. He did not turn people's suffering into an evangelistic opportunity, although most of the people were won over to his way of thinking. Fifth, Paul 'gives hope to the hopeless' by his conviction that God will save them and by celebrating this hope by breaking bread before them and encouraging them to eat also. In the end, Selvanayagam points out, the Christians get to safety by the same means as everyone else – by swimming or clinging to planks of wood as the ship breaks up: 'There is no special providence for Christians although they may feel it in mysterious ways', and this Selvanayagam believes, 'could become a witness far more powerful than a miraculous escape'. Finally, Selvanayagam contrasts this story of a boat with an earlier one: Noah's ark, in which the chosen few in the ark are saved while everyone else drowns, and which he fears is the message more commonly preached in Indian churches. Comparison with the story of Jonah, the reluctant missionary, is also instructive: whereas Jonah's presence was deemed to be the cause of the terrible storm that engulfed his ship, so that it ceased only when he was thrown overboard, in Acts 27 Paul's presence and wise intervention, were salvific. Selvanayagam concludes that 'the presence of Paul and his companions in a troublesome sea voyage and shipwreck provides a model for effective Christian witness in a multi-faith context'.[51]

6.6 Rethinking Christian witness among other faiths

Christians in India are called to show that they have at heart the this-worldly interests of all the communities on the ship that is India and are not going to jump ship. They are required to prove their Indianness. As a member of the St Thomas Christian community, Mathew argues that Christianity is also an Indian religion of long standing and, with his colleague Roger Hedlund, he has encouraged the study of other more recent indigenous forms of Christianity to show that Christianity is not always the result of foreign mission activity.[52] But commitment to the ship of India does not mean meekly submitting to the direction of the captain. Indian Christian political involvement on behalf of dalits, for example, and the performance of their own Christian religious practices should not be construed as disloyalty. Nor should the motives of converts be impugned as driven by hope of social or material gain. Those oppressed by the caste system rightly seek a better life. However, those who call others to conversion do bear a great responsibility (Matt. 23.15). In view of this, the World Council of Churches has been working with Roman Catholics, Evangelicals and Pentecostals on a code of conduct on conversion which would set guidelines for ethical witness.[53] Initially to be agreed among Christian leaders, it could also be shared with leaders of other faiths.

While the story in Acts 27 speaks particularly to the Indian context, not all multi-religious contexts are identical, and so it may be that others may find different passages instructive. Moonjang Lee argues convincingly that, because of distinctive Korean religious experience and socio-cultural norms, Korean Christians have a perspective on the other religions of the country that is significantly different from that which has recently become dominant in the West.[54] Christianity is a new and minority religion which other religions have found difficult to tolerate, and so Korean Christians do not feel the same guilt toward other religions which is detectable in Western theologies of religion that carry with them a history of colonial domination. Furthermore, Lee argues, historically not only Christianity but also the traditional religions in Korea have been 'exclusive in their religious commitment and missionary in their practice'. Each religion, which is literally 'teaching' (*gyo*), represents a unique self-contained system which the disciple is expected to master. In Korean culture, loyalty is highly valued and demands total commitment in the family, the workplace, and also in religion. For the faithful believer to take an interest in another religion would be disloyal, and to use elements of one religious system to correct another would be misunderstood as diluting or compromising the tradition. Though personal religious freedom is constitutionally guaranteed nowadays, conversion from one religion to another may often cause expulsion from the family, so it is a decisive step not undertaken lightly. Lee concludes that pluralism in the sense of the influence of the different religions on Korean culture is undeniable, but not in the sense of individuals practising more than one religion. Korean religious identity is single, not multiple; it is based on personal commitment, and religious boundaries are clearly defined and respected. In Korea therefore it is difficult for any one religion to absorb the others.

Any theology and philosophy of religion must depend on the nature of the other religion(s) in view and on the cultural, historical and political situation of those framing it. It also depends on the understanding of 'religion', which is a highly contested term. Is religion 'duty' (India), 'teaching' (Korea) or 'private spirituality' (Britain)? Religions are always particular to a time and place. There can be no universally agreed philosophy or theology of religions. Hitherto theologians of religions have mostly looked on India as their laboratory. There are undoubtedly many parallels in Britain with the Indian context but equally there are differences; we may need to look at other models and consider our own context more carefully to bear authentic witness to the Spirit of Jesus Christ in contemporary Britain.

Notes

1 Jong Chun Park, *Crawl with God, Dance in the Spirit! A Creative Formation of Korean Theology of the Spirit* (Nashville, TN: Abingdon Press 1998), p. 41.

2 P. Chenchiah, 'Religion in contemporary India', in G. V. Job, P. Chenchiah, V. Chakkarai, D. M. Devasahayam, S. Jesudason, Eddy Asirvatham and A. N. Sudarisanam, *Rethinking Christianity in India* (Madras: A. N. Sudarisanam, 1938), pp. 201–15, at p. 214; P. Chenchiah, 'Jesus and non-Christian Faiths', in Job et al., *Rethinking Christianity in India*, pp. 47–62, at pp. 55, 49.

3 John Macquarrie, *Jesus Christ in Modern Thought* (London: SCM Press, 1990), pp. 394–6.

4 Aloysius Pieris, *An Asian Theology of Liberation* (Maryknoll, NY: Orbis Books, 1988), pp. 45–50.

5 Chenchiah, 'Jesus and Non-Christian Faiths'; Chenchiah, 'Religion in Contemporary India', p. 214.

6 John Hick, *God Has Many Names* (Philadelphia: Westminster Press, 1982).

7 John Hick, *God and the Universe of Faiths* (Basingstoke: Macmillan, now Palgrave Macmillan, 1988). For a biography of Hick, see David Cheetham, *John Hick: A Critical Introduction and Reflection* (Aldershot: Ashgate, 2003).

8 Alan Race, *Christians and Religious Pluralism: Patterns in the Christian Theology of Religions* (London: SCM Press, 1983); cf. Paul F. Knitter, *No Other Name? A Critical Survey of Christian Attitudes toward the World Religions* (Maryknoll, NY: Orbis Books, 1985).

9 S. Mark Heim, *Salvations: Truth and Difference in Religion* (Maryknoll, NY: Orbis Books, 1995), pp. 6–7.

10 John Hick, *The Myth of God Incarnate* (London: SCM Press, 1977); *God and the Universe of Faiths*, pp. xi–xii.

11 John Hick, 'The Non-absoluteness of Christianity', in John Hick and Paul F. Knitter (eds), *The Myth of Christian Uniqueness: Toward a Pluralistic Theology of Religions* (Maryknoll, NY: Orbis Books, 1987), pp. 16–36, at pp. 18–20, 30.

12 See the following articles in Gavin D'Costa (ed.), *Christian Uniqueness Reconsidered: The Myth of a Pluralistic Theology of Religions* (Maryknoll, NY: Orbis Books, 1990): Kenneth Surin, 'A "Politics of Speech"', pp. 192–212; Wolfhart Pannenberg, 'Religious Pluralism and Conflicting Truth Claims', pp. 96–106; Paul J. Griffiths, 'The Uniqueness of Christian Doctrine Defended', pp. 157–73; J. A. DiNoia, 'Pluralist Theology of Religions', pp. 119–34.

13 Lesslie Newbigin, 'Religion for the Marketplace', in D'Costa, *Christian Uniqueness Reconsidered*, pp. 135–49, at pp. 141–3.

14 Rowan Williams, 'Trinity and Pluralism', in D'Costa, *Christian Uniqueness Reconsidered*, pp. 3–15; cf. Raimundo Panikkar, *The Trinity and the Religious Experience of Man: Icon–Person–Mystery* (London: Darton, Longman and Todd, 1973).

15 Paul F. Knitter, *One Earth Many Religions: Multifaith Dialogue and Global Responsibility* (Maryknoll, NY: Orbis Books, 1995), p. 157.

16 Julius Lipner, *Hindus: Their Religious Beliefs and Practices* (London and New York: Routledge, 1994), pp. 1–21.

17 For example, Stanley Samartha, 'The Cross and the Rainbow: Christ in a Multireligious Culture', in Hick and Knitter, *Myth of Christian Uniqueness*, pp. 69–88; Vinoth Ramachandra, *The Recovery of Mission: Beyond the Pluralist Paradigm* (Carlisle: Paternoster, 1996), pp. 120–5.

18 Sebastian C. H. Kim, *In Search of Identity: Debates on Religious Conversion in India* (Delhi: Oxford University Press, 2003), p. 56.

19 Ishita Banerjee-Dube (ed.), *Caste in History* (Oxford: Oxford University Press, 2008).

20 V. Devasahayam, *Frontiers of Dalit Theology* (Delhi: ISPCK, 1997); John Parratt, 'Recent Writing on Dalit Theology: A Bibliographical Essay', *International Review of Mission* 83/329 (1994), pp. 329–37.

21 John C. B. Webster, *The Dalit Christians: A History*, 2nd edn (Delhi: ISPCK, 1994).

22 Duncan B. Forrester, *Caste and Christianity: Attitudes and Policies on Caste of Anglo-Saxon Protestant Missions in India* (London: Curzon Press, 1980).

23 A. P. Nirmal, 'Towards a Dalit Christian Theology', in R. S. Sugirtharajah (ed.), *Frontiers in Asian Christian Theology: Emerging Trends* (Maryknoll, NY: Orbis Books, 1994), pp. 27–40.

24 Knitter, *One Earth Many Religions*, pp. 157–80, see p. 166;

'Stanley Samartha's *One Christ – Many Religions*: Plaudits and Problems', *Current Dialogue* 21 (December 1991), pp. 25–30, at p. 29; Stanley Samartha, 'In Search of a Revised Christology: A Response to Paul Knitter', *Current Dialogue* 21 (December 1991), pp. 30–7, at p. 35; Vandana, 'Introduction' (to Part IV, Hinduism section), *Shabda, Shakti Sangam* (Bangalore: NBCLC, 1995), p. 190.

25 Compare Knitter, *No Other Name?*, with Knitter, *One Earth Many Religions.*

26 Quoted in Amos Yong, *Discerning the Spirit(s): A Pentecostal-charismatic Contribution to Christian Theology of Religions* (Sheffield: Sheffield Academic Press, 2000), p. 73; see also pp. 71–7; Jacques Dupuis, *Toward a Christian Theology of Religious Pluralism* (Maryknoll, NY: Orbis Books, 1999 [1997]), pp. 143–9.

27 *Nostra Aetate* ('Declaration on the Relation of the Church to Non-Christian Religions') (1965), para. 4 – available at <www.vatican.va>.

28 Dupuis, *Toward a Christian Theology of Religious Pluralism*; Jacques Dupuis, *Jesus Christ and His Spirit* (Bangalore: Theological Publications in India, 1977).

29 See articles by Jacob Tomko, in Paul Mojzes and Leonard Swidler (eds), *Christian Mission and Interreligious Dialogue* (Lewiston: Edwin Mellen Press, 1990): 'Missionary Challenges to the Theology of Salvation', pp. 12–32, see pp. 22–4; 'Christian Mission Today', pp. 236–62, at p. 240. The named theologians were Michael Amaladoss and Joseph Kavunkal.

30 Samuel Rayan, 'Religions, Salvation, Mission', in Mojzes and Swidler, *Christian Mission and Interreligious Dialogue*, pp. 126–39.

31 John Paul II, *Redemptoris Missio* ('On the Permanent Validity of the Church's Missionary Mandate') (1990), paras 21–30 – available at <www.vatican.va>. Augustine Kanjamala, '*Redemptoris missio* and mission in India', in William R. Burrows (ed.), *Redemption and Dialogue: Reading* Redemptoris Missio *and Dialogue and Proclamation* (Maryknoll, NY: Orbis Books, 1993), pp. 195–205, see pp. 202, 203; see also p. 244 in the same volume.

32 Dupuis, *Toward a Christian Theology of Religious Pluralism*; Congregation for the Doctrine of the Faith, 'Notification on the Book *Toward a Christian Theology of Religious Pluralism* (Orbis Books: Maryknoll, New York 1997) by Father Jacques Dupuis, S.J.', 24 January 2001. The doctrine of the uniqueness and universality of salvation in Jesus Christ is attested in the CDF Declaration *Dominus Iesus* (2000) – both documents available at <www.vatican.va>.

33 Stanley J. Samartha, *Between Two Cultures: Ecumenical Ministry in a Pluralist World* (Geneva: WCC Publications, 1996), pp. 3–6; Hendrik Kraemer, *The Christian Message in a Non-Christian World* (London: Edinburgh House, 1938).

34 Stanley Samartha, 'The Cross and the Rainbow'.

35 Raimundo Panikkar, *The Unknown Christ of Hinduism: Towards an Ecumenical Christophany*, rvsd edn (London: Darton, Longman and Todd, 1981); Stanley J. Samartha, 'The Unknown Christ Made Better Known. Review of Raimundo Panikkar, *The Unknown Christ of Hinduism* 2nd edn', *Religion & Society* 30/1 (March 1983), pp. 52–61. M. M. Thomas, *The Acknowledged Christ of the Indian Renaissance*, 3rd edn (Madras: CLS, 1991 [1970]); Stanley J. Samartha, *The Hindu Response to the Unbound Christ: Towards a Christology in India* (Bangalore: CISRS, 1974), pp. 183–4, 119.

36 Available at <www.oikoumene.org>.

37 Stanley J. Samartha, *One Christ – Many Religions: Towards a Revised Christology* (Maryknoll, NY: Orbis Books, 1991), p. 57.

38 Paul Knitter, 'Stanley Samartha's *One Christ – Many Religions* – Plaudits and Problems', *Current Dialogue* 21 (December 1991), pp. 25–30, see p. 28; Stanley J. Samartha, 'In Search of a Revised Christology: A Response to Paul Knitter', *Current Dialogue* 21 (December 1991), pp. 30–7, see p. 34.

39 Lesslie Newbigin, *The Open Secret: An Introduction to the Theology of Mission* rvsd edn (Grand Rapids, MI: Wm. B. Eerdmans, 1995), pp. 56–65; *The Light Has Come: An Exposition of the Fourth Gospel* (Edinburgh: Handsel, 1982), pp. 216–17.

40 Lesslie Newbigin, *The Household of God*, 2nd edn (London: SCM Press, 1964), p. 26; *The Gospel in a Pluralist Society* (London: SPCK, 1989), pp. 155–83, quote from p. 183.

41 Ramachandra, *Recovery of Mission*, pp. 3–37; Sunand Sumithra (ed.), *Doing Theology in Context* (Bangalore: Theological Book Trust, 1992), pp. 79–97; Ken R. Gnanakan, *The Pluralistic Predicament* (Bangalore: Theological Book Trust, 1992), pp. 149–71.

42 'Report from Section I', para. 26, in F. R. Wilson (ed.), *The San Antonio Report: Your Will Be Done: Mission in Christ's Way* (Geneva: WCC Publications, 1990), p. 32.

43 Samartha, *Between Two Cultures*, pp. 138–9.

44 For background, see Christophe Jaffrolet, *The Hindu Nationalist Movement in India* (New Delhi: Viking, 1996).

45 Marcus Braybrooke, *Pilgrimage of Hope: One Hundred Years of Global Interfaith Dialogue* (London: SCM Press, 1992).

46 C. V. Mathew and Charles Corwin, *Area of Light: The Indian Church and Modernisation* (Delhi: ISPCK, 1994); C. V. Mathew, *The Saffron Mission: A Historical Analysis of Modern Hindu Missionary Ideologies and Practices* (Delhi: ISPCK, 1999); C. V. Mathew (ed.), *Jubilee Reflections: Essays on Selected Theological Issues* (Delhi: ISPCK, 2000).

47 Kim, *In Search of Identity*, pp. 59–87. For Hindu perspectives, see

Arun Shourie, *Missionaries in India: Continuities, Changes, Dilemmas* (New Delhi: ASA Publications, 1994).

48 Stanley J. Samartha, 'Milk and Honey – Without the Lord?', *National Christian Council Review* 101/12 (December 1981), pp. 662–71, at p. 670.

49 Israel Selvanayagam, *A Second Call: Ministry and Mission in a Multifaith Milieu* (Madras: CLS, 2000), pp. 338–53; *A Dialogue on Dialogue: Reflections on Interfaith Encounters* (Madras: CLS, 1995), pp. 123–37 – the latter volume is endorsed by Stanley Samartha.

50 Selvanayagam, *Dialogue on Dialogue*, pp. 110– 22.

51 Selvanayagam, *Dialogue on Dialogue*, pp. 117, 121, 122.

52 Roger E. Hedlund (ed.), *Christianity Is Indian: The Emergence of an Indigenous Community* (Delhi: ISPCK, 2000).

53 Information at <www.oikoumene.org>.

54 Moonjang Lee, 'Experience of Religious Plurality in Korea: Its Theological Implications', *International Review of Mission* 88/351 (October 1999), pp. 399–413.

7

WISDOM OF THE SPIRIT

Mission in Scientific and Secular Society

> The popular notion that Darwin had 'disproved the Bible' was to convince many that the authority of something called 'Science' was weightier than the authority of something called 'Religion'.[1]
> Mary Heimann

'World' mission has generally concerned itself with only a part of the world: the part where the greatest needs are perceived to be, and where missionaries have been sent since colonial times. In the British case this is mainly South Asia ('India') and East Asia (the 'Far East'), some Pacific Islands, Anglophone Africa, the Caribbean, and the 'Middle East'. British mission links with Francophone Africa, Central Asia and with Latin America are weak. Russia and Central and Eastern Europe – the Orthodox lands – came to European attention as mission fields only with the fall of the Ottoman Empire around the turn of the twentieth century. There are some very obvious gaps in this map of the world which 'world' mission – and often 'world' Christianity – does not cover: Western Europe is one and the European-dominated former colonies of North America and the Antipodes are another. These blind spots demonstrate the closeness of European relations with these countries and the extent to which 'the West' is regarded as an extension of European identity.

The origins of modern Western culture are found in the social, philosophical and industrial revolutions which inaugurated what we call 'modernity' and gave it its characteristic scientific and secular nature. Since the end of World War Two,

Western culture – and Western Christianity – has been dominated by the USA, which has had a great influence on almost all aspects of post-war popular society and thought in the UK.[2] The first aim of this chapter will be to discuss US American Christian experience to explain its extremes: the fundamentalistic tendencies of American Evangelicalism on the one hand and the liberalism of those who embrace social and scientific development on the other. Second, we will discuss the common challenges of doing mission in the West, in particular in view of its cultures of modernity and postmodernity. Modernity reduces Christianity to filling in the diminishing number of gaps that science cannot explain, and postmodernity regards it as merely one of a number of spiritual alternatives for personal fulfilment. The chapter will conclude by discussing the nature of Christianity as a public faith and the potential of the theology of wisdom to suggest a mission paradigm in the contemporary West.

7.1 Faith and modernity

The term 'modern' is popularly used to mean 'new', 'fashionable' or 'contemporary' but in scholarship 'modernity' refers to the kind of society and culture which developed in the West as the result of a combination of revolutionary changes after the Middle Ages.[3] These could be divided into three revolutions: technological-industrial, socio-political and intellectual-cultural. In the first case, rapid social change was stimulated by the arrival in Europe from Asia of printing by moveable block type, and its refinement in Germany in about 1450, together with the growth of literacy. Britain was the first to experience industrialization, a complex of changes in agriculture, manufacturing and transport which enabled the building of factories and mass production of products by machine. These processes demanded large amounts of raw material which increased the need for exploration and colonization of other parts of the world. At home they necessitated the migration of most of the population from the countryside into urban areas over a 150-

year period. Many other social changes took place alongside this, including rapid population increase aided by better diet, hygiene and eventually, by the late nineteenth century, advanced medical care. In France social revolution went further in the first successful attempt to completely overturn the political system of the Middle Ages, including the monarchy and the church, and replace it with a new republican and secular political system. Both the American and the French revolutions drew on powerful democratic ideas that the people should be represented in government, that individuals were citizens of a nation rather than subjects of a king, and that all human beings had rights which should be protected by government.

One the most significant socio-political developments in modernity was the separation of church from state and the rise of religious plurality. The new nation of the USA led these developments. The US was born out of religious persecution in seventeenth-century Europe when, in the wake of the Protestant Reformation, Catholic rulers persecuted Protestants, Protestants persecuted Catholics, and both persecuted the Anabaptists. In the seventh century the 'New World' became a refuge particularly for groups escaping Europe in search of religious freedom and the opportunity to establish the kind of society envisaged in their tradition. One of the earliest and the most well-known symbols of this migration, the Plymouth Brethren, sailed in the *Mayflower* in 1620 and were soon joined by other Puritans (or Congregationalists) who colonized New England. Soon Maryland was founded in 1629 as a Roman Catholic haven. The states of Virginia and Carolina were developed by trading companies whose workers were pastored by the Church of England, and the remaining 'Middle Colonies' welcomed various dissenting groups. Those who fought for the independence of the colonies from their British masters in 1776 wanted independence not only from the British crown but also from the Church of England, whose Act of Uniformity threatened their hard-earned religious freedom. When independence was achieved, a formula had to be found to bring together a varied collection of former colonies with different religious foundations or none. This was achieved by a federal constitution which forbade the government to make any laws to establish religion or inhibit its free exercise, and which afforded a high degree of autonomy to each new state to run its own affairs according to the traditions already established in that locality. The 13 states soon expanded southwards and westwards to include the Mississippi corridor which was predominantly French Catholic, the south-eastern and south-western parts of the present United States which were already Spanish Catholic, and what was later to become the state of Alaska which was partly evangelized by the Russian Orthodox Church.[4] All these different forms of Christianity coexisted in one nation which no longer legislated about religion, so religious practice became no longer a social obligation but a personal matter of conscience.

Intellectually and culturally Europeans were stimulated in the late Middle Ages by intellectual exchange with Arab scholars, who had preserved classical Greek scholarship with its humanist thinking and had developed their own sophisticated art and science that was highly mathematical. The accommodation of these new ideas led to a distinction in knowledge between what could be known only through revelation of God and what could be deduced by other means by anyone (regardless of faith). Mathematics became the foundation of this 'natural' reason, and was to replace theology as 'queen of the sciences' in the modern period. Philosophy, drawing heavily on classical Greek culture, became separated from theology, and attention shifted from theology – knowledge about God based on God's revelation – to anthropology – study of the nature of the human self and study by human beings. The human knower, it was believed, stood somehow outside the natural world to observe its operation and to classify what was in it, for example, in new encyclopaedias. Scientific knowledge became that knowledge deduced by the modern method of repeated and controlled experiments and scientific theory. It was developed by using mathematically based methods of logic. In 'the Enlightenment', the intellectual revolution of the modern period, this kind of reasoning was taken as the basis of all knowledge and argument. In the aftermath of the wars between religious groups in Europe, reason was promoted for its unifying effect. Reason, it was felt (by the elite males of the time), could be agreed on by all 'rational' human beings regardless of their religious affiliation and, as scientists began to make great progress in understanding how the world worked by universally applicable natural laws, there seemed less and less need to invoke the name of God to explain it. Many of the leading Enlightenment figures were Deists who compared the universe to one of their great machines, designed by its maker but now functioning mostly without any further need for him. Eventually in 1859 Charles Darwin published his theory of evolution by natural selection, which explained the very processes of creation itself in a way that seemed to obviate the need for God altogether. Science, it now seemed, offered an alternative grand or metanarrative, which could explain everything and deliver a superior civilization; religion was no longer needed by the elite, and so the German thinker Friedrich Nietzsche pronounced God 'dead'. Although in the same period, European church life was thriving and the gospel was being exported around the world, the intellectual foundations for faith and its place in modern life were under threat.

Modern society became highly problematic for religion, partly because specific scientific approaches and discoveries undermined biblical and church authority. But there was also a more basic problem: in the 'age of reason', 'religion' was defined as that which is not founded on reason but on faith. Furthermore, 'faith' was seen as blind and unreasonable, and associated with discredited traditions which were blamed for dividing Europe and holding back its development. In this situation Western Christians found themselves on the defensive for the first time in many centuries. Whereas Christian faith had been assumed to be true unless proved otherwise, now the onus was on Christians to justify their faith in terms acceptable to modern science.[5] In the twentieth century, modernist or progressive Christians attempted to do so in different ways: for example, justifying continued faith by pointing to the moral benefits of Christian teaching or by demonstrating Christian compassion. Others attempted to refound Christianity on what could be discovered scientifically about the historical Jesus. Some tried to make Christianity scientifically acceptable by finding natural explanations for miracles and pointing to the principles or meaning behind them as of ongoing relevance. Or they re-expressed God as part of the evolutionary processes of the universe. Still others found a place for faith in psychological and community experience which was less susceptible to analysis by science.[6] While it was necessary for Christians to engage contemporary thought, there was a tendency to fit Christianity into what was acceptable within the straitjacket of modernity, and in this the fullness and comprehensiveness of Christian tradition was lost.

7.2 Revival religion in the USA

During the nineteenth century the focus of interest in the development of Protestantism gradually shifted across the Atlantic from north-western Europe to US America, where its dominant form became Evangelicalism. David Bebbington has summarized the main characteristics of Evangelicalism as demanding conversion, activism in mission and evangelism, having the Bible as their sole basis of authority, and having the Cross at the centre of their theology.[7] Its origins lie among the Puritans, whose strongly biblically based religion demanded individual conversion and participation in a gathered community in which responsibility was shared. Their strong desire for independence and belief in God's sovereignty over national affairs was founded on the exodus narrative. They saw themselves as a nation rescued from tyranny and established in a promised land by divine right. Salvation was thus central to Puritan theology and, following the Reformed tradition, this was understood to be by faith in the efficacy of the cross of Jesus Christ. However, in a situation of religious choice, belief was voluntary and so Evangelicals needed to persuade people to participate. A means to encourage this was found in revival movements.

The first Great Awakening (known in Britain as the Evangelical Revival) resulted in the birth of Methodist churches. The Second Great Awakening, 1800–40, was associated with the name of Charles Finney and produced more Baptist churches. Both were transatlantic phenomena but had greatest effect in the south and west of the USA, among both the white and black communities. The comparative lack of hierarchy and loose denominational structure of the US Methodist and Baptist denominations suited the needs of the expanding nation.[8] Periodically, the scattered population gathered in large 'camp meetings', which were characterized by wild or ecstatic behaviour, such as is associated with certain charismatic revivals in our own day. The Revivalists expounded the offer of salvation and sought to deepen commitment. Finney regarded numbers of conversions as a measure of the success of the revival and developed the pragmatic approach to achieving them, informed by sociological and psychological methods and making full use of available technology, which is widespread today.

The conversion of large numbers in revival movements brought moral transformation to American society and many optimistic entrepreneurial attempts to improve the lives of individuals, to change society and to evangelize the world. Evangelicals were leaders in the economic and social development of the United States up to the middle of the century. However, after this they underwent a 'great reversal' and largely withdrew from public life.[9] The reasons are partly to do with the Civil War (1861–5) in which North fought South, ostensibly over the issue of slavery. Evangelicalism was strongest in the defeated states and after their victory Northern Christians gained the moral high ground. The late nineteenth and early twentieth centuries saw enormous social change in the USA as industry took over from the agricultural economy, and Northern society, where most industry was based underwent rapid modernization and secularization. Theologians in the great Northern universities became increasingly liberal in accommodating to modern thought, accepting biblical criticism and the latest scientific theories. They paid less attention to religious matters such as conversion and doctrinal orthodoxy and the initiative in mission was taken by the 'social gospel' movement (see Chapter 8). Christians became confident they were at the forefront of the inexorable march of progress. They were buoyed up by the kind of hopes expressed in the victorious Civil War anthem, 'The Battle Hymn of the Republic', that as Christ 'died to make men holy' they could 'live to make men free'.

White Evangelicals, especially in the South, felt profoundly threatened by these developments, by the freed slave population, and also by new waves of immigration. Many were increasingly pessimistic and hoped for revival that would bring back the certainties associated with the 'old time religion' as the only solution for a sick society. Their introspection and plain reading of the Bible encouraged millennialist expectations about the return of Christ. Instead of trying to build the kingdom on earth, many believed that true ('believing' or 'born again') Christians would be spared the tribulations to come and 'raptured' from the earth to begin a new life in heaven. Some became convinced that their future had to do with the establishment of a Jewish state and supported the Zionist cause. As they focused on more strictly religious concerns, Holiness movements looked for a 'second blessing' of spiritual perfection and Restorationist (or primitivist) churches rejected any religious practices that could not be justified by the New Testament.

7.3 Fundamentalism

Evangelicals fixed on the Bible as the only anchor in the storms of life and believed, in the Puritan tradition, that American society had been based upon it. But now, it seemed even the Bible was under threat from biblical criticism, and with it traditional Christian doctrines about Jesus Christ.[10] Wishing to keep a Christian world-view, they refused to make any conscious accommodation to the scientific mindset of modernity, at least in matters of faith. In the early twentieth century they became labelled as 'Fundamentalists' after the publication from 1909 of a series of books written by leading conservative theologians, some from Britain as well as North America, defending what were considered to be 'the Fundamentals' of Christian faith, such as the inspiration of the Bible, the deity of Jesus Christ, his unique role in atoning for sin, and the universality of the Christian gospel. They made the test of true faith belief in right doctrine, rather than some other aspect of faith such as right worship, moral uprightness or social work, and their efforts were directed to protecting it. 'Fundamentalists' not only condemned higher criticism of the Bible, they argued for the Bible's historical and scientific accuracy as well as its spiritual authority. They denounced liberal theology and also other threats they associated with the 'social gospellers', including socialism. However, Southern Christianity, along with rural Southern society, was held up to ridicule by the social elite and by liberal theologians of the North, who portrayed it as backward and bigoted.

After World War Two, Evangelicals tried to distance themselves from fundamentalism and rebuild a broader Evangelical coalition which could influence society as the Evangelicals of the Second Great Awakening had done. They supported a young evangelist named Billy Graham, originally from a fundamentalist background. Graham became a hugely popular figure who gradually moved toward centre ground and developed a wider social vision. Through his mass rallies, which were held in cooperation with a wide spectrum of churches, he helped Evangelicalism to become respectable again and to recover its social conscience.[11] Evangelicalism continues to be the mainstream of American Protestantism but its political involvement has been manipulated by politicians and some religious leaders, such as fundamentalist televangelists like Jerry Falwell and Pat Robertson. They serve a right-wing political agenda, which is intensely patriotic, vehemently anti-Socialist, anti-Islamic and against any form of moral liberalism, especially with regard to traditional family and sexual morality. Other Evangelicals, such as Jim Wallis of the network Sojourners, argue this is a travesty of the Christian gospel which is concerned above all with justice and peace.[12]

In theological terms, Christian fundamentalism is a rejection of the role of the Spirit in creation, which renders it impossible to appreciate what lies outside the inherited tradition, and therefore denies any goodness or any salvation beyond its own parameters. When Canadian Evangelical theologian Clark Pinnock discovered 'a wideness in God's mercy' and developed a theology of the Holy Spirit beginning with creation,[13] some other North American Evangelical leaders were very uncomfortable that this challenged the biblical confession that 'salvation is by no other name' (Acts 4.12), which they understood to mean the cognitive and explicit conversion demanded by their tradition.[14] Those of a fundamentalist tendency find it hard to appreciate that, not only are there multiple ways to respond to Jesus Christ – as the re:jesus website beautifully illustrates[15] – but there are many ways in which the Spirit of Christ is at work. Condemning fundamentalist belief as 'spiritless' is not a solution either. We need to understand it and engage with Fundamentalists, as far as they are willing.

Although Fundamentalists regard themselves as being true to Christian tradition, their faith is inevitably redefined in response to modernity. Fundamentalist emphasis on the authority of the written word to the extent of treating it as a textbook or handbook, for example, was influenced by scientific models of scholarship. The emphasis on conversion as an individual and intellectual decision is in keeping with the individualism and democratic systems of modernity. While rejecting the moral liberalism of modernity, fundamentalist Christians in the West do not generally criticize economic liberalism or the global capitalist system created by modernity. And they make full use of modern technology and communications for organizing and promoting their cause. The Southern Baptists are the largest Protestant denomination and representative of the fundamentalistic tendency. Separated from the Northern Baptists due to the Civil War, Southern Baptists are made up of independent local churches which are the mainstay of the so-called

'Religious Right', taking a strongly conservative moral stance against abortion and homosexuality, and advocating traditional female roles and family patterns. The umbrella body, the Southern Baptist Convention,[16] which is based in Nashville, Tennessee, is strongly evangelistic and has mission programmes targeting the Islamic world. It withdrew from the World Baptist Alliance in 2004 because it found it drifting toward liberalism. The Episcopal Church,[17] the successor to the pre-independence Church of England in the USA, is one of the most liberal. With its headquarters in New York, the church has campaigned on social issues of peace, economic justice, race and gender. Its ordination of an openly gay man, Gene Robinson, as bishop provoked a worldwide backlash, including among a minority of its own members who have split away.

The chief enemy of contemporary Fundamentalists is not 'liberal' Christians but secularists and secular society, whom they see as God-less. The most acute clash between Fundamentalists and modernity was – and continues to be – on the subject of creation or the origins of the universe. Christians of a fundamentalist inclination read the creation narratives as a superior scientific textbook and see Darwinian evolution as directly contradicting what they believe to be the facts about the origins of the universe. The Creationist stance is not only an intellectual one; it is also a political resistance to the cultural dominance of science, which in the Southern USA is perceived to be centred in the Northern cities. The chief form of protest of the Creationists is home-schooling their children, supporting faith-schools and promoting creationism in schools. However, the vehemence with which some scientists refute religion and promote science as the only possible way of looking at the world suggests that fundamentalism is not just a religious phenomenon but is found among scientists as well. The language of science often suggests it is a religion,[18] which people are expected to 'believe in', and which is equally fundamentalist. And some scientists, of whom the Oxford geneticist Richard Dawkins is the prominent contemporary representative in the UK, demand that people choose between science and religion, which they define in a way that bears little resemblance to any particular living religion, as if no dialogue is possible between the two world-views.[19] Pushed into a corner like this it is no wonder that people of faith may feel threatened.

The study of Christian fundamentalism was later extended to cover similar tendencies in other religions.[20] There are striking parallels between the way Christian Fundamentalists treat the Bible and the way many Muslims treat the Qur'an as the pre-eminent authority which cannot be subjected to historical, literary or any other form of criticism. This rejection of hermeneutics may extend to a general concern for certainty, consistency, simplicity and clarity and an inability to cope with doubt. There are parallels with Islam and with nationalist Hinduism in the way each seeks to reinstate a religious framework for society by political militancy. This involves the need to create an enemy by invoking symbols of evil and demonizing the other. Fundamentalists of all kinds tend not to take a historical perspective but to jump straight from a golden past – the New Testament church, the Golden Age of Islam, or the days of Lord Ram in India – to the evil present. This also means they reject notions of evolution and development. Finally, Fundamentalists seek to establish their particular tradition or belief-system and reject secularism or any other compromise that will allow different traditions to coexist within society. They are absolutist and therefore refuse any form of dialogue; they are also authoritarian and unable to sympathize with the views or situations of others.[21]

These are symptoms of fundamentalism; to use them as definitions would be sometimes to overstretch them to cover what are very diverse movements. The main common ground between fundamentalist groups is their root cause, which is the threat perceived to be posed by modernity, or in global terms the modernizing project of the Western elite, to which some react with extreme violence.[22] The revolutions which created modernity also had enormous implications for the world's people in terms of exploitation of the world's resources. Furthermore, for modernity to advance, the world had to modernize and be brought into what was becoming a global economic and cultural system. While most people appreciate the material benefits of modernity, they do not wish to be subject to Western control and may resist the values which accompany it. Modernization is not a neutral term for improving people's material lives but has political, cultural and anti-religious overtones.

7.4 From religion to spirituality

Until recently social theories of modernization have assumed that it will always be accompanied by decline in religious adherence and the rise of secularism. This was not only because modern education would make religious doctrine no longer believable but also on the grounds, first predicated by Karl Marx, that religion thrives on material deprivation and insecurity. It is not uncommon to suppose that when people's needs are met, they will no longer look to God to provide (cf. Deut. 8.12–18), and missionary work often assumes that it is the poor who are most likely to respond to the gospel message (cf. Matt. 11.28–30). The Western project of modernizing the rest of the world, therefore, was not only a necessity for continued economic growth but could also be expected to pay political dividends in depressing religious movements. However, particularly since the Iranian Revolution in 1979 many scientists and sociologists have been startled by what is often described as a 'resurgence of religions'.[23] Whether there has been a global increase in religious practice is questionable but there has certainly been an increase in the political visibility of religions. This is not only true in the case of radical Islam, but also for conservative Christianity (Evangelical, Roman Catholic and Orthodox), political Hinduism, engaged Buddhism and others. As a result secularization theories of religion have had to be revised to recognize the extent to which religions are expressions of cultural identity and a vehicle for political mobilization.[24] The rise of Pentecostal-charismatic forms of Christianity across the world has attracted scholarly attention because these seem to be a way either of resisting modernity or of coping with it. African

Initiated Churches – see next chapter – are an example of the former, and Pentecostalism in Latin America of the latter.

The case of Western Europe has seemed to prove the modernization theory of religion, at least if the statistics showing the decline of traditional churchgoing are taken at face value. Material prosperity does seem to work against traditional religious faith and practice here. But Grace Davie, Professor of Sociology at the University of Exeter, has argued that Europe is an exceptional case and that a global perspective does not show a correlation between modernization and the decline of religions.[25] The most obvious counter-example is the USA, where levels of churchgoing continue to be high and where, despite the constitutional separation of church and state, God is frequently invoked in political life. Davie suggests that although traditional patterns of religious practice have changed, Western Europeans continue to believe. They have rejected membership of religious organizations but they continue 'believing without belonging' and have a vicarious approach to faith, giving tacit support to traditional religious practice, which they see as beneficial to the wider society.[26] This view is partly corroborated by Nottingham zoologist David Hay who finds that religious or spiritual awareness is 'hard-wired' into human nature for reasons of survival. His interviews with British people over more than a decade showed that the number of people reporting spiritual experience, such as transcendent providence or awareness of a sacred presence in nature, remained remarkably constant. He concluded that, despite vocal anti-Christians like Richard Dawkins, the majority of British people are allies of Christian faith in this respect.[27] Davie's and Hay's research seems to be born out by the census figures for 2001, which showed that 72 per cent of the British people identify as Christian.[28]

Another explanation for the continued prevalence of religious values and spiritual concerns in Western society is advanced by American sociologist Ronald Inglehart. On the basis of a global survey of religious values, he concludes that wealth and wellbeing do not necessarily equate with spiritual satisfaction. In 'secure' societies people's overall sense of wellbeing ceases to increase with per capita income but people may continue to try to improve their lives by developing a 'spiritual' dimension.[29] It may also be said that, despite wealth and political stability, people in Western societies do not always feel secure. What may be happening in the West is that people are changing the way in which they exercise faith, and one way of expressing this is as a shift from 'religion' to 'spirituality'. This was the suggestion of 'the Kendal project' led by Paul Heelas and Linda Woodhead of the University of Lancaster.[30] They understand 'spirituality' as a subjective experience in contrast with the external and objective nature of (organized) religion. Whereas religion is practised through membership of a congregation, spirituality is an individual pursuit only loosely associated with others. Their study of the Lake District town of Kendal showed that, while traditional churches ('congregations') were numerically declining, other movements offering an alternative 'holistic', therapeutic religious experience of a neo-Pagan or New Age type were growing. They believe this indicates a 'spiritual revolution', spelling the end for organized religion, and they see it as symptomatic of other changes in modern culture (see below).

An alternative explanation to the secularization theory is based on religion's ability to appeal to another aspect of modernity: consumerism, which we discussed in Chapter 3. The 'supply-side' or 'market' theory denies that there is a negative relation between religion on the one hand and economic prosperity and existential security on the other. Instead the argument is that, like the market, religiosity is related to the supply of religious 'goods'. Like consumers, people looking for religious services will be more likely to 'buy' if they are presented with a range of attractively packaged religious options.[31] Consequently churches are tempted to the 'MacDonaldization' of the gospel and the church for the sake of the efficiency, calculability, predictability and control so valued in the market.[32] Following this line of thinking, competition between Christian denominations and religious pluralism is therefore good for the religious 'economy' and will result in increased religious participation. Of course, even if it is true that people tend to behave in this way, it does not justify multiplying churches to compete for 'customers' in a way that is contrary to the spirit of Christian unity. Nevertheless, churches do need to take into account that we live within a religious marketplace and find their place within it, as well as outside it.

7.5 Postmodernity and religious plurality

Modernity is not a static condition. Especially since the 1960s, there has been a recognized shift in Western culture from a centralized and compartmentalized society, based on stated foundations, to a more fragmented and rapidly changing society with greater allowance for difference and a variety of lifestyles. This has been accompanied by many other political, economic, aesthetic and intellectual changes. As a result, contemporary society is sometimes described as 'postmodern', or sometimes 'late modern', by those who see it as an extension of modernity rather than a rejection of it. Postmodernity is a cultural condition to be distinguished from postmodernism, which is a philosophical theory.[33] A brief summary of the new situation is called for here.

The language of modernity is of unity, uniformity and universality. Modern science searches for a unified theory that is universally applicable, believing that the behaviour of all bodies can be deduced from certain principles. Scientific facts are expected to be universally acknowledged and Western (modern) civilization is expected to represent the future of humankind. Hegemonic governments aim to bring the whole world into one global village, to conform to one uniform civilization with unified systems of trade and communication, and to be governed by universally applicable law. In contrast, postmodern thinking is sceptical of such claims and aims. From a postmodern world-view, the world is fragmented rather than whole. It defies classification under one system of thought, or explanation by one overarching theory or 'metanarrative', whether it be Christian or scientific. Scientific theory itself now recognizes that what was once assumed to be universal may depend on circumstances. The theory of relativity shows that human beings are not objective observers without any effect on what they observe, and that where a person stands affects the view. Knowledge may be arrived at by processes of induction, working from the bottom up rather than the top down. And histories of science now recognize shifting paradigms of scientific thought in different eras.[34] Absolute claims and universal applications are suspect in postmodernity because the emphasis is on subjective experience and diversity. It is now possible to appreciate a variety of cultures, perspectives and ways of life; and it is difficult to promote any one of them over any other.

Modernity uses the language of certainty and expects that truth can be known, but postmodernity is characterized by doubt and we are no longer sure that there is a world to be known outside the reality we have constructed for ourselves in our own minds. Consequently, postmodern thinkers are less concerned with knowledge itself than with ways of knowing (epistemology). Academic discussion is less about what actually happens and more about questions of interpretation (hermeneutics), less about quantitative measurement and more about qualitative assessment. In this there is a shift from mathematical and rational discourse to the use of literature and imagination. Reacting against a world of numbers, facts and calculation, postmodernity deals in images, impressions and speculation. Recognizing no absolute foundations for knowledge, or any one particular system for acquiring it, postmodernity is comfortable with lyrical, story-telling approaches, with pastiche and bricolage. It is not worried by contradiction, juxtaposition and inconsistency. There is not one Truth but many truths; it is not a question of either/or but of both/and – or of indifference or apathy to any.

The deistic leaders of the Enlightenment, in so far as they concerned themselves with God, envisaged an absolute power above and beyond the world, the distant originator of a mechanistic universe. Rather than focusing on a vertical relationship between God and man, postmodernity encourages thinking about the interconnectedness of the world as a self-contained entity. This idea, which is referred to as the Gaia hypothesis, is the foundation of modern ecological movements.[35] It regards the earth as a closed system which is self-regulating but fluctuating and fragile, and in which human beings are regarded as just one species among many. From a postmodern perspective, the world is not like a machine but a living organism, an ecosystem better described by biology than physics. Unlike the deistic pioneers of modernity, leaders of postmodernity are more likely to be pantheists who are aware of multiple interconnecting forces within the world (immanence) but lack a sense of transcendence. The postmodern world is not centralized and externally directed but many different hubs are connected together in a worldwide web. Indeed, the internet provides a useful image for describing the world of postmodernity, which is imaginary, a virtual world that does not necessarily touch the material one. Whereas modernity encourages us to think in words and numbers arranged in straight lines and discrete sections – like a book, postmodernity is a world of icons and windows which overlap and are hyperlinked. Modern ways of thought start from the beginning and work toward the end, but in postmodernity – like a website – there are multiple points of entry and multiple conclusions, and conclusions may not be needed.

Postmodernity has not superseded modernity; the two coexist in contemporary society, and it is not clear that the postmodern world-view has escaped the world which modernity defined. Although it rejects all metanarratives, postmodern thought is itself an alternative world-view, and by its own nature it cannot claim to be the only alternative. Ironically, the view that there is no absolute truth may be just as dogmatic, and many movements that claim to embrace diversity deflect criticism by invoking political correctness. Postmodernity's scepticism and encouragement to disconnectedness from material realities do not suggest it as a practical way of life. By definition, its impetus toward diversity and plurality militates against any constructive action toward a unified goal. In a world faced with challenges such as poverty, global warming and culture clashes, postmodernity appears as a luxury indulged in by the elite. Relativized visions offer no solution to our common human predicament. More worryingly, it may be used to encourage apathy, a laissez-faire attitude and political quietism among those with influence who could be working together to improve the life of the masses. The internet may appear to be polycentric and free but it is also highly controlled, not in terms of censorship of its content but by powerful commercial interests which seek to manipulate surfers' choices, and to whom a great deal of personal information about 'netizens' is readily available. The hiddenness of the forces at work and the lack of clear lines of authority do not make them any less dangerous to human wellbeing than conventional forces. The global and social systems initiated by modernity continue to dominate today's world for good and ill.

However, postmodern thought does offer a powerful critique of modernity. It relativizes modernity, revealing it as one particular world-view among many others in human history. In rejecting grand theories of everything, it recognizes the naturally existing chaos and disorder of the universe and the heterogeneity or variety of human existence. It allows for different versions of history which do not necessarily correspond to the perspective of the West that the world is developing towards a higher human life through globalization and technology. It rightly raises important questions about whether these metanarratives are simply stories told by the powerful to legitimize their version of 'the truth'. While it may equally be indifferent, it may also celebrate diversity and difference. It encourages the arts as well as scientific approaches to knowing, and it questions scientific fundamentalism. And the organic and complex views of the world which it supports are an improvement on some of the mechanistic and simplistic visions of modernity.

The prevalence in the West of the new world-view represented by postmodernity demands a rethinking of mission approaches and a new inculturation, or recontextualization, of the Christian gospel. Whether we regard postmodernity as a threat or an opportunity, we are called to do mission in an age of uncertainty, questioned authority, competing visions and an emphasis on subjective experience. In particular, we find ourselves in Europe in a – for us – novel situation where the Christian gospel is one story among others. On the one hand, in a culture of postmodernity the Christian story can be told more authentically, without having to fit it into the constraints of a modern scientific mindset. On the other hand, there is no reason for it to be accepted as Truth and little incentive for people to make a choice for Christianity over any other truth. The same applies to any other religion, ideology or truth claim. Indeed Western society seems to be undergoing a crisis of knowledge in which it is difficult to stake any kind of truth claim.[36]

7.6 Public faith in the West

Whereas in modernity, Christian claims to absolute and universal truth are resisted as contrary to scientific fact, in the postmodern West they are more likely to be met with indifference or incredulity and dismissed. Both cultural contexts encourage the shift from 'religion' to 'spirituality' described above. In the face of secularization there is privatization of faith, and in reaction to rationalism there is an interest in story, narrative and art, encouraged by the context of postmodernity. Christian faith may still thrive as private spirituality but it may not be taken seriously in the public sphere. Christians who make a public statement of faith are likely to be put down as 'Fundamentalists'. Now Christians and churches are called to witness to the truth of the gospel in the context of plurality without buying into relativism on the one hand or fundamentalism on the other.

To achieve this, Christians need to consider what kind of truth claim is constituted by the gospel. Is belief in Christian faith like Richard Dawkins's belief in science, which cannot be sympathetic to other perspectives because it cannot countenance any other truth than what is encompassed in his philosophy? Does believing in Christ mean believing a body of knowledge and adopting an exclusive way of thinking by which everyone else is wrong? Or is it the culture of modernity which has encouraged us to make Christianity a version of modernity in which 'faith' replaces 'rationality'?[37] Christians have struggled to find a place for Christian testimony in the public sphere and come up with various different approaches. One of the most well known is Lesslie Newbigin's challenge to 'a genuinely missionary encounter between the gospel and [modern Western] culture'.[38]

Returned from India to the UK in 1974, Newbigin saw more acutely the decline in influence of the churches, such as the URC of which he was a minister, and the mission challenges of the British context. He decided that the root of the missionary problem caused by modernity lay in the division made between (scientific) 'facts', which are agreed on in public to be true, and 'values', which are regarded as private opinions. He insisted that, although it might be 'foolishness to the Greeks', the gospel is 'public truth' intended not just for church but for the wider society, and relevant to social issues.[39] Newbigin's background in India, in which Hinduism accommodates many different spiritual visions under one umbrella, made him concerned about the danger of postmodern relativism. Since Christianity is a religion based on God's action in public events in history, and the church is a community in history which has also shaped history, he argued that it cannot be one option of many. So Newbigin sought to inspire Christians with 'proper confidence' that the Christian gospel is a plausible view of history which challenges modern thinking, and he urged them to claim their place in Western history and to seek to continue to change and influence Western society by the gospel.[40]

Newbigin's ideas resulted in a number of different initiatives, and especially 'The Gospel and Our Culture Network' (GOCN). Its goal is the 're-Christianization of the West'; it 'aims to stimulate and assist the Church's witness in and to Western culture, with a view to transforming the basic premises of that culture in the light of the reality of Jesus Christ'.[41] In the United States, GOCN has stimulated the missional church movement, which recognizes the USA as a distinct mission field and encourages local churches to reshape themselves in a way compatible with their sending into society.[42] Although Newbigin, as the returned missionary suffering re-entry culture shock, seemed to say little positive about Western society, he did not intend to encourage a communal (sectarian) church which sees itself as holding out against society. He urged participation in cultural development. This engaged approach was facilitated by his Trinitarian understanding of mission, which set the mission of Jesus Christ within the intention of the Father and the mission of the Spirit.[43]

However, the weakness of Newbigin's theology in relation to postmodernity is his modernist appeal to history as the basis of the church's claim to truth. While it is true that Christianity has a unique history, and it is to that particular story that Christians testify, this does not give it any more weight than any other tradition in plural society where each community has its own narrative. The power of Christian truth is not in its history but in the quality of the life of the churches here and now. One of the leading theologians of missional church, Darrell L. Guder, argues that the US church has failed to 'translate' the gospel into every human culture because it has reduced the gospel. In particular, it has separated the 'benefits' of the gospel (eternal salvation, forgiveness etc.) from missionary responsibility, and majored on the former – understood in an individualistic sense – at the expense of the latter, which is the calling of the community. These, he argues, must be reconnected by the 'continuing conversion of the church'. The change to 'missional church' is not merely structural but a deep transformation to enable churches to become witnessing local communities and have incarnational integrity as institutions.[44] In this way the churches may win the right to a voice in the public sphere which they cannot expect merely on the basis of history.

7.7 Secular and spiritual wisdom

The shift from 'religion' to 'spirituality' discussed above has not just been forced on the churches by changes in modernity;

it is also the result of active missionary engagement of Western Christians with contemporary modern and postmodern society. Heelas and Woodhead do not predict the end of Christianity. Among the examples of the new spirituality they looked at were Christian churches or groups which have adapted to the needs of the new generation by offering alternative forms of worship and gathering. Such innovations are encouraged by initiatives such as 'Fresh Expressions', 'Church in a Spiritual Age' and 'Sense Making Faith'.[45] Engagement with contemporary spirituality is a necessary part of Christian mission in contemporary society. Cultivating spirituality in its charismatic, Celtic and mystical forms has been a way of deepening church life which is called for in Christian witness today. In part this is a necessary corrective and a proper recognition of the holistic nature of Christian faith, and its concern not only with intellectual and public life but also with domestic and personal affairs, with the emotions and with the senses. It is also a recognition of women's religious experience, which may differ from men's,[46] and gives opportunities for women to practise religious leadership so long denied to them in churches. Nevertheless, many of the people in the Hay and Heelas-Woodhead interviews did not see Christianity as offering the kind of spirituality they were looking for but were attracted to alternative forms such as Neo-Paganism and New Age spirituality. In their affirmation of the material world, Neo-Pagans see indigenous religions as an antidote to religious otherworldliness, and to New-Agers Eastern religions appear less self-centred or anthropocentric than traditional Christianity.[47] There is more that Christians can do to challenge these perceptions but it is also important to recognize that there is more than one kind of spirituality, and people may not choose what Christianity stands for.

Christian spirituality differs from contemporary Neo-Paganism and New Age spiritualities in at least two ways. First, the latter very often describe a privatized religion, where the emphasis is on personal experience and a search for fulfilment. If Christian spirituality is reduced to this, Christianity becomes pushed into the 'body, mind and spirit' sector of the bookshop and no longer engages with public life. But the basis of Christian confession of fullness of life is not the practice of spiritual techniques or the acquisition of spiritual knowledge. It is identification with the passion of Jesus Christ, who suffered and was raised for the sake of the whole world. Second, contemporary New Age spiritualities express a belief in the wholeness of creation or the 'circle of life', and the Gaia hypothesis captures this religious instinct, especially among feminist theologians.[48] Unlike Christianity, there is no sense of an overall controlling God; their spirituality is immanent rather than transcendent, and intimately related to the local environment. Christianity affirms creation as good but maintains that, although God is involved in creation, God also transcends creation as the Creator. So the earth is not worshipped but it is cherished as a divine gift. Nor is creation a closed system; it is open to God and moving toward a goal. This is the basis of Christian hope and the motive for the exercise of responsibility for other creatures and the whole creation.

What is meant by 'spirituality' very much depends on what is understood by 'spirit'.[49] Christians have a particular understanding of spirituality derived from the Spirit of God, which is breathed into us, moving in the whole creation (Rom. 8.18–25). Contemporary spirituality reminds us that the Holy Spirit is not just another name for the authority of the church or personal sanctification. The biblical Spirit is holistic in connecting heaven with earth (Mark 1.10), mind with body (Phil. 2.1–7), and in promoting ecological integrity (see Chapter 8). But neither is the Spirit merely a cosmic force or life principle. The Christian testimony is that the Holy Spirit is sent from the transcendent God (Acts 2.17) and is most fully expressed in Jesus Christ (Rom. 8.11). Spirituality for Christians is primarily life lived in the Spirit of Jesus Christ (Rom. 8.12–17). The Holy Spirit is the grace of God, granting empowerment and fullness of life (1 Cor. 12.7–11; John 4.13–14; 7.37–9), but the Spirit of Jesus Christ also puts demands on Christians to practise holiness and love – or Christlikeness (Gal. 5.22–3). The gifts of the Spirit are not for selfish use but to be shared for the building up of others (1 Cor. 12.7; 14.26) and the reconciliation of the whole creation (Rom. 8.19–23). The freedom of the Spirit is not license but an opening to love (Rom. 6.1–2; 1 Cor. 12.31—13.8). The truth of the Spirit convicts the world and brings about liberation and justice (John 16.8–13; Rom. 8.19–23; Gal. 5.5). And the power of the Spirit is for testimony to Jesus Christ who gives the Spirit (John 14.26; 15.26–7).

The Christian spirit is not only religious, in the narrow sense of that word since the Enlightenment; the Spirit is also 'the mind of Christ' (Phil. 2.1–2) and 'the wisdom of God' (1 Cor. 2.6–16). We are accustomed to associating the Spirit with emotional or mystical religion, and with the unusual rather than the mundane. In the first case, the outpouring of the Spirit in the Pentecostal-charismatic movement may produce impulsive and irrational behaviour, such as in the 'Toronto Blessing', which has no clear objective.[50] In the second, the meditative practices of mystical spirituality may tend to 'ethereal euphoria' rather than result in 'committed historical action'.[51] The prophetic tradition of the Bible is purposeful but associates the Spirit particularly with 'spontaneity and suddenness of appearance'.[52] Such overattention to the extraordinary means we may connect the Holy Spirit only with the supernatural or paranormal, the miraculous and surprising, or the counter-cultural. Yet if the Holy Spirit is life, then the Spirit must be encountered in the regular patterns and mundane systems which are the framework for our existence, and also in human attempts to understand them. The Spirit of God surpasses the human Spirit not only in power but also in wisdom (Matt. 13.54, cf. Mark 6.2; 1 Cor. 1), and so must help us to understand the universe and explain it. The Holy Spirit, and the Christian faith, is therefore related to philosophy and science as well as religion. And if this were not the case, Christian faith would not have anything to say to the scientific and secular societies of modernity and postmodernity.

The Holy Spirit is the Spirit of Wisdom (*hokma*, *sophia*), known from the wisdom literature of the Hebrew Bible (e.g. Prov. 8—9), evident in the boy Jesus (Luke 2.40, 52), lived out in his adult ministry (James 3.17), proclaimed in the manner of his death (1 Cor. 1–2) and shared through his resurrected life (Eph. 1.17; 3.10). Each community has its accumulated wisdom, expressed by its sages, artists, philosophers, muses and scientists, and very often it can be shared between communities. It may be religious or secular. Wisdom traditions are concerned with 'the long-term shaping of life in many dimensions, including the common good and the formation of the whole person'.[53] Wisdom embraces the intellectual and also relates it to the imaginative, the passionate and the practical. David F. Ford, Regius Professor of Divinity at the University of Cambridge, has promoted wisdom as the best description of what theology is seeking. Christian wisdom may be a scandal to the Jews and foolishness to the Greeks (1 Cor. 1.22–4), but it is a reasoned way in which Christians understand the world as they see it in the light of Christ. As such, it has a contribution to make to the sum-total of human wisdom both by what it teaches and also by its challenges to other forms of wisdom.[54]

Christians have introduced their distinctive wisdom in public and political life in 2,000 years of European history. Sometimes it has been accepted by the wider society; for example, in the case of just war theory, social covenants, community service, charitable giving and human dignity. At other times Christian perspectives have been sidelined and Christians have been ridiculed; but the servants of Jesus Christ can expect no less. Celia Deane-Drummond, Professor of Theology and the Biological Sciences at the University of Chester, urges Christians to contribute from their tradition of wisdom to scientific debate. She sees the Christian contribution as most helpful not when it is closely tied to the latest scientific theories but when it offers a distinctive Christian perspective drawing from Christian tradition. Mindful of the danger of science becoming 'scientism', a mythology that takes over all other ways of perceiving the world, Deane-Drummond argues that science needs to be saved from itself, and that 'the future of science is too critical a phenomenon to be left just to scientists themselves'. What she hopes Christian wisdom will offer to science is a broader sapiential framework which affirms scientific 'values of wonder, beauty, reason, truth and imagination' but rejects attitudes of 'arrogance, closed mindedness and irresponsibility'.[55]

It is not Neo-Pagan and New Age spiritualities but the scientific and secular outlook which dominates the contemporary West. The challenge of the Christian gospel to the wisdom of the Greeks is not the doctrine of creation according to Genesis 1—3 but the cross and resurrection of Jesus Christ (1 Cor. 1—2), which sadly is bypassed in the creationist discussion, and in alternative movements may be downplayed in favour of ahistorical spirituality. For Christians, the Spirit of Christ, the Holy Spirit is the key to the universe, and the Spirit is both a scientific and spiritual and also an ethical key. The Spirit not only moves the heart and inspires the head, but also shapes attitudes. The Spirit is the spirit of Wisdom which, if heard, can enrich all aspects of modern society.

Notes

1 Mary Heimann, 'Christianity in Western Europe since the Enlightenment', in Adrian Hastings (ed.), *A World History of Christianity* (London: Cassell, 1999), pp. 458–507, at p. 497.

2 As shown in cultural histories of Britain such as Peter Leese, *Britain since 1945: Aspects of Identity* (Basingstoke: Palgrave Macmillan, 2006).

3 Useful introductions to modernity in a mission context can be found in David J. Bosch, *Transforming Mission: Paradigm Shifts in Theology of Mission* (Maryknoll, NY: Orbis Books, 1991), pp. 349–62; Lesslie Newbigin, *Foolishness to the Greeks: The Gospel and Western Culture* (London: SPCK, 1986); Heimann, 'Christianity in Western Europe since the Enlightenment'.

4 Michael Oleska, 'Orthodoxy in Mission: the Alaskan Experience', in George Lemopoulos (ed.), *Your Will Be Done: Orthodoxy in Mission* (Geneva: WCC Publications, 1989), pp. 217–19.

5 Heimann, 'Christianity in Western Europe since the Enlightenment'.

6 For example (respectively): J. A. T. Robinson, *Honest to God* (London: SCM Press, 1963); *But That I Can't Believe!* (London: Collins, 1967); Ernst Käsemann, *New Testament Questions of Today* (London, SCM Press, 1969); Rudolf Bultmann, *Faith and Understanding*

(Philadelphia: Fortress Press, 1969); John B. Cobb, *God and the World* (Philadelphia: Westminster Press, 1969); Don Cupitt, *The Sea of Faith* (London: BBC, 1984).

7 David W. Bebbington, *Evangelicalism in Modern Britain: A History from the 1730s to the 1980s* (London: Unwin Hyman, 1989), pp. 2–17.

8 Edwin S. Gausted and Leigh E. Schmidt, *The Religious History of America*, rvsd edn (New York: HarperCollins, 2002), p. 166.

9 George M. Marsden, *Fundamentalism and American Culture*, 2nd edn (Oxford: Oxford University Press, 2006), pp. 85–93.

10 Michael Moore's 2002 film *Bowling for Columbine* captures well this feeling of threat.

11 Mark A. Noll, *American Evangelical Christianity* (Oxford: Blackwell, 2001), pp. 44–55.

12 Jim Wallis, *God's Politics: Why the Right Gets It Wrong and the Left Doesn't Get It* (New York: HarperCollins, 2005).

13 Clark H. Pinnock, *A Wideness in God's Mercy: The Finality of Jesus Christ in a World of Religions* (Grand Rapids, MI: Zondervan, 1992); *Flame of Love: A Theology of the Holy Spirit* (Downers Grove, IL: InterVarsity Press, 1996).

14 For example, Norman L. Geisler, *Options in Contemporary Christian Ethics* (Grand Rapids, MI: Baker Book House, 1981), p. 32; see also John Sanders, *No Other Name: Can Only Christians Be Saved?* (London: SPCK, 1994), pp. 152–64.

15 Re:jesus, a site supported by a wide variety of British churches and agencies: <www.rejesus.co.uk>.

16 <www.sbc.net>.

17 <http://ecusa.anglican.org>.

18 Mary Midgley, *Science as Salvation: A Modern Myth and Its Meaning* (London: Routledge, 1992).

19 Richard Dawkins, *The God Delusion* (London: Bantam Press, 2006), p. 31.

20 For Christian fundamentalism, see James Barr, *Fundamentalism*, 2nd edn (London: SCM Press, 1981). Wider introductions include: Hans Küng and Jürgen Moltmann, *Fundamentalism as an Ecumenical Challenge* (London: SCM Press, 1992); Steve Bruce, *Fundamentalism* (Cambridge: Polity, 2000). See also Martin E. Marty and R. Scott Appleby (eds), *Fundamentalism Project* (Chicago: University of Chicago Press): Vol. 1, *Fundamentalisms Observed* (1991); Vol. 2, *Fundamentalisms and Society: Reclaiming the Sciences, the Family and Education* (1993); Vol. 3, *Fundamentalisms and the State: Remaking Polities, Economies, and Militance* (1993); Vol. 4, *Accounting for Fundamentalisms: The Dynamic Character of Movements* (1994); Vol. 5 *Fundamentalisms Comprehended* (1995).

21 Küng and Moltmann, *Fundamentalism as an Ecumenical Challenge*.

22 Karen Armstrong, *The Battle for God* (New York: Alfred A. Knopf, 2000); Mark Juergensmeyer, *Terror in the Mind of God: The Global Rise of Religious Violence* 3rd edn (Berkeley, CA: University of California Press, 2003).

23 For example, Scott M. Thomas, *The Global Resurgence of Religion and the Transformation of International Relations: The Struggle for the Soul of the Twenty-first Century* (New York: Palgrave Macmillan, 2005).

24 For example, Peter L. Berger, *A Rumour of Angels: Modern Society and the Rediscovery of the Supernatural* (London: Penguin, 1970); Harvey Cox, *Fire from Heaven: The Rise of Pentecostal Spirituality and the Reshaping of Religion in the Twenty-first Century* (London: Cassell, 1996); David Martin, *On Secularization: Towards a Revised General Theory* (Burlington, VT: Ashgate, 2005).

25 Grace Davie, *Europe: The Exceptional Case. Parameters of Faith in the Modern World* (London: Darton, Longman and Todd, 2002).

26 Grace Davie, *Religion in Britain since 1945: Believing without Belonging* (Oxford: Blackwell, 1994); *Religion in Modern Europe: A Memory Mutates* (Oxford: Oxford University Press, 2000), p. 177.

27 David Hay 'The Spirituality of the Unchurched', in Howard Mellor and Timothy Yates, *Mission and Spirituality: Creative Ways of Being Church* (Sheffield: Cliff College Publishing, 2002), pp. 11–26.

28 National Statistics Website, 2001 Census, <www.statistics.gov.uk>.

29 World Values Survey, <www.worldvaluessurvey.org>.

30 The Kendal Project, <www.kendalproject.org.uk>; Paul Heelas and Linda Woodhead, *The Spiritual Revolution: Why Religion is Giving Way to Spirituality* (Oxford: Blackwell 2004).

31 Rodney Stark and Roger Finke, *Acts of Faith: Explaining the Human Side of Religion* (Berkeley, CA: University of California Press, 2000).

32 John Drane, *The McDonaldization of the Church: Spirituality, Creativity, and the Future of the Church* (London: Darton, Longman and Todd, 2000).

33 Introductions to postmodernism from Christian theological perspectives include: Stanley J. Grenz, *A Primer on Postmodernism* (Grand Rapids, MI: Wm B. Eerdmans, 1996); J. Richard Middleton and Brian J. Walsh, *Truth Is Stranger Than It Used to Be: Biblical Faith in a Postmodern Age* (Downers Grove, IL: InterVarsity Press, 1995); Graham Ward, 'Introduction', in Graham Ward (ed.), *The Postmodern God* (Oxford: Blackwell, 1997), pp. xv–xliii; 'Introduction', in Graham Ward (ed.), *Postmodern Theology* (Oxford: Blackwell, 2001), pp. xii–xxvii; Kevin

J. Vanhoozer, 'Theology and the Condition of Postmodernity', in Kevin J. Vanhoozer (ed.), *Postmodern Theology* (Cambridge: Cambridge University Press, 2003), pp. 3–25.

34 Thomas S. Kuhn, *The Structure of Scientific Revolutions* (Chicago: University of Chicago Press, 1962).

35 'Gaia' is the ancient Greek earth goddess or 'Mother Earth'. The Gaia Hypothesis was formulated by British independent scientist James Lovelock in 1979; J. E. Lovelock, *Gaia: A New Look at Life on Earth* (Oxford: Oxford University Press, 1979). See Celia Deane-Drummond, *A Handbook in Theology and Ecology* (London: SCM Press, 1996), pp. 98–114.

36 J. Andrew Kirk and Kevin J. Vanhoozer (eds), *To Stake a Claim: Mission and the Western Crisis of Knowledge* (Maryknoll, NY: Orbis Books, 1999).

37 Bert Hoedemaker, 'Mission beyond Modernity: A Global Perspective', in Simon Barrow and Graeme Smith (eds), *Christian Mission in Western Society* (London: CTBI, 2001), pp. 212–33, see pp. 214–16.

38 Newbigin, *Foolishness to the Greeks*, p. 1. For more examples, see Barrow and Smith, *Christian Mission in Western Society.*

39 Newbigin, *Foolishness to the Greeks*; *The Other Side of 1984: Questions for the Churches* (Geneva: WCC Publications, 1983).

40 Lesslie Newbigin, *Proper Confidence: Faith, Doubt, and Certainty in Christian Discipleship* (Grand Rapids, MI: Eerdmans, 1995); *The Gospel in a Pluralist Society* (London: SPCK, 1989).

41 UK site at <www.gospel-culture.org.uk>.

42 George Hunsberger and Craig Van Gelder (eds), *The Church between Gospel and Culture: The Emerging Mission in North America* (Grand Rapids, MI: Eerdmans, 1996); Darrel L. Guder (ed.), *Missional Church: A Vision for the Sending of the Church in North America* (Grand Rapids, MI: Eerdmans, 1998); Craig van Gelder, *The Ministry of the Missional Church: A Community Led by the Spirit* (Grand Rapids: Baker Books, 2007). See <missionalchurchnetwork.com>.

43 See the following articles in Thomas F. Foust, George R. Hunsberger, J. Andrew Kirk and Werner Ustorf (eds), *A Scandalous Prophet: The Way of Mission after Newbigin* (Grand Rapids, MI: Wm. B. Eerdmans, 2001): Werner Ustorf, 'The Emerging Christ of Post-Christian Europe', pp. 128–44; Duncan B. Forrester, 'Lesslie Newbigin as Public Theologian', pp. 3–12. See also Michael W. Goheen, *As the Father Has Sent Me* (Zoetermeer: Boekencentrum, 2000); George R. Hunsberger, *Bearing the Witness of the Spirit: Lesslie Newbigin's Theology of Cultural Plurality* (Grand Rapids, MI: Wm B. Eerdmans, 1998).

44 Guder, *Missional Church.*

45 'Fresh Expressions', see <www.freshexpressions.org.uk>. 'Church in a Spiritual Age', The Group for Evangelization (Churches Together in

England), see <www.churchinaspiritualage.org.uk>; and Steve Hollinghurst, Yvonne Richmond and Roger Whitehead, with Janice Price and Tina Adams, *Equipping Your Church in a Spiritual Age* (London: Church House Publishing, 2005). 'Sense Making Faith', The Mission Theological Advisory Group, see <www.spiritualjourneys.org.uk>; and Anne Richards (ed.), *Sense Making Faith: Body, Spirit, Journey* (London: Churches Together In Britain and Ireland, 2008).

46 See Joann Wolski Conn, *Women's Spirituality: Resources for Christian Development*, 2nd edn (Mahwah, NJ: Paulist Press, November 1996); Nicola Slee, *Praying like a Woman* (London: SPCK, 2004).

47 David Tacey, *The Spirituality Revolution: The Emergence of Contemporary Spirituality* (New York: Brunner-Routledge, 2004).

48 Celia E. Deane-Drummond, *Creation through Wisdom: Theology after the New Biology* (Edinburgh: T&T Clark, 2000), pp. 36–8, 138–9.

49 Kirsteen Kim, *The Holy Spirit in the World: A Global Conversation* (Maryknoll, NY: Orbis Books, 2007).

50 Martyn Percy, *Words, Wonders and Power: Understanding Contemporary Christian Fundamentalism and Revivalism* (London: SPCK, 1996), pp. 151–4.

51 Samuel Rayan, *Come, Holy Spirit* (Delhi: Media House, 1998), p. 7.

52 Deane-Drummond, *Creation through Wisdom*, p. 121.

53 David F. Ford, *Shaping Theology: Engagements in a Religious and Secular World* (Oxford: Blackwell, 2007), p. xvii.

54 David F. Ford, *Christian Wisdom: Desiring God and Learning in Love* (Cambridge: Cambridge University Press, 2007).

55 Celia E. Deane-Drummond, *The Ethics of Nature* (Oxford: Blackwell, 2004), pp. 228–31; quotations from pp. 181, 45.

8

SPIRITUAL GROWTH

Mission and Development

Poverty is 'alienation from the wholeness of life' by being cut off from the life-sustaining gifts of God that we receive and share with others.[1]
Manas Buthelesi

Lucy lived in Ethiopia 3.2 million years ago and the discovery of her skeleton in 1974 confirmed the growing consensus that human beings originated in Africa.[2] A transitional figure with both human and ape features, Lucy was a distant ancestor of all human beings, who are understood to have originated in Africa and migrated out of there across the world in more recent times. The correlation of the scientific evidence of the Ethiopian origin of humanity and the fact that Ethiopia also fits the criteria for the location of Eden in the biblical story has tempted some – Rastafarians for example – to combine the two, inspiring a sense of pride in their African or black heritage. The thought that the command to Adam and Eve to 'Be fruitful and multiply, and fill the earth and subdue it; and have dominion over the fish of the sea and over the birds of the air and over every living thing that moves upon the earth' (Gen. 1.28) was given to Africans is revolutionary for people whose ancestors were enslaved and transported.[3]

In the biblical narrative, the first human beings were created when God breathed his Spirit into the body he had formed from the dust of the ground (Gen. 2.7; Job 33.4). The ground itself had been created when God spoke and his Wind, or Spirit, moved across the face of the waters (Gen. 1.1–2). It is the creative Spirit of God who continues to sustain the earth

(Job 34.14–15; Ps. 104.29) and renew the creation (Ps. 104.30; Rom. 8.22–23). The new creation in Jesus Christ is another body, the Church, indwelt by the Spirit. Like the first human beings, the Church has a mandate to grow and promote growth (Matt. 28.18–20; Acts 1.8) and in the Spirit it has a key role in the redemption of the whole created order (Rom. 8.19). Adam and Eve were gardeners and the Bible is replete with images of biological growth: the church, abiding in Christ, is a vine, alive by the Spirit, dressed by the Father and growing – although sometimes by harsh pruning – upwards toward God (John 15.1–6). The kingdom of God is like a tree – the result of the seed of faith (Mark 4.30–2). In this chapter we will try to recover the relationship between spiritual growth and the flourishing of the whole creation, between the Great Commission given to the disciples and the creation mandate to the first human beings, which African theologians particularly help us to appreciate.

8.1 The Bible and African life

The location of the Garden of Eden is not the only link between Ethiopia and the biblical story. The kings of Ethiopia – a line which ended when Emperor Haile Selassie was deposed by Communists in 1974 – trace their ancestry from King Menelik I in about 1000 BC. Menelik is held to be the offspring of a liaison of King Solomon with the Queen of Sheba when she visited his court (1 Kings 10). As we saw in Chapter 4, Ethiopia has an ancient Christian heritage, and there are many parallels between cultures of the Old Testament and aspects of traditional African society, not only in Ethiopia but also in black Africa in general. One of these is a strong belief in a creator God and in the unity of the whole creation, including the invisible world of the ancestors and of the spirits of rocks, forests, mountains and roads. There are 'recurring, though not universal' patterns of belief and practice in Africa, sometimes grouped under the heading of African traditional religion. Its practice varies greatly but a major aim is maintaining the wholeness of life, which consists in a proper balance within the created order and in human communities.[4] Human wellbeing depends on community co-operation and living in harmony with natural forces, and poverty is due to alienation. According to African Orthodox priest Kwame Labi, in many African societies and other indigenous communities, 'the ultimate penalty or punishment is not death but banishment' because, in death, a person remains part of the community as an ancestor but in banishment he or she is totally cut off; and he notes the similarity in the banishment of Adam and Eve from the garden (Gen. 4.13).[5]

Despite the biblical affirmation of the wholeness of life, those who carried the Bible to Africa were also implicated in the banishment of many Africans from their communities through the slave trade and the disruption of the natural systems by land-grabbing and exploitation. At the conference in Berlin in 1884–5, the remaining parts of Africa were carved up by the European powers, and in 1941 even the proud Christian kingdom of Ethiopia was briefly occupied by Italian armies. Whereas the first Portuguese probably had a similar standard of living to Africans and were impressed by inland African empires such as that of the Ashanti in modern Ghana, the rapid economic development of Europe, partly at the expense of Africa, meant that later colonists from Britain and France felt themselves economically superior to Africans. They also perceived themselves as racially superior, owing to their theories of human cultural development; and religiously also, post-Enlightenment Europeans regarded Africans as 'primitive'. They dismissed African beliefs in the supernatural and the spirit world as superstition, and there was a tendency to demonize African gods and spirits.[6] Increasing disdain for African life in the colonial period led to the 'withdrawal upwards' of missionaries away from contact with the people and into their institutions, such as hospitals and schools.[7]

Today there are an estimated 400 million African Christians, the majority of whom worship in churches founded by missionary societies in the colonial period.[8] However, there are also many churches and denominations founded by Africans.

These fall broadly into two groups: African Initiated Churches (AICs) and neo-Pentecostals. We will look at neo-Penteostal churches later. AICs emerged first as breakaway groups from colonial Protestant churches from the 1890s onwards – such as the Ethiopian Church in South Africa (1892) and the Aladura Churches in Nigeria (from 1918) – although 'breakaway' is something of a misnomer as many were prayer groups that were forced out of mission churches because of disagreement with the leadership. These were the first independence movements against white rule.[9] The authority with which these African Christians preached the gospel was not from the colonial church but from the Bible, which they recognized as an African book and took as the ultimate authority at a time of social upheaval.[10]

As they read the Bible for themselves Africans identified with biblical characters and rejected much of the practice of the mission churches as 'extra-biblical' and foreign to the Christian message.[11] African prophets arose who led worship using African music, dance and symbols. Such African churches include the Harrist churches, founded by William Wade Harris in Ivory Coast and Ghana, 1913–15, and the Kimbanguists, a denomination begun by the preaching of Simon Kimbangu in Congo in 1921. Many other churches – often calling themselves Zionist or Spirit churches – were founded in the late colonial period, which in Africa continued into the 1970s.[12] AICs were not just another option to attend on Sunday but formed distinct communities or 'church tribes' who adopted a particular style of dress and separated themselves from colonial society, acquiring their own land, and supporting one another to be independent of government bodies, including state education and Western-style medicine.[13]

The distinctive Christian life of the AICs draws particularly on sections of the Old Testament and Hebrew culture, such as the food and purity laws of Leviticus, in some cases the practice of polygyny (polygamy) by the patriarchs, genealogies and veneration of ancestors, the use of dancing, percussion and musical instruments (like King David), and the revelation of

God through dreams, visions, prophetic messages and miraculous signs. In the AICs, the New Testament is understood in the light of the Old rather than through a Hellenistic or European lens[14] so that Jesus Christ is understood primarily as a prophet, the culmination of a line of prophets (cf. Heb. 1.1–2). The church tends to be seen as an extended family, incorporating the dead as well as the living and those yet to be born. New Testament texts dealing with invisible yet powerful entities such as ancestors (e.g. Heb. 1.1; 11.4—12.1), spirits, powers and demons come alive in the context of African awareness of the spirit world.

As a result of European dismissal of African world-views and suspicion of African religiosity, many African leaders felt 'the Western God was spiritually inadequate and irrelevant to deal with the reality of many aspects of our lives'. They found it necessary to address concerns about the spirit world, which they knew Jesus Christ himself dealt with, because otherwise their church members would continue to visit the caretakers of the African traditional religions.[15] Yet AICs were swiftly condemned by many Westerners as 'syncretistic' for supposedly indiscriminately combining African and Christian religious beliefs and practices. There have been serious problems in some AICs but AICs are best regarded as representing a rediscovery of Christianity by Africans who, because of their African religious heritage, emphasize the practices of prophesy, healing and spiritual power which they find in the Bible.[16] The popularity of AICs and later neo-Pentecostal movements has had a profound effect on the majority of established churches, many of which have incorporated indigenous and charismatic worship forms, and deal more explicitly with traditional African concerns. As a result the former mission churches are also unmistakably African in worship and community life, and increasingly in their reading of the Bible.[17]

Reading of the Bible is a key issue in the current debate in the Anglican Communion over issues of sexuality, in which African leaders have been prominent. The debate reveals how different the context of African Anglicans is and how their issues and the priorities of African Christians differ from many in the North. As Kevin Ward, a specialist in African Christianity explains, the issue of homosexuality is not one with which African church leaders are often confronted in their ministry. They are far more preoccupied with issues of sexuality arising from traditional African society and Islam in Africa such as polygamy, marital infidelity and the position of women, and with the scourge of AIDS and its implications for sexual behaviour. The sense in African culture of the worth of children and their importance for the continuity of human society is one of many other factors which make the suggestion that homosexual behaviour may be acceptable especially difficult for the majority of African Christians to agree with.[18] That there is great suffering among people of a homosexual orientation in Africa due to discrimination is without doubt, and there are many African Christians struggling sensitively with this question in their context,[19] but for most Africans the Bible appears to support their view and Western church leaders seem to be twisting passages which appear to condemn homosexual practice, to suit their particular cultural circumstances.[20] The solution is crucially dependent on questions of biblical authority or, more directly, of whether the power to interpret the Bible lies with Europeans or Africans.[21]

8.2 The Spirit of life and healing

Almost all commentators note the stress on healing in AICs.[22] The prevalence of endemic diseases such as malaria, the recent HIV/AIDS pandemic, a generally low life expectancy and high infant mortality make healing a major concern of ordinary Africans. Healing is one of the main roles of the prophets in African Traditional Religions, so it is not surprising that AIC Christians see Jesus primarily as a prophet-healer in the African tradition, who confronted the spirits with the power of the Holy Spirit.[23] Indeed healing by dealing with the spiritual powers believed to be responsible for suffering and death was central to Jesus' ministry (Luke 7.11–17; John 11.11; Mark

5.35–43). Jesus commonly performed exorcisms (Matt. 8.16; Mark 1. 23–8; 5.9; 7.32–5; Luke 4.33–7; John 5.1–8) and the demons 'shuddered' when they saw him (James 2.19; 1 John 3.8; see Col. 2.15). Through Christ's resurrection and ascension, all evil powers have been defeated and his disciples are commissioned to 'Heal the sick, raise the dead, cleanse the lepers, cast out demons' (Matt. 10.8; Mark 6.13; Luke 9.1).[24] Whatever the scientific view of evil spirits, they are real in the sense that they have a hold over people and therefore they cannot be ignored. A recent World Council of Churches study concluded that the churches' ministry of proclaiming the gospel should 'consciously address and name the powers, taking up the struggle with evil in whatever way it presents itself'.[25]

Since God is master of all the cosmic powers, for African writers healing disease is only a specific example of the wider life-giving work of the God by the Spirit.[26] The Nicene Creed describes the Holy Spirit as 'the Giver of Life'. The Holy Spirit is the fountain of life (John 7.37–9) who groans with the creation and the people of God to bring about the promised new creation (Rom. 8.22–3). The World Council of Churches' study points out that the Spirit 'actualises Christ's solidarity with the suffering and so witnesses to the power of God's grace that may also manifest itself paradoxically in weakness or illness (2 Cor. 12.9)'. The life which the Spirit brings, and the blessing of the Spirit poured out on the church in many gifts, empowers her for life-giving mission, which includes all aspects of holistic healing, such as prayer, pastoral care, professional medicine, prophetic denunciation of the causes of suffering, and scientific research.[27]

Within this cosmic setting, healing in the African context is holistic. Restoring life, just as healing in African traditional medicine – and in the Bible, is not a matter of treating the illness but of treating the person in their body and in all their relationships,[28] including those with the 'natural world'. 'The African', wrote Lutheran Bishop Manas Buthelezi, 'has a sense of the wholeness of life', meaning that the living are in fellowship with the dead, the supernatural and natural interrelate and the sacred and secular are not separated.[29] As Ghanaian theologian Mercy Amba Oduyoye has written, 'the cry for salvation/liberation in Africa is primarily a cry for health and wholeness'.[30] Illness is disharmony in human and cosmic relations so there is no discontinuity between healing and reconciliation, or between healing and creation.[31] 'Health is a dynamic state of wellbeing of the individual and society, of physical, mental, spiritual, economic, political, and social wellbeing – of being in harmony with each other, with the material environment and with God.'[32]

8.3 The international development agenda

Since the fifteenth century, Christian mission in Africa has been carried out not in the context of holistic healing but of the exploitation of African resources. Arabs, Portuguese, Dutch, British, Americans and now Chinese have all come to Africa in search of resources for their economic development, and through this means Africans have been incorporated into what is now a global economic system. This has allowed countries in the West, and now many in Asia, to develop economically and technologically and achieve a high material standard of living for the majority of their citizens. However, the centres of power in this system do not lie in Africa and this continent has, on the whole, been bypassed by development, or what is worse, suffered for the development of others.[33] In this section we will look briefly at the involvement of Christian mission in international development.[34]

The industrial revolution ushered in a social revolution, or 'great transformation', which turned people and nature into commodities – labour and land – which could be bought and sold in the market.[35] Capitalists focused on the economic system, rather than the ecological system, and regarded it as self-regulating and the driving force of human development. Seeing the growth of capitalism as inevitable, even desirable, and seeking the best outcome for Africans within it, many Christians have encouraged commerce and economic development in Africa (as we saw in Chapter 4). In doing so they also facilitated Africa's incorporation into European empires, which took place in the 'scramble for Africa' at the end of the nineteenth century.[36] The 'civilization' of labour forces and education of a local elite to supply the civil service of colonial governments were largely carried out by well-meaning missionaries who, being close to the people, were 'ideal allies' of the colonial government.[37]

The historian Niall Ferguson sums up the fall of the British Empire thus: in the colonial period, the British Empire controlled the global markets in raw materials, manufactured goods and labour. To protect the global economy the British exercised political power over most of the globe by their military supremacy. But they were not able to do so in Europe, where British attempts at intervention led to two world wars which bankrupted the empire and led to the transfer of global power to the United States.[38] In 1944 at Bretton Woods, New Hampshire, USA, the Allied nations agreed to peg their currencies to the American dollar and decisions were made to shift the global market from nation-centred economies to the internationally co-ordinated finance and trade we know today. Three institutions were planned to regulate the new system, which are now known as the World Bank, the IMF (International Monetary Fund) and the WTO (World Trade Organization). A fourth institution – the United Nations – was intended to provide international security for trade through its Security Council, whose permanent members were the USA, Britain, France, Russia and China. It was only due to the intervention of US churches in the negotiations[39] that the UN Charter also provided for a General Assembly where all nations could participate on the basis of one nation, one vote.

The famous 'Accords' signed at Yalta in the Crimea in 1945 by the leaders of the USA (Franklin D. Roosevelt), Britain (Winston Churchill) and the USSR (Joseph Stalin) determined who would occupy which of the defeated lands at the end of the war but could not agree on a political system. The preference of the United States and its allies for capitalism combined with liberal democracy and of the USSR and its allies for communist systems of government led to the creation of two separate political blocs in the post-war period: the capitalist First World and the communist Second World. In the ensuing stand-off between them, known as the 'Cold War', the blocs did not confront one another directly but played out their political tensions through propaganda and 'proxy wars' in the divided nations of Korea and Vietnam, and in other countries caught between the interests of the two, several of them in Africa: Ethiopia, Congo, Angola, Mozambique and Namibia.

As European nations gradually let go of their imperial possessions, the nations of Africa were among the last to be decolonized, beginning with Libya in 1951 and finishing with Zimbabwe in 1980. In the context of the Cold War, the new nations were faced with difficult choices about what political and economic system to adopt. By forming the Non-Aligned Movement, leaders of many independent countries in Africa and Asia were able to gain some advantage from East–West divisions by exercising their bloc voting power in the UN. These nations described themselves as 'the Third World'. The term was a political one, suggesting an alternative society, a 'third way'. On independence several African nations drew up their own plans for development, which looked back to pre-colonial Africa for their inspiration. One such was Julius Nyrere of Tanzania, whose vision for *ujamaa* was derived from a traditional African concept of 'familyhood', and partly from his Roman Catholic background.[40] This communal and spiritual ideal was so different from the prevailing Western norms that Nyrere felt its application required delinking Tanzania from the world system and its self-reliance.

In this new post-war world order, the term 'development' was coined by US President Harry S. Truman as 'a bold new program for making the benefits of our scientific advances and industrial progress available for the improvement and growth of underdeveloped areas'.[41] In the immediate post-war period, 'development' was mainly directed at Europe in the form of grants and support for state-managed economic growth to reconstruct the ravaged continent. Then, as the Cold War intensified, development was applied to the former colonies in programmes of modernization, according to either democratic or socialist models, depending on which superpower was promoting it. US President John F. Kennedy particularly expressed great confidence in human technology and goodwill, and optimism that humankind could work together to overcome obstacles to development. The historic Western churches and their successors in newly independent countries largely supported these efforts, engaging in humanitarian work as they had done in the colonial period. The chief difference was that modernization came with a secularist agenda, which assumed that increased material wellbeing would obviate the need for dependence on God. This secularization thesis marginalized the churches in development and obliged Christian agencies to distinguish social responsibility from evangelism in order to work with governments.

The Cold War continued until the gradual liberalization of the Chinese economy from 1978 onwards lessened the Asia–Pacific tension and the collapse of European communist regimes after 1989 dissolved the 'Iron Curtain' in Europe. The apparent triumph of the capitalist and democratic model by 1990 was celebrated by many in the USA as 'the end of history' since it left no socio-political alternative.[42] We are living in an American empire in all but name, and commentators argue about whether this is for good or ill.[43] Without the division between the First and Second Worlds, the term 'Third World' has lost its political edge and is used simply to refer to the poorest countries, in which sense it is often understood as a term of numerical proportion, in which case the alternatives 'Two-Thirds World', 'Three-Quarters World', 'Majority World' are to be preferred. But since 1990 the main division in the world has been the economic one of 'global North' and the 'global South'.

It could be argued that *ujamaa* in Tanzania failed because it was unsustainable as a development project for the large population of modern Tanzania and also because the indigenous spirituality on which it drew was ethnocentric and anachronistic.[44]

But the greatest difficulty for Nyrere and other African leaders in achieving their indigenous visions did not lie in Tanzania or in Africa but outside in the global economic system. *Ujamaa* foundered on the oil crisis of the late 1970s and the collapse of commodity prices. Like other African nations, Tanzania was forced to apply to the IMF for a loan in the 1980s. The condition for Tanzania and other poor nations was that the country undergo a Structural Adjustment Programme (SAP) by which its economy was remodelled, cutting back welfare programmes and opening up markets to foreign competition.

8.4 Mission and development

In sub-Saharan Africa since the application of SAPs, which cut spending on health and education, the poorest have again, as in the colonial period, been looking to the churches to meet their needs. Today some estimate that more than half the health care in Africa and much of the education is delivered by faith-based organizations.[45] As the money available from the declining historic European churches has contracted, African churches have sought funding from other churches in North America, and more recently from South Korea, Singapore and other wealthy Christian nations. Secular international donor organizations are also looking for channels to distribute aid, and the churches often present themselves as better organized, wider reaching and more reliable than governments. Donors also realize the advantages of tapping into the spiritual power generated by religious movements. For example, since 2000 the World Bank has enlisted the help of the Council of Anglican Provinces of Africa to alleviate poverty because the Bank recognized the Church's 'ability to influence constructively, based on its numbers, its position as the moral conscience of nations, its closeness to the poor, and its own accountability to God'.[46]

The shift from state-centred to liberalized, deregulated and privatized economic growth in the 1980s provided opportunities for faith-based organizations not only in poorer countries but also in 'developed' ones. The British government, for example, has been trying to involve religious communities in the provision of various social services at home as well as in channelling aid abroad. The willingness to work with and through faith groups is a sign that the secularization thesis has been revised (see Chapter 7). Not only for reasons of effectiveness but also because of the danger of the subversion of development by religious groups have development theorists urged co-operation. The use of participation methods by which local people are involved in the planning and implementation of development projects is itself a result of the influence of liberation theology and the educational theories of Paulo Freire (see Chapter 5) on mainstream development theory.[47] Subsequent research into the role of religions in development recognizes that religion is a key factor in the way many people (at all standards of living) live their lives, that religious organizations are among the most important social organizations in many societies (and not only poor ones), that the major world faiths also have global influence, and that religions may have a constructive effect in public life.[48] The result of these changes is a level of co-operation between religions and governmental organizations that has not been seen since the colonial period. While this is welcome in many respects, it also makes it all the more important for Christian development agencies to learn from mission history.

Christians have responded to the post-war development agenda in a number of different ways but always stressing that human welfare is not only about economics but about a joining of heaven with earth in such a way that God's will is done and God's kingdom comes. The main forms of that response have been social Christianity, Ecumenical social thought, Evangelical social responsibility and Catholic social teaching.[49] Each of these envisages the relationship between heaven and earth in a different way. Protestant social Christianity could be characterized as *building heaven on earth*. Developed from the social gospel movement of the late nineteenth century, social Christianity emphasizes Jesus' ethical teaching to love God and neighbour and stresses the incarnation of Jesus Christ and the continuing immanence (presence) of God on earth, uniting sacred and secular, God and humanity, and church and state. This results in an optimistic view of the human condition, downplaying human sinfulness and doctrines of judgment and eternal punishment and believing it is possible to build the kingdom of heaven on earth and by social compassion to bring fullness of life (John 10.10) to all. In its stress on the continuity between church and society, the social gospel movement has a tendency to secularize Christianity and to fuse civilization with the purposes of God in Christ. Social Christians work with governments, and with groups which do not share their Christian belief, in an altruistic way and with an ethos of service in the fulfilment of human aspirations.

Social Christians worked most closely with colonial governments and were therefore most susceptible to post-colonial criticism of mission. In the post-World War Two era, the idealism of the social gospel was tempered by the criticism of Reinhold Niebuhr, an American Protestant theologian (and brother of H. Richard Niebuhr – see Chapter 3) who translated Christian ideals into a pragmatic agenda for a free and democratic post-war world.[50] Many socially concerned Christians switched their support from the older mission societies to newly created Christian NGOs such as Christian Aid.[51] Christian Aid does not use the term 'mission' for its activities but emphasizes service, and works alongside the local churches and other bodies in Britain and overseas, 'wherever the need is greatest'. Its aim – as expressed in its ingenious slogan, 'we believe in life before death' – is not religious but humanitarian. Christian Aid arguably has taken a more critical stance toward British government activities than the colonial missionary societies did but like most other NGOs it is prepared to use Western government money and so pursue (Western) government projects of development. Although it is not explicit, there is considerable continuity between European NGO activities – whether Christian or not – and the social gospel of pre-colonial missionaries. The dangers of a close relationship between Christian agencies and secular governments include several factors.

First, as Evangelicals and other conservatives particularly point out, religious bodies may be diverted by secular interests from their primary religious goals. Second, not only do donors use faith-based organizations because they are more effective, they are also cheaper and therefore their altruism may be exploited. Third, religious bodies may be tainted by association with political interests. Fourth, states may be threatened by active and well-resourced civil groups and react by suppressing them when they are able – thus co-operating with aid and development agencies may be dangerous for local Christians.[52]

The central vision of Ecumenical social thought could be expressed as *heaven is earth's future*.[53] It was born as a product of deliberations between churches, for which the embryonic World Council of Churches was the central forum, in the destruction caused by Nazism and World War Two. The first assemblies of the Council rejected the social gospel optimism about the possibility of building the kingdom of God on earth and accepted the prophetic challenge of Karl Barth and the Confessing Church in Nazi Germany to take the reality of evil more seriously and recognize the discontinuity between God and the world. Focusing on the cross of Christ, they rediscovered eschatology, recognizing that the kingdom is 'already' but 'not yet', and consequently the provisional nature of all human endeavour.[54] In the context of the Council of Churches, Ecumenical social thought established a strong emphasis on the role of the Christian community as a 'sign' and 'instrument' of the kingdom. Mission is therefore 'an invitation to God's future' in the dual sense that it is a call to join the Christian community and also a participation in God's transforming activity.[55] In Britain, the Methodist Church, in which each member is also a member of the Methodist Missionary Society, probably best expresses the ecumenical vision that you cannot be a member of the church (understood more as the Christian community than as the institution) without also sharing in God's purposes for the world, and that it is in the life of the church where the future reign of God is inaugurated now.[56]

Where Evangelicals exercise social responsibility their vision could perhaps be described as *from heaven to transform earth*. The Evangelical withdrawal from corporate social involvement during the late nineteenth and early twentieth century was due to a number of factors (for the US American case see Chapter 7) which encouraged an increasingly pessimistic view of human nature. The 'pre-millennialist' view that the world is destined for destruction and that Christian hope lies only in a future life elsewhere – the 'pie in the sky when you die' attitude – discouraged action for social reform. Fundamentalistic Evangelicals were further alienated from the Ecumenical movement particularly in the 1960s and 1970s when they saw Ecumenical leaders preoccupied with 'social action' and apparently neglecting 'evangelism' in the sense of verbal proclamation of the Christian message. The recovery of Evangelical social conscience owed a great deal to the challenge of René Padilla of Argentina, Samuel Escobar of Peru, Orlando Costas of Puerto Rico and other Third World Evangelicals at the 1974 Lausanne Congress to work for the poor.[57]

The Lausanne Covenant (1974) expresses regret for the separation of 'evangelism' from 'social concern' and affirms that 'socio-political involvement' is part of the Christian duty to love one's neighbour, and that God's kingdom begins in this world. The Lausanne Covenant's statement that evangelism is 'primary' in the church's mission does not necessarily imply that social action is a secondary activity to be used only where evangelism is not possible, or to create opportunity for it.[58] The rationale behind it is that the conversion of individuals will change behaviour and improve society, the belief is that faith in Christ not only helps a person temporally but also secures an eternal destiny, and that, whereas any human being can engage in social action, evangelism is a uniquely Christian activity.[59] Many who align themselves with the Lausanne Covenant regard evangelism and social action as interrelated and interdependent. This view is upheld by the British relief and development charity Tearfund, which was founded in 1968 as 'The Evangelical Alliance Relief Fund' to distribute funds given spontaneously in response to war and natural disaster.

Tearfund has developed a vision for 'integral mission', which means 'giving practical help alongside hope, through emotional and spiritual support'.[60] Unlike Christian Aid, Tearfund has an explicitly Christian agenda and works only with and through churches.

The final example of a Christian approach to development, and the most fully articulated, is Catholic social teaching. This can be characterized *as in heaven, so on earth* because it begins from the basis that there is a divinely appointed 'natural law', which can be known through human reason, and therefore a universal framework for human societal behaviour and relations. Its application to issues of development has been a subject of church teaching since 1891 and is well discussed and documented.[61] Central to Catholic social teaching is the fundamental and equal dignity of all human beings because they are made in the image of God. They have a duty and the potential to develop themselves to become fully human and they are social beings, who live in community with others as children of the same heavenly Father, and in relationship with the whole creation.[62]

Catholic social teaching starts with economics and then draws political conclusions. The economic starting point is concern for the poor on the basis that 'the goods of this world', given by God, 'are originally meant for all'. Under the influence particularly of Pope John Paul II, the Roman Catholic Church stresses solidarity between God, humanity and the natural world, and also the special solidarity of the church with the poor. Private property is regarded as 'valid and necessary' but only because it is the best means of safeguarding the earth and its fruit for all.[63] The church aims to take a middle position between socialism and Marxism, on the one hand, which fail to recognize the sacredness of the human person, and liberalistic capitalism, on the other, which neglects the social aspects of the human person. It does not set out a new economic system, and does not oppose the present capitalist system as a whole, but aims to strike a medium between upholding a basic minimum for everyone and offering the opportunity for individual accumulation of wealth as part of human development. Such economics has political implications, which were worked out in resistance to the twentieth century extremes of Communism and Fascism. The state is said to exist to bring about both 'public wellbeing and private prosperity'. In order to achieve this, without becoming totalitarian, the state must recognize the primary importance of the human person and family, and the power of the state is limited to dealing only with matters that exceed the capacity of individuals and intermediate bodies such as neighbourhoods, social, cultural, educational organizations, churches and voluntary associations.[64]

Since the Second Vatican Council of 1962–5, the Roman Catholic Church has accepted democracy as the preferred political system and championed human rights because they are understood to contribute to upholding the fundamental principle of human dignity. In its teaching, human rights include economic and social as well as political and civil rights, and they are related to duties and values such as truth, justice and charity. In 1967, the church embraced 'development' as 'the new name for peace' with the potential to overcome economic disparity between nations. It should not be restricted to the economic sphere alone but represents all aspects of humanity's 'transition from less than human conditions to truly human ones'.[65] Catholic social teaching is applied by CAFOD, the Catholic Agency for Overseas Development, which is the official overseas development and relief agency of the Roman Catholic Church in England and Wales, founded in 1962.[66] Agency workers may find it difficult to agree with all aspects of Catholic social teaching, which raises controversial development issues. For example, women's roles are generally only considered in relation to home and family, and artificial methods of birth control, including condoms, were officially proscribed by Paul VI in 1968, although many Catholic ethicists believe they should be allowed, at least between spouses where one has HIV/AIDS.

8.5 Defining development

Since 1945 the word 'development' has been used in several different ways. For neo-liberals who regard development as a consequence of free-market growth, development means the development of capitalism by individual entrepreneurs. However, most development theorists recognize the limits of the free market to solve the problems of poverty and advocate some form of intervention by governments and non-governmental organizations (NGOs) to ameliorate its ill-effects. In this view development takes place alongside capitalism to achieve basic social and environmental goals. Others believe that true human development is not possible within the capitalist system and propose changing global structures and creating an alternative system, usually some form of communism or socialism. Still others, critical of capitalism, advocate an alternative approach to development which is centred on the achievement of the potential of each person or group rather than driven by the forces of the global economy. Post-developmentalists reject development altogether as a hoax which only serves to strengthen US hegemony.[67]

Despite notable successes in terms of control of disease and increased life expectancy, in many parts of the world, and especially in Africa, development has manifestly failed to improve the overall standard of living of the world's poor. In light of this, theories of development have become more critical of development driven by economic models, and development studies have focused more on the causes of poverty and ways to alleviate and reduce it. Consequently, since the 1990s there has been greater recognition of the need for human development if economic targets are to be met. The emphasis is on sustainable development in the context of an intensification of global co-operation.[68] In an attempt to deal with global poverty, in September 2000 the United Nations declared eight 'Millennium Development Goals', addressing poverty and related issues of education, gender inequality, child mortality, maternal ill health, disease and environmental degradation, and encouraging global partnership for development.[69] Progress toward these goals has been hampered by new issues of terrorism and failed states, climate change and the growing competition for natural resources, and global economic crisis. Nevertheless in the 2007 Reith Lectures, eminent US economist Jeffrey Sachs expressed a Kennedy-esque optimism in the power of technological advancement and social mobilization to solve the problems and create a world of plenty for all. At the same time, he also recognized that in the twenty-first century the initiative in development seems to be passing away from the United States, towards the emerging and hugely populous nations of China and India particularly.[70]

In the Christian social theory we have looked at, the dominant theological motif for development is the kingdom of God. The kingdom of God was the terminology of the social gospel movement which in keeping with the imperial period was regarded as the ideal human society, gradually coming into being through processes of Christianization. The eschatological vision of the early Ecumenical movement was supported by a more apocalyptic understanding of the kingdom or reign of God which stressed the sovereignty of God over human affairs and the contingency of all human efforts at progress. Dewi Hughes, Theological Secretary for Tearfund, discusses development in terms of the kingdom in the sense of God's just rule in the world, which brings blessing to the poor here and now – a view which is greatly influenced by liberation theology.[71] Catholic social teaching differs in that it speaks to all people and therefore uses secular terminology but the Roman Catholic Church understands itself to be 'the initial budding forth of that kingdom', which was present in Jesus Christ on earth and grows in the world mysteriously and incompletely until the final consummation.[72] No church is identified with the kingdom but Jesus did apply his teaching about the kingdom to the community of his disciples (Matt. 13) and so all churches are expected to offer a model of the kingdom life which is for all society.

However, the imagery of the kingdom may not be the most suitable to a post-colonial and post-monarchical era. There is an alternative image which may better express a Christian theology of development for today: the Holy Spirit. Whereas the kingdom of God or kingdom of heaven is preferred for expressing the Christian vision by the synoptic writers Matthew, Mark and Luke, the parallel idea of 'life in the Spirit' is more commonly used by John and Paul. The meaning of God's purposes is more fully illuminated by this parallelism.[73] Samuel Rayan demonstrates how the writer of the Fourth Gospel, sometimes known as the 'spiritual gospel', shows much the same concrete concern for the poor as does Luke in his Gospel but he does so by using the theme of new life in the Spirit, which Jesus Christ gives to all who ask (John 4.13–14). In the Spirit there is 'wine for the wineless' (2.1–11), 'bread for the breadless' (6.1–14), the power of resurrection from the dead (11.38–44) and the love which binds the new community of justice and peace (14.15—16.15).[74] According to Paul, being 'in the Spirit' is participating in a new creation only just coming into being (Rom. 8). The Spirit is the foretaste, guarantee or downpayment (2 Cor. 1.22; 5.5; Eph. 1.13–14; Rom. 8.23) of the life that is to come. In other words, in the church we begin to experience a new life: eternal life, the life of the new age, spiritual life. Fullness of life is yet to come, but it is anticipated in the Spirit. In view of the political sensitivity of the language of 'kingdom' on the one hand and of contemporary interest in discourse on spirit(s) and spirituality on the other, it would seem wise to re-express our theologies of development in terms of the Holy Spirit. Liberation theologians have already done this to a great extent (see Chapter 5), and Mark Lewis Taylor shows how it is particularly appealing in the context of African beliefs in spirits.[75]

8.6 Development as community growth

In all the discussion about churches servicing the international development agenda, what tends to get lost is that churches are agents of human development in and of themselves. Sociologists have noted that Pentecostal-type churches particularly often have a transformational effect on the lives of church members. Indeed Pentecostalism worldwide could be described as the most successful *social* movement of the last century.[76] Although Pentecostal-style churches are often criticized by their co-religionists as 'happy clappy', insular and lacking social concern, David Martin and others have argued from a sociological point of view that such groups bring benefits to their members in terms of personal and community development. These members are often poor but 'new social and cultural capital is being created' in the churches, leading to the upward social mobility of individuals, families and whole communities.[77] The AICs are a case in point. The contribution of AICs to development is not unambiguous. On the one hand, in their push for independence, the AICs rejected the colonial authority, and in many cases remain suspicious of government. In the government's eyes this hinders their development, especially as they often refuse to take modern medicine and sometimes fail to send their children to school. But, on the other hand, members of AICs resist corruption and their refusal to play the game is a political protest against bad governance. They also have advantages in negotiating the push towards individualism in modern life by imbuing each individual with a sense of equality and worth, providing social security through pooling of resources and access to help, and encouraging ethical discipline which pays dividends in employment and family life. In so far as they have brought dignity and increased human wellbeing, then, the AICs can be regarded as development movements.[78]

The human development which takes place through Pentecostal churches echoes aspects of the biblical narrative. First, the experience of empowerment from the Holy Spirit at Pentecost led to the formation of a community which shared its goods and looked after the poor (Acts 2.44–5; 6.1–6). From the beginning, therefore, Pentecostal movements have had a strong missionary spirit[79] and churches have networks of giving that may extend into the wider community. Second, in the version of Jesus' commission to his disciples in Mark's Gospel (16.14–18) mission is a 'power encounter' in which signs and wonders transform the world. In Pentecostal churches these verses are taken particularly to refer to deliverance ministry, speaking in tongues, divine protection from evil and divine healing. Third, the 'gifts of the Spirit' that appear in the New Testament (Rom. 12.6–8; 1 Cor. 12.8–10; Eph. 4.11), and which are intended for the building up of the body (1 Cor. 14.1–33) are definitive of Pentecostalism.[80] Receipt of gifts is a great encouragement to individual believers as well as the community and provides valuable opportunities for leadership. Finally, the holiness of the Spirit attested to in Scripture is applied to people's personal lives in Paul's teaching of the fruit of the Spirit (Gal. 5.22). In many Pentecostal churches today those who join therefore have an incentive to live reformed, upright lives, which benefits their families and communities.[81]

Since the 1970s a new wave of Pentecostal-type Christianity has been growing in Africa. This stresses that among the blessings poured out by God is material prosperity. One justification for this is 2 Corinthians 8.9: 'For you know the generous act of our Lord Jesus Christ, that though he was rich, yet for your sakes he became poor, so that by his poverty you might become rich.' The new churches are not rural and anti-modern as the AICs were but are found in the cities, among the middle classes, and equip their congregations for success in a globalized and postmodern world.[82] They are partly the result of globalized communications systems, which make the broadcasts of Western 'televangelists' available to African audiences, and share the general characteristics of worldwide neo-Pentecostalism with its focus on prosperity and personal success. In Africa they also have a particular emphasis on deliverance from demonic forces associated with traditional religion. The most dramatic growth has been in West Africa, and some of the most prominent churches, such as Deeper Life Bible Church, the Redeemed Christian Church of God, Winners Chapel and the Church of Pentecost, also have branches in Britain and elsewhere among the African diaspora, and can be easily found online. Professor Paul Gifford of the School of African and Oriental Studies (SOAS), London, has raised concerns that the tactics of many of the 'prophets' who lead the churches abuse the trust of those who attend and that they do not address the underlying problems of West African society. However he singles out one church leader, Dr Mensa Otabil of the International Central Gospel Church in Ghana, who preaches about success brought about by hard work, assuming responsibility and obtaining education, rises above fears of witchcraft to address social ills and makes calls for political reform, and whose personal integrity and careful negotiation of politics has won him widespread respect.[83]

At the time of writing, Kingsway International Christian Centre (KICC), in London, has the largest congregation in the UK.[84] It is an example of a neo-Pentecostal church, and is led by Nigerian, Revd Matthew Ashimolowo. The church encourages personal growth and worldly success on the basis that 'the Word of God . . . states that God wants us to prosper and be in health even as our souls prosper' (cf. Deut. 8.18). The KICC has a vision statement, which would impress any development agency. For example, it aims to grow the church from about 10,000 to 25,000 members by 2010, 'pioneer city churches around the world', 'open a KICC Bank to empower God's people economically', and 'build a 5,000-seater church building and a four floor office'. Although there may be reservations about its message and its theology, from a sociological point of view there is little doubt that KICC has created a dynamic community that offers encouragement, support and hope to many who may be otherwise marginalized and disadvantaged in British society.

KICC encourages its members to 'grow up', 'grow big' and 'grow together'. In some such churches, whether in London, the USA, South Korea or other countries, development is chiefly understood in terms of 'grow big'. They look back to the growth of the first church in Jerusalem on the day of Pentecost when 'about three thousand persons were added' (Acts 2.41) and other references in the book of Acts to the numerical growth of the early church (6.1, 5, 7; 12.24). Church growth and its causes has become a popular field of study with pastors and those concerned with world evangelization in the sense of bringing all the peoples of the world to explicit Christian faith. Different theories have been developed to bring about numerical growth. The church growth school of Donald McGavran and C. Peter Wagner advanced the 'homogeneous unit principle': churches are more likely to grow if they are composed of people of the social class, caste or subculture where the social barriers to commitment are at a minimum. The homogenous unit principle may be an observable fact, but its use as a mission strategy was strongly criticized for making the end justify the means and encouraging social segregation.[85]

Another theory of church growth has been the cell group method pioneered by Pastor David Yonggi Cho at Yoido Full Gospel Church in Seoul, which grew from a handful of displaced North Koreans in 1958 to more than 800,000 today.[86] Cho divided his congregation according to where they lived and organized them into small groups, led by lay women, meeting for prayer and bible study during the week in each locality. Members are expected to bring along their friends and the leader trains an assistant. Once the group reaches a maximum number it is divided into two and the process is repeated, following a biological pattern of exponential growth. The groups are closely supervised by pastors appointed for larger areas of the city; all members are expected to join the main church and gather there on Sundays. The method has been developed and varied in different countries. It reached the UK in the 1990s and has been promoted through CellUK and other bodies. There is much to be said for cell groups as long as the concern for quantitative growth does not override qualitative development and is the result of a comprehensive spiritual vision.

8.7 Creation and ecology in mission

The interpretation of the Great Commission mainly in terms of growth in church membership is a little like interpreting the creation ordinance primarily in terms of population growth. The command to Adam and Eve to 'Be fruitful and multiply, and fill the earth and subdue it; and have dominion over the fish of the sea and over the birds of the air and over every living thing that moves upon the earth' (Gen. 1.28) includes numerical increase but this is only part of a more comprehensive vision. That vision, as Paul interprets it, is about the new life in the Spirit (Rom. 8.18–25). This life does not pertain only to humanity but to the whole creation, which has also been suffering in bondage and is longing for redemption, 'that the creation itself . . . will obtain the freedom of the glory of the children of God' (Rom. 8.21). The ecological dimensions of salvation run through the New Testament, which continues a salvation history that begins with the creation and culminates in Christ, 'the firstborn of all creation', in whom 'all things in heaven and on earth were created', and through whom 'God was pleased to reconcile to himself all things' (Col. 1.15, 16, 20; cf. Eph. 1.10).

Christians have been waking up to the cosmic scope of the goal of mission since 1967 when an article in a scientific journal argued that Judeo-Christian tradition is fundamentally exploitative of creation and responsible for the 'environmental crisis', of which scientists were then becoming aware.[87] The argument was on the basis of the creation stories of Genesis, in which human beings are superior to the rest of creation and have the right to 'dominion' over it. Biblical scholars have pointed out that 'dominion' does not mean 'domination' or exploitation but that 'stewardship' of creation is a better representation of the role of human beings in the biblical creation stories, and especially in the second one (Gen. 2.4–25) where Adam and Eve are gardeners in Eden. But stewardship alone may still be used to serve only human interest, unless it is accompanied by an awareness of the earth and all its creatures as having value in themselves.[88] The Bible affirms that earth, and everything in it, belongs to God (Ps. 24.1) and the land, not just the people, is at the centre of his concern. Furthermore, God has covenanted with Noah and his descendants to preserve the creation.[89] But the strongest biblical argument that creation has value in or of itself is the incarnation of the heavenly *Logos* in the material world (John 1.1–18). As Dave Bookless, UK Director of the Christian environmental charity A Rocha, concludes, 'From creation to [the book of] Revelation, God's purposes are far wider than human salvation or human welfare – although the place of humanity within those purposes is critical.'[90] The blame for environmental catastrophe cannot be laid on the Bible but it is nevertheless the case that, particularly since the late Middle Ages, European Christians have been complicit in policies and actions that have had a hugely degrading and destructive effect on human, animal and plant life of the earth and on the balanced ecosystem in which they exist.

In the Ecumenical movement, concerns about the environment and the land were raised most forcefully not by scientists but by theologians from Africa, the Pacific Islands and others representing indigenous peoples, who were living more closely with the land and seeing their life and environment suffer.[91] Those who are now known as 'First Nations' in Canada, 'Native Americans' in the USA, 'Amerindians' in Central and South America, 'Aborigines' in Australia, 'Maoris' in Aotearoa-New Zealand and 'Adivasis' in India, together with many black Africans were referred to in the colonial period as 'primitives', 'savages' and 'uncivilized', and their wishes, and even their rights were ignored. The Nigerian theologian Bolaji Idowu has commented that Westerners define 'the natural world' as 'the remainder of the world, when Europe and America have been subtracted from it', which they regard as theirs to use for resources, settlement and tourism.[92] Being mostly non-literate societies, indigenous peoples were (and are) cheated of their land by colonists who determined that ownership was by legal documents which those actually living there did not have. Their land was not only the source of their material welfare but also of their spirituality, and the result in many cases was the destruction of the society, the culture and even the person. As Maori theologian Rob Cooper writes, 'Huge expanses of sea, ice and supposedly barren wastelands are home to people' who have profound links with the creator and creation which cannot be grasped by outsiders.[93] The result of the deprivation of their lands, which was also an invasion of their religion and culture, was in many cases despair. Still today displaced indigenous peoples have high rates of alcoholism, heart disease, diabetes and suicide. They describe themselves as a 'Fourth World . . . oppressed by the powerful nations and the so-called developing nations' and 'insist on being recognized as "peoples", even nations, with a claim to national sovereignty based on ancient title to our land'.[94] Native American theologians have raised difficult questions about the use of the Exodus story by Christians because they read it 'with Canaanite eyes' and are worried that 'As long as people believe in the Yahweh of deliverance, the world will not be safe from Yahweh the conqueror.'[95]

The Anglican Consultative Council, which developed the 'five marks of mission' between 1984 and 1990, included as number five the aim 'to strive to safeguard the integrity of creation and sustain and renew the life of the earth'.[96] In retrospect this aspect of mission is a noticeable omission from David Bosch's 'ecumenical consensus' in mission in 1991. However, its incorporation means rethinking Bosch's whole biblical basis for mission, which begins with re-creation and hardly refers to the first creation. Such rethinking began in the 1990s with the development of 'eco-theology', much of which is grounded in a theology of the work of God's Spirit in the creation – a theme which is also absent from Bosch's mission paradigm.[97] Eco-theologies combined four main strands of reflection on creation and the environment. The first was social ecology which extended the socio-political struggle for justice of liberation theology to the whole creation to bring about eco-justice. The second strand was creation theology, which aimed to recover the creation motif in the biblical narrative to counter human-centred domination of the earth. The third was eco-feminism, which linked the rape of women to rape of land and sought to overcome dualisms of male and female, spiritual and material, to heal the whole cosmos. The final strand was eco-spirituality which reworked the mystical traditions to facilitate participation with the Spirit in creation.[98]

Although both drawing on theology of the Holy Spirit, two

prominent eco-theologians have come out with different agendas for eco-mission. German Protestant pastor, academic and activist, Geiko Müller-Fahrenholz sees the Spirit as the power of truth, consolation and endurance in a world of violence, who maintains the covenant of God with creation. In faithfulness to this covenant, he argues for 'respectable poverty' for the majority of the world's population, frugal living for the rich, population control, the empowerment of women and the strengthening of civil society as the way forward for a sustainable future.[99] However, Samuel Rayan would disagree with most of this agenda not only for theological reasons but also because of his different economic context. Working with outcastes in India, Rayan would be highly suspicious of Müller-Fahrenholz's attempts to limit the prosperity of the poor world and to control its population. He argues for common ownership of all the world's land and a sharing of all its resources, which would include changing immigration laws to equalize population distribution, giving access to under-populated land in the West to people from the Majority World. He also calls for an end to destructive technologies, including arms manufacture, and regards the rejection of unjust social institutions as integral to dealing with abuse of the environment. Rayan derives his views not from a theology of covenant but from a sacramental theology of the presence of the Spirit in all creation, so that living in the Spirit means knowing 'we are the earth'.[100] He believes that respect for indigenous people means learning from their spiritualities, in which, as George Tinker writes, 'God reveals God's self in creation, in space or place', rather than in time and history.[101]

Environmental issues are nowhere more pressing than in sub-Saharan Africa, which has always been prone to drought and is likely to be hit most by climate change. Sustainable development here and everywhere has become the key issue. M. L. Daneel has described how for AICs in South Africa it is natural to think of the Holy Spirit as the 'earthkeeping Spirit' who heals, protects and gives life, and therefore the AIC prophets condemn acts harmful to the environment as sin, and promote an understanding of baptism and the Eucharist as affirming the elements of creation.[102] In this they follow the example of the prophet Joel, 'prophet of the environment and development', who warns of the coming environmental disaster when 'the sun shall be turned to darkness and the moon to blood' (2.1–11, 30–31) but also holds out hope of restoration and renewal when 'you shall eat in plenty and be satisfied' and 'the mountains will drip with sweet wine' (2.26; 3.18). They, and the leaders of churches of other indigenous peoples, fight 'not for survival, not for conquest and domination but in defence and protection of basic human rights' in what are 'critical and decisive times in history, as the very existence of humanity and of the whole earth is threatened'.[103]

Notes

1 Manas Buthelezi, 'Salvation as Wholeness', in John Parratt (ed.), *A Reader in African Christian Theology*, 2nd edn (London: SPCK, 1997; article first published in 1972), pp. 85–90, at p. 89.

2 See the documentary at <www.becominghuman.org> made by the Institute of Human Origins, Arizona State University.

3 It may lead on to attempting to prove other far-reaching theories about African origins: e.g. Paul C. Boyd, *The African Origin of Christianity* (London: Karia Press, 1991).

4 Lamin Sanneh, *West African Christianity: The Religious Impact* (London: C. Hurst, 1983), pp. 236–41; J. N. K. Mugambi, *Christianity and African Culture* (Nairobi: Acton Publishers, 2002), pp. 57, 62; Elizabeth Isichei, *A History of Christianity in Africa, from Antiquity to the Present* (Grand Rapids, MI: Wm B. Eerdmans, 1995), p. 96; Buthelezi, 'Salvation as Wholeness'; Diane B. Stinton, *Jesus of Africa: Voices of Contemporary African Christology* (Maryknoll, NY: Orbis Books, 2004), pp. 55–6.

5 Kwami Labi, 'Environmental Justice from the View of the Poorest', paper delivered to the day conference of the British and Irish Association for Mission Studies, 4 October 2006.

6 Birgit Meyer, 'Modernity and Enchantment: The Image of the Devil in Popular African Christianity', in Peter van der Veer (ed.), *Conversion to Modernities: The Globalization of Christianity* (New York: Routledge, 1996), pp. 199–230, at p. 222; Isichei, *History of Christianity in Africa*, pp. 53–4; Andrew F. Walls, *The Cross-cultural Process in Christian History: Studies in the Transmission and Appropriation of*

Faith (Maryknoll, NY: Orbis Books, 2002), p. 92; Kevin Ward, 'Africa', in Adrian Hastings (ed.), *A World History of Christianity* (London: Cassell, 1999), pp. 192–237, at p. 202.

7 Ward, 'Africa', p. 221.

8 Figure extrapolated from David B. Barrett, George T. Kurian and Todd M. Johnson (eds), *World Christian Encyclopedia* (Oxford: Oxford University Press, 2001), p. 13.

9 For a short introduction, see John S. Pobee and Gabriel Ositelu II, *African Initiatives in Christianity* (Geneva: WCC Publications, 1998). See also, Allan Anderson, *African Reformation: African Initiated Christianity in the Twentieth Century* (Trenton, NJ: Africa World Press, 2001); Inus Daneel, *Quest for Belonging: Introduction to the Study of African Independent Churches* (Harare: Mambo Press, 1987); Deji Ayegboyin and S. Ademola Ishola, *African Indigenous Churches: An Historical Perspective* (Lagos: Greater Heights Publications, 1997).

10 John Mbiti, *Bible and Theology in African Christianity* (Nairobi: Oxford University Press, 1986), p. 29.

11 Mbiti, *Bible and Theology in African Christianity*, p. 29; Philip Jenkins, *The New Faces of Christianity: Believing the Bible in the Global South* (Oxford: Oxford University Press, 2006), p. 35; Paul Gifford, 'A View of Ghana's New Christianity', in Lamin Sanneh and Joel A. Carpenter (eds), *The Changing Face of Christianity: Africa, the West and the World* (Oxford: Oxford University Press, 2005), pp. 81–96, at p. 86.

12 Anderson, *African Reformation*, pp. 69–166.

13 One example is the Holy Ghost Church of East Africa (HGCEA), the largest of the *Akurinu* or Gikuyu Spirit Churches of Kenya, which originated in the East African revival of 1927–30. The HGCEA combines millennialist and biblicist doctrine with a strong work ethic and a simple, communal lifestyle. Philomena Njeri Mwaura, 'African Instituted Churches and Socio-economic Development', in Grace Wamue and Matthew M. Theuri (eds), *Quests for Integrity in Africa* (Nairobi: Acton Publishers, 2003), pp. 75–94.

14 Allan Anderson, *Zion and Pentecost: The Spirituality and Experience of Pentecostal and Zionist/Apostolic Churches in South Africa* (Pretoria: UNISA, 2000), pp. 133–4.

15 Pobee and Ositelu, *African Initiatives in Christianity*, p. 68.

16 Ayegboyin and Ishola, *African Indigenous Churches*, pp. 156–7; Anderson, *African Reformation*, pp. 16–18; Pobee and Ositelu, *African Initiatives in Christianity*, pp. 43, 34.

17 Gerald West and Musa Dube (eds), *The Bible in Africa: Transactions, Trajectories and Trends* (Leiden: Brill, 2000).

18 Kevin Ward, 'Marching or Stumbling towards a Christian Ethic? Homosexuality and African Anglicanism', in Terry Brown (ed.), *Other Voices, Other Worlds: The Global Church Speaks Out on Homosexual-*

ity (London: Darton, Longman and Todd, 2006), pp. 129–41, at pp. 129, 132, 139.

19 See, for example, Esther Mombo, 'Kenya Reflections', pp. 142–53; Rowland Jide Macaulay, 'Homosexuality and the Churches in Nigeria', pp. 154–67; Kawuki Mukasa, 'The Church of Uganda and the Probelm of Human Sexuality: Responding to Concerns from the Ugandan Context', pp. 168–78; David Russell, 'Putting Right a Great Wrong: A Southern African Perspective', pp. 179–92, in Terry Brown (ed.), *Other Voices, Other Worlds.*

20 Emmanuel Egbunu, 'To Teach, Baptize, and Nurture New Believers', in Andrew Walls and Cathy Ross (eds), *Mission in the 21st Century: Exploring the Five Marks of Mission* (London: Darton, Longman and Todd, 2008), pp. 25–36, at pp. 28–9.

21 Philip Jenkins, *The Next Christendom: The Coming of Global Christianity* (Oxford: Oxford University Press, 2002).

22 Gifford, 'View of Ghana's New Christianity', p. 87; Andrew F. Walls, *The Missionary Movement in Christian History: Studies in the Transmission of Faith* (Maryknoll, NY: Orbis Books, 1996), pp. 97–100; Andrew A. Kyomo, 'Faith and Healing in the African Context', in Mika Vähäkangas and Andrew A. Kyomo (eds), *Charismatic Renewal in Africa: A Challenge to African Christianity* (Nairobi: Acton Publishers, 2003), pp. 145–56, at p. 151; Pobee and Ositelu, *African Initiatives in Christianity*, pp. 70–1.

23 J. Ade Aina, 'The Church's Healing Ministry', in Parratt, *Reader in African Christian Theology*, pp. 104–8; Stinton, *Jesus of Africa*, pp. 71–5, 80–103; Allan Anderson, *Moya: The Holy Spirit in an African Context* (Pretoria: UNISA, 1991), pp. 120–5.

24 Chad N. Gandiya, 'Mission as Healing: Reconciling Spirit and Body', in Kirsteen Kim (ed.), *Reconciling Mission: The Ministry of Healing and Reconciliation in the Church Worldwide* (Delhi: ISPCK, 2005), pp. 23–42; World Council of Churches, 'The Healing Mission of the Church' (2005), para. 30 – published in Jacques Matthey (ed.), *'You Are the Light of the World': Statements on Mission by the World Council of Churches 1980–2005* (Geneva: WCC Publications, 2005), pp. 62–89, also available at <www.mission2005.org>.

25 WCC, 'Healing Mission of the Church', para. 45.

26 Kyomo, 'Faith and Healing in the African Context', p. 148; Omega Bula, 'Women in Mission – Participating in Healing', *International Review of Mission* 71/322 (1992), pp. 247–52, at p. 247; cf. Stinton, *Jesus of Africa.*

27 WCC, 'Healing Mission of the Church', paras. 40, 41.

28 Stinton, *Jesus of Africa*, pp. 54–61; Walls, *Missionary Movement in Christian History*, p. 98.

29 Buthelezi, 'Salvation as Wholeness', pp. 85–6.

30 Mercy Amba Oduyoye, *Hearing and Knowing: Theological Reflections on Christianity in Africa* (Maryknoll, NY: Orbis Books, 1986), p. 44.

31 Jean-Marc Ela, *My Faith as an African* (Maryknoll, NY: Orbis Books, 1988), pp. 50–1; Kyomo, 'Faith and Healing in the African Context', p. 149; Bula, 'Women in Mission', p. 247.

32 Quoted in WCC, 'Healing Mission of the Church', para. 41.

33 Martin Meredith, *The State of Africa: A History of Fifty Years of Independence*, 2nd edn (London: Free Press, 2006).

34 For a comprehensive introduction to the study of international development, see: Tim Allen and Alan Thomas (eds), *Poverty and Development into the Twenty-first Century* (Oxford: Oxford University Press, 2000).

35 Michael Polanyi, *The Great Transformation* (New York: Farrar & Rinehart, 1944).

36 Scottish missionaries in Nyassaland and CMS missionaries in Uganda called for these countries to be incorporated into the British Empire. Ward, 'Africa', pp. 216–17.

37 David J. Bosch, *Transforming Mission: Paradigm Shifts in Theology of Mission* (Maryknoll, NY: Orbis Books, 1991), p. 303.

38 Niall Ferguson, *Empire: How Britain Made the Modern World* (London: Allen Lane, 2003).

39 O. Frederick Nolde, 'Ecumenical Action in International Affairs', in Harold E. Fey (ed.), *The Ecumenical Advance: A History of the Ecumenical Movement, Vol. II, 1948–1968* (Geneva: WCC Publications, 1993), pp. 261–85; 'History and Overview of WCC Relations with the UN', at <www.oikoumene.org>.

40 Julius Nyrere, 'The Church's Role in Society', in Parratt, *Reader in African Christian Theology*, pp. 109–19.

41 Quoted in Tim Allen and Alan Thomas (eds), *Poverty and Development into the Twenty-first Century* (Oxford: Oxford University Press, 2000), p.5.

42 Francis Fukuyama, *The End of History and the Last Man* (London: Penguin, 1992).

43 Compare Niall Ferguson, *Colossus: The Rise and Fall of the American Empire* (London: Penguin, 2004), with Noam Chomsky, *Hegemony or Survival: America's Quest for Global Dominance* (London: Penguin, 2003).

44 Frans Wijsen, 'Indigenous Spirituality and Sustainable Development: A Critical Appraisal of African Renaissance', paper presented at the conference on religion and development at the Free University of Amsterdam, 14–15 June 2007 – available at <www.religionanddevelopment.nl>.

45 Carole Rakodi, 'Understanding the Roles of Religions in Devel-

opment: The Approach of the Religions and Development Programme' (Birmingham: University of Birmingham, 2007), p. 14 – available at <www.rad.bham.ac.uk>.

46 D. Belshaw, R. Calderisi and C. Sugden (eds), *Faith in Development* (Oxford: Regnum, 2001), pp. 8, 9.

47 Robert Chambers, 'Power, Knowledge and Policy Influence: Reflections on Experience', in K. Brock and R. McGee (eds), *Knowing Poverty* (London: Earthscan, 2002), pp. 140–58; Tim Allen, 'Taking Culture Seriously', in Allen and Thomas, *Poverty and Development into the Twenty-first Century*, pp. 443–67; Paulo Freire, *Pedagogy of the Oppressed*, trans. Myra Bergman Ramos (New York: Seabury Press, 1970 [1968]).

48 Rakodi, 'Understanding the Roles of Religions in Development', p. 11.

49 Kirsteen Kim, 'Concepts of Development in the Christian Traditions'. Background paper for the Religions and Development Research Programme (Birmingham: University of Birmingham, 2007) – available at <www.rad.bham.ac.uk>; see also Michael Taylor, *Poverty and Christianity* (London, SCM Press, 2000); Duncan B. Forrester, 'Social Gospel and Social Teaching', in Adrian Hastings, Alistair Mason and Hugh Pyper (eds), *The Oxford Companion to Christian Thought* (Oxford, Oxford University Press, 2000), pp. 675–6.

50 William Werpehowski, 'Reinhold Niehbuhr', in Peter Scott and William T. Cavanaugh, *Blackwell Companion to Political Theology* (Oxford: Blackwell, 2007), pp. 180–93.

51 <www.christian-aid.org.uk>.

52 See, for example, Philip Quarles van Ufford, 'Religion and Development: Transforming Relations between Indonesian and Dutch Churches' (2007). Paper presented at the conference on Religion and Development, Free University of Amsterdam, 14–15 June 2007 – available at <www.religionanddevelopment.nl>.

53 For a helpful digest of ecumenical social thought, see Mark Ellingsen, *The Cutting Edge: The Churches Speak on Social Issues* (Geneva, WCC Publications, 1993).

54 Norman Goodall (ed.), *Missions under the Cross* (London: Edinburgh House Press, 1953).

55 Bosch, *Transforming Mission*, pp. 374–6; Jürgen Moltmann, 'The Mission of the Spirit: The Gospel of Life', in Timothy Yates (ed.), *Mission – an Invitation to God's Future*, papers of the conference of the British and Irish Association for Mission Studies, Oxford, 1999 (Sheffield: Cliff College Press, 2000), pp. 19–34.

56 <www.methodist.org.uk>.

57 Ross Langmead, *The Word Made Flesh: Towards an Incarnational Missiology* (Lanham, MD: University Press of America, 2004), p. 94.

58 Lausanne Committee for World Evangelization, *The Lausanne Covenant* (1974) – available at <www.lausanne.org>.

59 Lausanne Committee for World Evangelization and the World Evangelical Fellowship, *Evangelism and Social Responsibility: An Evangelical Commitment*, Lausanne Occasional Paper 21 (1982), pp. 24–5 – available at <www.lausanne.org>.

60 John Stott, *Christian Mission in the Modern World* (London: Church Pastoral Aid Society, 1975). Tearfund website, <www.tearfund.org>; see also Dewi A. Hughes and M. Bennett, *God of the Poor: A Biblical Vision of God's Present Rule* (Carlisle: OM Publishing, 1998).

61 Charles E. Curran, *Catholic Social Teaching, 1891–Present* (Washington DC: Georgetown University Press, 2002); Donal Dorr, *Option for the Poor: A Hundred Years of Vatican Social Teaching*, rvsd edn (Maryknoll, NY: Orbis Books, 1992); Rodger Charles, *Christian Social Witness and Teaching: The Catholic Tradition from Genesis to* Centesimus Annus (Leominster: Gracewing, 1998); E. P. Deberri and J. E. Hug, with P. J. Henriot and M. J. Schultheis, *Catholic Social Teaching: Our Best Kept Secret*, 4th edn (Maryknoll, NY: Orbis Books, 2003).

62 Paul VI, *Populorum progressio* ('On the development of peoples') (1967), paras. 15–16 – available at <www.vatican.va>; Curran, *Catholic Social Teaching*, pp. 127–36.

63 John Paul II, *Sollicitudo Rei Socialis* ('On Social Concern') (1987), para. 42 – available at <www.vatican.va>.

64 Leo XIII, *Rerum Novarum* ('The Condition of Labour') (1891), para. 32; Pius XI, *Quadragesimo Anno* ('After Forty Years') (1931), para. 80 – both available at <www.vatican.va>.

65 Paul VI, *Populorum progressio*.

66 <www.cafod.org.uk>

67 Allen and Thomas, *Poverty and Development into the Twenty-first Century*, pp. 23–49.

68 Emmanuel Nkurunziza, 'An Overview of Development Studies: Background Paper' (Birmingham: University of Birmingham, 2007) – available at <www.rad.bham.ac.uk>; Alan Thomas, 'Poverty and "the End of Development"', in Allen and Thomas, *Poverty and Development into the Twenty-first Century*, pp. 3–22.

69 <www.un.org/millenniumgoals>.

70 BBC Reith Lectures of 2007 – available at <www.bbc.co.uk>.

71 Hughes and Bennett, *God of the Poor*.

72 Vatican II, *Lumen Gentium* ('The Dogmatic Constitution on the Church') (1964), para. 5 – available at <www.vatican.va>.

73 Timothy J. Gorringe, *Redeeming Time: Atonement through Education* (London: Darton, Longman and Todd, 1986), pp. 71–111.

74 Samuel Rayan, 'Jesus and the Poor in the Fourth Gospel', *Bible-*

bhashyam 4/3 (September 1978), pp. 213–28; see also, Rayan, *Come, Holy Spirit* (Delhi: Media House, 1998), pp. 43, 102.

75 Mark Lewis Taylor, 'Spirit', in Scott and Cavanaugh, *Blackwell Companion to Political Theology*, pp. 377–92.

76 Jenkins, *Next Christendom*, p. 8.

77 David Martin, *Pentecostalism: The World Their Parish* (Oxford: Blackwell, 2002), p. 74; Allan H. Anderson, *An Introduction to Pentecostalism* (Cambridge: Cambridge University Press, 2004), pp. 139–44.

78 Mwaura, 'African Instituted Churches and Socio-economic Development'.

79 Allan H. Anderson, *Spreading Fires: The Missionary Nature of Early Pentecostalism* (London: SCM Press, 2007).

80 Anderson, *Introduction to Pentecostalism*, p. 13.

81 Martin, *Pentecostalism*, pp. 74, 50.

82 Walls, *Missionary Movement in Christian History*, pp. 92–3; Anderson, *African Reformation*, pp. 167, 170.

83 Gifford, 'View of Ghana's New Christianity'.

84 <www.kicc.org.uk>.

85 Donald A. McGavran and C. Peter C. Wagner, *Understanding Church Growth*, 3rd edn (Grand Rapids, MI: Wm B. Eerdmans, 1990). Lesslie Newbigin, *The Open Secret: An Introduction to the Theology of Mission*, rvsd edn (Grand Rapids, MI: Wm B. Eerdmans, 1995), pp. 121–59; David J. Bosch, *Witness to the World: The Christian Mission in Theological Perspective* (London : Marshall, Morgan and Scott, 1980).

86 <www.fgtv.org>. Actually the latter figure is arrived at by including satellite churches; that is, congregations which gather outside Seoul under the supervision of a local pastor but which participate in the main Sunday worship by broadband link.

87 Lynn T. White Jr, 'The Historical Roots of Our Ecologic Crisis', *Science* 155/3767 (1967), pp. 1203–7.

88 Celia Deane-Drummond, *A Handbook in Theology and Ecology* (London: SCM Press, 1996), pp. 18–20.

89 Samuel Rayan, 'The Earth Is the Lord's', in David G. Hallman (ed.), *Ecotheology: Voices from South and North* (Maryknoll, NY: Orbis Books, 1994), pp. 130–48; Margot Kässman, 'Covenant, Praise and Justice in Creation', in Hallman, *Ecotheology*, pp. 28–32.

90 Dave Bookless, 'Christian Mission and Environmental Issues: An Evangelical Reflection', *Mission Studies* 25/1 (2008), pp. 37–52; see also Dave Bookless, *Planetwise* (Leicester: Inter Varsity Press, 2008).

91 Especially at the Vancouver Assembly (1983) and the Canberra Assembly (1991). David Gill (ed.), *Gathered for Life: Report of the 6th Assembly of the World Council of Churches, Canada, 24 July–10 August 1983* (Geneva: WCC Publications, 1983); Michael Kinnamon

(ed.), *Signs of the Spirit: Official Report of the Seventh Assembly of the World Council of Churches, Canberra, 1991* (Geneva: WCC Publications, 1991).

92 E. Bolaji Idowu, 'The Spirit of God in the Natural World', in Dow Kirkpatrick (ed.), *The Holy Spirit* (Nashville, TN: Tidings, 1974), pp. 9–19.

93 Rob Cooper, 'Through the Soles of My Feet: A Personal View of Creation', in Hallman, *Ecotheology*, pp. 207–12.

94 George Tinker, 'The Full Circle of Liberation', in Hallman, *Ecotheology*, pp. 218–24.

95 Robert Allen Warrior, 'Canaanites, Cowboys and Indians', in R. S. Sugirtharajah (ed.), *Voices from the Margin: Interpreting the Bible from the Third World*, rvsd edn (Maryknoll, NY: Orbis Books, 1995), pp. 277–85, 284.

96 The 'five marks of mission' are available at <www.anglicancommunion.org>.

97 Bosch, *Transforming Mission*; Kirsteen Kim, 'Postmodern Mission: A Paradigm Shift in David Bosch's Theology of Mission?', *International Review of Mission* 89/353 (April 2000), pp. 172–9.

98 Adapted from Sebastian Kim, 'Eco-theology and Mission', in Krickwin C. Marak and Atul Y. Aghamkar (eds), *Ecological Challenge and Christian Mission* (Delhi: ISPCK, 1998), pp. 211–31.

99 Geiko Müller-Fahrenholz, *God's Spirit: Transforming a World in Crisis* (Geneva: WCC Publications, 1995).

100 Samuel Rayan, *Come, Holy Spirit* (Delhi: Media House, 1998); *Renew the Face of the Earth* (Delhi: Media House, 1998); 'Earth Is the Lord's'.

101 George Tinker, 'The Full Circle of Liberation', in Hallman, *Ecotheology*, pp. 218–24.

102 M. L. Daneel (1993) 'African Independent Church Pneumatology and the Salvation of all Creation', in Harold D. Hunter and Peter D. Hocken (eds), *All Together in One Place: Theological Papers from the Brighton Conference on World Evangelization* (Sheffield: Sheffield Academic Press), pp. 96–126.

103 Jose Pepz M. Cunanan, 'The Prophet of Environment and Development', in Hallman, *Ecotheology*, pp. 13–27.

9

SPIRITUAL VISIONS

Reconciliation and Mission Spirituality

Mission without vision, is like words without an inner spirit.[1]
Jyoti Sahi

One of the expectations of the outpouring of the Holy Spirit at Pentecost was that 'your young men shall see visions, and your old men shall dream dreams' (Acts 2.17). A vision directs and energizes persons and communities in mission and it could be argued that all Christian mission begins with vision. It is now common practice for secular as well as religious organizations to have 'mission statements' that are based on 'vision statements', because they recognize the power of the imagination to shape behaviour, bind groups and motivate action. Samuel Rayan writes, 'It is by dreams that people live and by visions that hope is sustained' and 'Jesus is . . . the dreamer of humankind's dreams and the seer of our visions'.[2] Jesus' human mission started at his baptism, when 'the heavens were opened' to him (Matt. 3.16). He reinterpreted the messianic expectations of the Old Testament prophets and contemporary Jewish apocalyptic visions in his preaching of the kingdom (or reign) of God.[3] According to the narrative in Acts, it was through a series of visions, appearances and revelatory experiences that this gospel was handed on to the apostles and spread through the Gentile world. We can count among these the resurrection appearances of Jesus recorded in each of the Gospels, Stephen's vision of heaven as he was being stoned to death (Acts 7.56), Paul's encounter with the risen Christ on the Damascus Road (9.3 and parallels) and his dream of the Macedonian calling him to 'Come over and help us' (16.9). The New Testament ends with the visions of John in the book of Revelation, which portray the goals of God's mission and also reveal the contemporary spiritual state of the churches and the true nature of forces with which they are contending.[4]

The missionaries gathered from all over the world at Edinburgh in 1910 heard that Christianity is 'the final and universal' religion; that it is the duty of the Christian citizens of the colonizing nations to act to ensure that the policies of their governments advance the kingdom of Christ throughout the world; and that 'The end of the Conference is the beginning of the conquest.'[5] The vision articulated at Edinburgh 1910 has been criticized both for its content and its method. First, the aim seemed to be to make the world in the image of Christendom: the Christian empires of Europe and North America. Second, the way many of the missionary leaders of the time sought to bring the vision about was aggressive; the use of the militaristic language of empire (such as 'conquest') was prevalent at the conference. Colonial missionary methods (past or contemporary) which set out to 'conquer' others with the gospel are incompatible with the gospel we proclaim.

Edinburgh 1910 concentrated on the missionary task. Only the last of the eight commissions, on 'Co-operation and the Promotion of Unity', looked at the way it was to be carried out. Arguably, Commission VIII is the one that bore most fruit because it led to ongoing ecumenical work at local level, and to reconciliation of divisions through church unions and in the World Council of Churches, which is the most tangible result of Edinburgh today. Furthermore, it is arguable that the realization of the task of 'world evangelization' dreamt of at Edinburgh 1910, to the extent that it has happened, has not been achieved by the missionary strategy of John Mott or others but primarily by local initiative. This is particularly true in North-East Asia – China, Korea and Japan, where in the twentieth century foreign missionaries were forced by governments to withdraw. In this chapter we will focus particularly on the remarkable story of the Korean Church and its vision for revival, rebuilding and the reunification of the nation.

9.1 Spiritual visions in North-East Asia

North-East Asia is dominated by China as the 'elder brother' to Korea and Japan, which both look to China for their classical art and literature. After a relatively brief period in terms of East Asia's long political history in which Japan held sway in the twentieth century, China is regaining regional pre-eminence and re-emerging as a global power since the liberalization of its economy after Chairman Mao's death in 1976. Christianity has a long history in China,[6] dating back to the East Syrian or 'Nestorian' Christians in the seventh to the ninth centuries (see Chapter 4). Catholic missionaries reached the Mongol court in the thirteenth century and during the late Ming Dynasty (1368–1644) the great Matteo Ricci won the emperor's favour and a genuinely Chinese Church was established. But after the Pope forbade the 'Chinese rites' in 1715, there were episodes of severe persecution against Chinese Christians. After 1860, British and French missionaries took advantage of the forced opening of China to Western trade, and it became the largest mission field in the world. However, converts were frequently in danger from anti-Christian violence for being either 'anti-traditional' or 'cultural imperialists'. When the Chinese Communist Party won power in 1949, the government of the new People's Republic of China demanded that all Christian churches, Catholic and Protestant, should be Chinese run without any foreign links and expelled all foreign missionaries. But as links were re-established with the West in the 1980s, China-watchers were amazed to see how an indigenous Christianity had flourished, even during the Cultural Revolution. China is probably the fastest growth area in the world for Christianity at the moment, and is sometimes described as experiencing 'Christian fever'. Thousands of churches closed under Mao have reopened and others have emerged from the underground to register with the Three Self Patriotic Movement, the official

Protestant church. There are also underground Catholics and an official Chinese Catholic Patriotic Association, which had to separate from the Roman Church but is now hoping to restore all its links with worldwide Catholicism. There are 5 million registered Catholics and 16 million registered Protestants. The real figure may be more than 6 per cent of China's huge population – that is 90 million people.[7]

At the time of the Beijing Olympics in 2008, it was evident that the ideology of the People's Republic of China is no longer centred on Chairman Mao. In the new centres for religious studies at China's universities which have sprung up since the liberalization of anti-religious laws, other ancient traditions – Confucianism, Buddhism, Taoism and also Christianity, are being examined for what they can offer to the emerging China. Christian intellectuals are feeding in a Christian vision for society based on the kingdom of God,[8] and millions of ordinary Christians hope in the gospel of Jesus Christ as they struggle to cope in the new China. The Christian gospel has also been inspirational in Japan, where the gospel was first preached by the Jesuit missionary Francis Xavier in the sixteenth century. Despite episodes of severe persecution and never numbering more than 3 per cent of the population, the Christian contribution to Japanese society, especially through education, healthcare and ethics, has been considerable.[9] But it is in Korea where a Christian vision has been most widely embraced and it can be said to have energized the revival and rebuilding of the Korean nation.

The mountainous and tightly controlled Korean peninsula was difficult for foreign missionaries to penetrate and not generally high on their agenda and, in both the Protestant and the Catholic case, Koreans took the initiative to bring Christianity to their homeland.[10] In the twentieth century Korea experienced a religious revival as Christianity went from being the religion of a tiny persecuted minority to the dominant religious force on the peninsula.[11] Just 120 years later the 2005 census recorded that nearly 30 per cent of the population of South Korea professed to be Christian – the majority Protestant. In the same period what had been a technologically backward and politically unstable nation was colonized, divided and then (South Korea at least) was rebuilt to become the world's eleventh largest economy with a Human Development Index among the top 30 in the world. These two spectacular examples of human development – economic and religious – are not just a coincidence but are closely connected in the sense that Christianity provided a vision of human development which empowered Korean people through this difficult period.[12]

In the eighteenth and nineteenth centuries, Korean society was under great strain. Internal tensions weakened the monarchy and administration, and the country was threatened from outside by foreign powers. Unlike the traditional religions of Shamanism, Buddhism and Confucianism, Christianity presented itself as an alternative which held out hope for a modern outlook. Some Korean scholars believed the 'Western learning' – the name they gave to the Jesuit teachings they encountered in China – could reform Korean society, and that was why they adopted Catholicism as their faith.[13] Many of the first Protestant Christians were also attracted to Christianity because what they read in the Bible and heard from the missionaries seemed to offer political liberation and national salvation.[14] Protestants chose to translate the name of God in the Bible by the term *Hananim*, which was similar to the word for the Great Spirit of Korean traditional religion, the tribal God of Korea, but meant 'one Lord'. The effect of this was to identify the God of Israel and of Jesus Christ with the primal roots of Korean identity and with national aspirations, and at the same time emphasize monotheism, the supremacy of the one God.[15] Thus the high God of Korean religion was transformed and universalized, offering hope not only for Korea but for the world and laying the foundations for later missionary movements from Korea.

Converts understood the Christian message to be one of transformation, and this was applied socially as well as individually.[16] The first Protestant missionaries from 1884 onwards founded the first Western-style medical institution, the first modern schools – including the first ever school for girls, and the first Western-style publishing house. Korean Christians were quick to imitate the missionary initiatives and multiply churches, schools and hospitals around the country. This social work was accompanied by religious revival. The revival which broke out in 1907 in Pyongyang (now capital of North Korea) appealed both to Confucianists, who appreciated the study of the Bible, and to those used to the traditional Shamanistic or spirit-religion in its Pentecostal-style emotion and enthusiasm. It was interpreted by Korean Christians as an outpouring of the Spirit of God in power on the Korean people for the restoration of the nation in the face of the threat from Japan and other powers.[17] Koreans did not leave the evangelization of Korea to the missionaries, and they soon took responsibility for spreading the good news further afield; as early as 1913 Korean churches were supporting some of their number as missionaries to China.

Christianity had a transforming effect on Korean society in several ways. First, Christian teaching had a great influence on social relationships in Korea, especially on those relating to age and gender. In the hierarchical and patriarchal society of the time, Christian teaching introduced the principle of equality and the rights of women. The doctrine of conversion encouraged personal and social change and engendered a sense of responsibility for one's own destiny. In place of the Confucian father's expectation of devotion from his son, the church encouraged fathers to see their children as gifts from God, and they limited parental authority. Second, the churches accelerated the formation of modern culture. Education led to the breaking down of superstitions. Publications and literacy work disseminated new ideas and made them accessible to a much wider group. Through education and literature Korean culture was also opened up to outside influences, such as ideas of human freedom and universal rights. Third, reading the Bible nurtured a spirit of social justice in that all human beings are created in the image of God, the growth of a social conscience and a vision for the betterment of society.[18] It was Korean Christians who founded the first vernacular newspaper to apply Christian beliefs to national issues and generate popular support for reform. However, as Christians worked to build up their nation, the Japanese, who had a head-start in modernization and the support of the Western powers to develop an empire in the East, threatened Korea's sovereignty.

The aggression of Japan – the youngest brother – toward first Korea and then China itself in the first half of the twentieth century was a shocking aberration of the natural order for those of a Confucian frame of mind. Having defeated China in battle on Korean territory in 1895 and Russia at sea in 1905, in 1910 Japan was able to formally annex the Korean peninsula and use it as a bridge onto the rest of the Asian mainland. The movement of resistance to Japan was Christian-led with Buddhists and others also participating. Like the Israelite prophets, Christian nationalist leaders believed it was the sin of the Korean people which had allowed their defeat and they encouraged repentance of personal sin as part of national recovery.[19] The independence activities culminated in a declaration of Korean independence on 1 March 1919, which was brutally put down, Christians and churches suffering by far the greatest loss.

Despite the dire political situation, Christians continued to hold out hope of national salvation and resisted Japanese imperialism as the early Christians had resisted imperial Rome. As the Japanese grip tightened and focused on colonization of the Korean mind and culture, prayer and revival meetings became the main means of resistance used.[20] The policy of Japanese–Korean unity led to the imposition of Japanese language and names, and finally enforced worship at Shinto shrines. Despite the efforts of the Japanese government and Japanese theologians to portray Shinto worship as a civil rather than a religious ceremony, Korean Christian leaders saw it as compromising the command to worship only the one true God, *Hananim*, and therefore also contrary to serving the national Spirit. Some Christians defied the government at great cost. It is estimated that 2,000 were imprisoned and 50 people died for their resistance. Two hundred churches and many Christian schools were closed down.[21] The biblical logic of suffering leads from the suffering messiah to the coming of the messianic kingdom. This encouraged Christians to think that they were suffering on behalf of the whole Korean people and so Christianity developed the characteristics of a messianic movement.[22] However, they were unable to bring to an end the aggression of the Japanese authorities, who suppressed Korean culture and language, drained Korean resources for the war in the Pacific, and took away tens of thousands of women to 'comfort' Japanese soldiers.

Liberation finally came at the end of World War Two, when Korea was liberated from Japan by the USA from the South and the Soviet Union from the North. Liberation was an answer to prayer and, for Christians in the South, the fact that it came from the 'Christian' nation of the USA, from where most of the missionaries had also come, confirmed that God's hand was at work. But the Communists in the North, where Christianity had been strongest, persecuted Christians, and many fled south. The division of Korea in 1945, for the first time in 1,300 years, was a national tragedy, which was compounded when in 1950–3 the two Koreas fought each other in the first, and arguably the most devastating, of the proxy superpower wars of the Cold War era. Three million Koreans (10 per cent of the population) were killed, wounded or lost, and five million displaced.[23] At the end of the war Korea was much more deeply divided than before and both North and South were among the poorest countries in the world.

9.2 Korean dreams of reunification

During and after the Korean War (1950–3), Christians in the South were involved in bringing humanitarian assistance to the injured, bereaved and destitute both through international organizations and also at the local level of Korean churches. The largest Protestant denominations in Korea were Presbyterian and Methodist but they had the kind of Pentecostal (or charismatic) spirituality which encourages upward mobility and engenders attitudes consonant with success in the capitalist context of late- or postmodernity (see Chapter 8).[24] In the post-war period Pentecostal churches were founded as well, notably the Full Gospel Church of David Yonggi Cho. For displaced and wartorn communities, churches provided a community and support network. They encouraged education, discipline and hard work, and a strong moral code. They inculcated capitalist thinking, being run as businesses with buildings in a Western style and making full use of available technology. And their links with foreign missionaries, usually from North America, provided opportunities to learn English through bible study and sometimes the connections necessary for emigration to the United States.

But most of all, the churches developed a dream. Pastors sought to encourage their weary congregations with new vision and inspiration. Through their sermon illustrations, many drawn from a Western context, they opened up new vistas and gave Koreans a sense of the world beyond national borders. Although they aspired to democracy most, including Christian pastors, put a higher value on national security and economic growth, believing that, unless Korea became a powerful nation, it would once again be obliterated by outside powers.[25] So they supported the hard-line policies of the military dictators and the modernization goals set by the government. They encouraged their congregations to be disciplined and to work hard for the sake of their family, clan and nation.[26] Their vision was for a Christian nation whose prosperity would be a sign of God's blessing, and which would be a light to the rest of Asia and the world. With US help and great determination, South Korea built up its domestic economy and entered the world market, becoming now the thirteenth largest economy in the world. The main contribution of Christianity was to stimulate new visions and inject a new energy that enabled Koreans to transform their existing situation and revitalize – or redeem – their society.[27]

As the economy began to grow, many South Korean Christians saw the growth of Christianity and the growth in material blessings as two sides of the same coin. Popular prosperity teaching provided a rationale for this belief and was encouraged by the traditional Shamanistic spirituality of the Korean people. From inside the mainstream Protestant community, it was uncritically accepted that the outpouring of God's Spirit was responsible for both church growth and material blessing.[28] However, a minority of Christians actively opposed the military government in support of civil and workers' rights. They formed *minjung* (grassroots or people's) movements to struggle for civil and human rights. Christian intellectuals identified with farmers, workers and the urban poor in their experience of oppression and were dismissed from their posts, and sometimes imprisoned and tortured by the government. Their reflection on this experience laid the foundations for *Minjung* theology, a form of liberation theology which was widely disseminated through ecumenical networks, raising international support for the cause. *Minjung* theologians saw themselves in continuity with the leaders of the 1919 uprising and other popular movements and criticized the mainstream churches for supporting the government. They envisaged a country in which justice was done and there was political freedom and urged Christians to struggle for it, inspired by Jesus' preferential option for the poor and the liberating power of the Spirit in history.[29] Because of the tension with North Korea which has an extreme communist regime, the first generation of *minjung* theologians were labelled communists and imprisoned and tortured as enemies of the state. In this period, the Roman Catholic Church also came out on the side of the poor and made a powerful contribution to the cause of human rights and democracy.[30] The principled stand of the Catholic Church is one of the reasons that, according to the census results, it is now the fastest growing Christian denomination in Korea and about 40 per cent of Christians now belong to it. The actions of Christians supported a movement that culminated in the nationwide protests that ended military rule in 1987 and brought about the transition to democracy.

In 1988 a democratic South Korea proudly invited the

world to a spectacular Olympic Games in Seoul but the North Korean government boycotted the event. For 60 years the border between North and South has remained firmly closed. North Korea developed as an extreme Stalinist state in which the 'Great Leader' Kim Il Sung, who was a communist fighter against the Japanese, and his son the current 'Dear Leader' Kim Jong Il are revered as gods. Thousands of families have been separated, and many North Korean men who fled south during the war to avoid conscription into the Communist army have lived and died there without ever seeing their parents, wives and children again. It is not known how many Christians there are in North Korea today. It is at the top of Open Doors' list for religious persecution, although a few officially sponsored churches are allowed.[31] Churches in the South have contact with underground Christians in the North, but for obvious reasons they do not publicize this.

Today travelling north of Seoul the reminders of the tension between the two states are everywhere in the form of tank traps, anti-aircraft guns, military bases, tanks and military vehicles and mine fields. The mile-wide strip of land ironically called the '*de*militarized zone' bristles with service personnel who eye one another from afar with binoculars. North Korea has one million men under arms, all South Korean young men are conscripted for two and a half years, and the US army still has 30,000 troops on the Peninsula. Prime burial land in South Korea is on the mountainsides facing North Korea. Reunification is the fervent prayer of all Koreans, and both the *minjung* and the Evangelical churches are agreed on the reunification of the two Koreas as the next goal, but they differ greatly in their vision and method to achieve it.[32]

For the Evangelical churches, reunification is envisaged as a revival-type event of conversion to Christianity, mutual repentance and brotherly and sisterly embrace across the borders. In political terms this seems to mean the collapse of the North and the absorption of the North by the South. However Western political commentators do not see this as a likely or desirable scenario because North Korea will not admit any kind of defeat and because it will be extremely costly for the South.[33] On the one hand, their strongly anti-Communist stance has prevented Evangelicals from any dialogue with North Korea and from furthering the political process. On the other hand, they have always held up the hope that unification is possible. Evangelicals have prayed for reunification and worked by whatever means available to disseminate the gospel in North Korea, including by generous giving of food and other aid.[34] As part of their revivalist approach, Evangelicals rightly draw attention to the importance of the interpersonal dimension of reconciliation, and the need for repentance as part of the reconciliation process. However, they are less conscious that their own disunity may be a hindrance to reconciliation. Korean Protestant churches are so splintered into different groups in competition with one another that the reunification of Korea seems more achievable than the unity of the churches. Their rivalry is detrimental to Christian witness not only in Korea but also in other parts of the world where Koreans serve as missionaries.

Ecumenical Christians, by contrast, emphasize the importance of unity in mission and common witness. They also tend to be less vehemently anti-Communist, and for that reason also more willing to dialogue, although they risk accusations of betraying the nation. They are more willing to countenance a political compromise such as a federal system of unity where the two Koreas unite but maintain separate systems and gradually grow together. Sadly though, they do not have much respect for the popular Evangelical churches and therefore find it difficult to win widespread support for their efforts. Ecumenical theology of reconciliation has been expressed by the symbol of *han-puri*, the release by the shaman of pent-up feeling or repression by dealing with the spirits that cause it. Ecumenicals are aware that reconciliation is not a matter of brushing aside differences, or of finding common ground, but involves identifying the problems and dealing with them.[35] In 1988 through the auspices of the World Council of Churches, Christians of the National Council of Churches (which does not represent the majority Evangelical churches) met representatives of the official church in North Korea and bravely declared the mutual hatred of North and South and its justification to be idolatrous. They drew on Jesus' call for jubilee (Luke 4.18–19) and proclaimed 1995, the fiftieth anniversary of the liberation from Japan, a year of jubilee 'to bring about the restoration of the covenanted community of peace'.[36]

The year 1995 did not bring reconciliation but in 1997 Kim Dae Jung, a Roman Catholic with close links to *minjung* movements was elected president. He initiated a 'sunshine policy' toward the North. This changed the rhetoric completely by recognizing the humanity and dignity of North Koreans and engaging with them. It aimed at peaceful coexistence of the two Koreas, in which the South pledged neither to provoke North Korea nor to seek to absorb it. This initiative resulted in the first ever North–South summit, which took place in the North Korean capital Pyongyang in June 2000, and for which Kim Dae Jung received the Nobel Peace Prize.[37] Since then steps toward reconciliation have been halting but further progress has been made. There is limited tourism allowed by South Koreans to certain places in the North, and South Korean businesses have plants in the North. In all the political manoeuvrings of the last 60 years, the essential unity of the Korean people has not been questioned. The dream of reunification has yet to be realized but Korean Christians continue to dream and work toward it.[38]

9.3 Reconciliation as means and end of mission

South Korean Christians are not alone in working for reconciliation. Since about 1990 Christian mission has been increasingly concerned with conflict resolution and reconciliation. One of the reasons for this is that political liberation has been achieved in many countries formerly in the grip of Communist regimes or dictatorships of one sort or another.[39] The success of liberation movements in Latin America, South Africa and Poland, for example, has also helped to move theological interest forward to consideration of reconciliation. In the UK context, the cessation of hostilities and the Good Friday Agreement of 1998 in Northern Ireland was the culmination of years of attempts at peace-making.[40]

Robert Schreiter gives many other reasons for the contemporary interest in reconciliation among churches worldwide. Among these are: the challenge of the increasingly multicultural nature of most societies due to travel and migration, and the resulting ethnic conflicts; the prevalence of poverty and competition for scare resources; and the upsurge in interest in religion generally, especially in fundamentalist forms, also leading to violence. He concludes that the current awareness of violence and its harmful effects make peace-making and reconstruction a major priority for the world today, and all the more so for Christians, given that a link of violence with religion often gives it greater virulence.[41]

There is a tendency for globally influential scholars and international bodies to create an impression that the paradigm they are promoting at the time should be the overriding concern of every local church. Though, if challenged, they would probably be the first to recognize that issues may be very local and that no part of the Christian church can dictate the agenda of another part. The proper role of missiology is not to regulate, but to facilitate local discernment of mission priorities. Nevertheless, reconciliation can be said to be central to mission, not only as its goal but also because 'the ministry of reconciliation' is a biblical way of describing mission activity. The term 'reconciliation', with one important exception (Matt. 5.24), is confined to the letters of Paul, who uses the verb *katallasso* (reconcile) and the noun *katallage* (reconciliation) in some central passages of his theology, where he attempts to express what God has done in Christ and the meaning of the gospel. Paul applies the term reconciliation to the new relationship we have with God as a result of the death of Jesus Christ (Rom. 5.10–11; 11.15). He describes the reconciliation of Jew and Gentile with one another as an integral part of our reconciliation with God (Eph. 2.14–16). The reconciliation achieved by

Christ is cosmic in its scope, and the reconciled lives of faithful believers are set within it (Col. 1.19–22); the vision of *shalom* inherited by Jesus and Paul is not imposed uniformity and order but a world of diversity that 'holds together' as one body (Col. 1.17).[42] Finally, Paul describes the participation of the church in God's reconciling mission to the world as a ministry of reconciliation (2 Cor. 5.18–20).[43]

Many other passages in the Bible concerning settling, resolving, harmonizing and also healing are related to the theme of reconciliation. The resurrection appearances of Jesus are examples of reconciliation,[44] and the same could be said of all those moments in the gospel stories when something that has been lost is found, when new relationships are established and when salvation is declared. In the Hebrew Scriptures the story of the lifelong enmity between the twins Esau and Jacob and their meeting after many years of estrangement (Gen. 33) is paradigmatic for the biblical meaning of reconciliation. Israel Selvanayagam describes the essence of reconciliation in the light of this story as 'seeing the face of God in one's brother's face'. He notes that the hug between the brothers is not the only evidence of reconciliation. Esau was a longstanding victim of exploitation and injustice by Jacob, who had stolen his birthright. Jacob did not only embrace his brother but also offered reparation in the form of the gifts he brought him. The biblical story of Jacob and Esau is not only about individuals but about Israel/Jacob's relations with surrounding peoples. Looking at the contemporary world stage, and particularly the affluence of the West, Selvanayagam warns, 'there is no peace without justice, no justice without economic justice, no economic justice without self-sacrifice and reparation, and without this there is no true reconciliation and no stable future', emphasizing the key importance of the churches' work for justice.[45] However, although justice is a necessary condition for reconciliation it is not a sufficient one. The struggle for reconciliation continues after justice has been achieved.[46]

Many examples could be given of mission as reconciliation from churches worldwide. The consummation of the kingdom envisaged in the book of Revelation is described as a tree for 'healing of the nations' (Rev. 22.2). Pervaiz Sultan, Principal of St Thomas' Theological College in Karachi, Pakistan, summarizes the prerequisites for this as 'a long-term sustainable world political and economic system where no single political power or group of powers have sweeping rights to determine the discourse of world nations'. He believes the churches can help to bring this about by spreading the moral values of personal responsibility, social compassion and economic justice in their work for development.[47] Drawing on her long experience of interfaith dialogue in Birmingham, Ruth Tetlow shows that the practice of dialogue is an expression of reconciliation because it is a way of 'making friends'. The outcome that is hoped for in dialogue is that people of different faiths can live alongside one another, certainly without violence, and in an atmosphere of mutual respect and co-operation.[48] In times of conflict dialogue is exactly what is impossible, but dialogue has a preventative purpose in keeping doors of communication open so that tension does not escalate into violence. It is therefore part of the long-term process of reconciliation.[49] Lap Yan Kung, from the Chinese University of Hong Kong, is engaged in dialogue between China and Hong Kong since it was returned to China in 1997 after 150 years of separation under British rule. Kung sees a basic lack of trust in two groups of people: in the Chinese central government's relatively tight political control of Hong Kong and, on the other side, in the relatively antagonistic attitude to the central government taken by the people of Hong Kong. He believes a shift from suspicion to trust is essential to reconciliation because 'Trust realizes reconciliation, and reconciliation creates trust.' Kung argues that trust is a spiritual matter that cannot be created by patriotism or by economic prosperity, as the Chinese government hopes. However, he believes the church, though small in numbers, can play an important role in bringing about reconciliation by showing 'that trust is not measured by absence of conflict in relationship, but by openness to the differences and commitment to one another'.[50]

When 'healing' is added to the term reconciliation, as we saw in the African context (Chapter 8), the theme extends beyond reconciled relationships to include wholeness of body and mind and the wellbeing of the whole creation. This brings into the picture the healing ministry of Jesus and the disciples in the Gospels. This was not restricted to physical ailments but resulted in the healing of the whole person and their community. Furthermore, as Chad Gandiya, Bishop of Harare, points out, healing in the New Testament is a broad term that encompasses exorcism, restoration to the community, and forgiveness of sins (see also Chapter 8). So both 'reconciliation' and 'healing' point to peace with God, to personal wholeness and integrity and to right relationships in society.[51] Jesus' healing activity also included restoring sight to the blind. Indian artist and theologian Jyoti Sahi points out that this too was not only at the medical level but at the level of spiritual insight. Light gives vision and bridges between what lies within us and what lies outside us. When Jesus restores sight, 'something "other" than what we know becomes present to our understanding'. For example, the kingdom was something hidden, but in Jesus and in the mission of the disciples it became visible. The miracles of the walking on the waters (John 6.16–22) and the transfiguration (Matt. 17.2; Mark 9.2) give us a glimpse of the cosmic reality of Jesus. Sahi concludes that the transfigured vision that the blind receive through Jesus' ministry is to see the other in a new light. 'The great challenge of reconciliation today is to accept the truth of another' – and to do so 'even when that truth seems to contradict what we ourselves hold to be true'. True reconciliation may be thought of as 'a way of seeing, and accepting, and even celebrating, the fact that we are different'.[52]

Paul describes the purpose of God, for which he sends the Spirit and sent the Son, as to reconcile the whole creation (Col. 1.15–20). In the biblical story, the series of covenants God established with the chosen people of God show God's desire for reconciliation. The passion of Jesus Christ, as described in the Scriptures, was itself a reconciling act that resulted in the opening of a way of reconciliation for all humanity (Eph. 2.13–18). The church represents the first fruits of that act of reconciliation; it is the community of those who are reconciled with God; and in its life it also expresses the ongoing reconciling work of God (Rom. 5.9–11). Consequently, the lifestyle of the people of God, especially the quality of the reconciled relationships of Jew and Gentile, slave and free, male and female (Gal. 3.28) and the meaning of Christian love (John 17.20–3), can all be considered under the theme of reconciliation. This includes much of the Law of Moses, the prophetic books, Jesus' ethical and moral teaching, and that of the Epistles. Reconciliation characterizes the spirituality of the mission community as well as the goal of mission.

Churches, even when they are themselves implicated in conflict, also have an important role to play in the process toward reconciliation. Reconciliation is both a present reality and future goal that is integral to the church's work of mission and unity. It involves striving for unity among Christians and also responding in unity to the world's need for reconciliation. In some cases these aims are related because of the complex interaction between longstanding divisions within the church and the fracture lines that segregate people in the wider community – for example, in Northern Ireland or Rwanda. Christian consciousness of being part of the one mission of one triune God inspires and sustains movements for church unity and churches working together to serve the wider community. But realizing a common identity in Christ should not preclude diversity. So, as Colin Marsh, Ecumenical Officer for Birmingham, advises, 'the search for discovering common factors that unite across boundaries of division should be accompanied by a second journey: learning how to live with difference in a reconciled community' and exploring the limits to diversity.[53] This advice resonates within the Anglican Communion at the present time as deep divisions are revealed over approaches to human sexuality. Exploring Anglican perspectives on reconciliation and mission, John Corrie, a former adviser to the Archbishop of Canterbury, points out that nevertheless there are instances around the world where Anglican insights may have something to offer to other traditions. The Church itself was founded as a *via media*, which found a way for several sides to worship and work together with their differences. The fact that the Communion itself is in need of reconciliation does not disqualify Anglicans from helping others in their weakness.[54] 'We have this treasure in clay jars', writes the Apostle Paul as he explains the ministry of reconciliation, 'so that it may be made clear that this extraordinary power belongs to God and does not come from us' (2 Cor. 4.7). Like Paul, Christians have a responsibility to communicate the message of reconciliation. This may be done through personal testimony in a variety of media but Val Ogden, Director of the Selly Oak Centre for Mission Studies, reminds readers that, however fervently and intelligently we try to communicate, the message is unlikely to be heard unless our actions and lifestyle are observed to be reconciled with our theology of reconciliation.[55]

Reconciliation is not the last word in mission paradigms but it is a helpful step along the way toward a fuller understanding of what it means to participate in God's work in the world. Mission as reconciliation shapes the practice of mission by urging reconciliation within the mission community. Indeed, 'Reconciliation with others is the only convincing evidence that we are reconciled with God' (Matt. 5.23–4).[56] Those who are ambassadors of reconciliation (2 Cor. 5.20) are themselves being reconciled to God and to one another. Reconciliation is both means and end.

9.4 Mission spirituality

In continuity with its concern for justice, peace and the integrity of creation, and in consistency with its exploration of 'the purpose of Christian unity in a broken world', the World Council of Churches launched its Decade to Overcome Violence (DOV) in 2001 and affirmed the churches' commitment to the ministry of reconciliation.[57] The impulse to broaden ecumenism to include peace-making came at the instigation of the 'peace churches', which have historically taken a pacifist stance and opposed violence on any grounds. These include Church of the Brethren, Mennonites and Quakers or Religious Society of Friends. It also involved recognition that the liberation theologies and political messianism of the 1970s and 1980s were not free from violent overtones.[58] In keeping with this new approach, the World Council of Churches mission conference in Athens in May 2005 was called 'to empower participants to continue in their call to be in mission together and to work towards reconciliation and healing in Christ in God's world today'. Two preparatory papers explored the themes of healing and reconciliation in mission and, in recognition of the holistic nature of reconciliation, the conference itself was planned as an exercise in healing and reconciliation. The theme of Athens, 'Come, Holy Spirit, heal and reconcile' recognized the foundation of reconciliation in pneumatology and established it as a new paradigm in mission.[59]

Reconciliation is linked to spirituality. Mission as reconciliation implies a critique of mission models that do not take seriously the whole human being, body and soul, or that neglect human relationships, and particularly the need for just dealings, in their mission enterprise. The reconciled and reconciling community is at the heart of all mission activity; it is never perfect but its testimony has integrity because of its loving intention. The community demonstrates in its life how human beings can respect their differences, appreciate the other's point of view, and find ways of working together and staying together. Where reconciliation is in view, tensions do not explode into conflict but work together creatively for good. In this way mission reveals the heart of God, who as Trinity shows a model of difference with participation and without separation.[60]

God's mission is not only strategy. It is a therapeutic activity which ministers to all dimensions of human life; it takes place within, ministering to the fractured self; and it is operative at all the levels at which human beings relate, from interpersonal relationships within the family or neighbourhood to institutional structures and international affairs. It works toward a vision of peace and harmony in creation that comes about, not because everyone thinks and believes alike, but because justice is done and the voice of each member or group is heard. Seeing the face of God in our brother or sister's face, we will attend to the issues that concern them: their financial situation, their health, what makes them angry and what they treasure. Mission is a spiritual activity and reconciliation is a gift of God. Human activity can prepare the way for it, using tools that God has given, but unless God, by the Holy Spirit, moves in hearts, lives and communities, there can be no reconciliation, now or in the future. We do not ourselves overcome violence; we can only bear witness to the Overcomer of violence.[61] It is our testimony as Christians that Jesus Christ, by allowing himself to be broken, has brought about our reconciliation and that of the whole creation. The Spirit of Jesus Christ, who comes in peace as the source of forgiveness and life and who is breathed into us (John 20.21–3), makes us ambassadors of God's reconciliation (2 Cor. 5.20).

'Spirituality' is often used for a kind of religion that is not expressed in worldly activity, but in worship, meditation and often introspection (see Chapter 7). 'Mission', in contrast, is associated with activism, with goals and strategy, so 'mission spirituality' sounds like a contradiction in terms.[62] Liberation theologians soon became alert to the danger that the 'Nazareth manifesto' to 'bring good news to the poor' could degenerate into activism or even violence if it was not connected with spiritual anointing, 'the Spirit of the Lord is upon me' (Luke 4.18).[63] Considering contemporary mission, Irish Catholic missiologist Donal Dorr implies criticism of Christian efforts at social liberation that make the achievement of justice the aim without looking beyond it toward a reconciled society. He argues that 'reconciliation should accompany liberation from the start'. A commitment to reconciliation is shown by 'whether those who struggle for justice show a respect for human rights *during* their struggle'. Having a vision for future reconciliation with our enemy, Dorr's words suggest, we will not try to crush them but wage our struggle in a way that does not breed future resentment and bears witness to the rightness of our cause. Christian love is to be extended even to our enemies (Matt. 5.43–8).[64]

Any kind of mission activity must be accompanied by a mission spirituality if it is not to degenerate into activism. Mission spirituality is concerned with the spiritual resources from which mission springs: the experience of God that initiates, the reading of Scripture that guides, and the prayer life that sustains the missionary or the movement in mission. As spirituality of, or for, mission, mission spirituality draws attention to the motives and attitudes that accompany mission activity. It shifts the focus from the missionary task to the ethos and ethics of mission, to the way in which mission is carried out, to the praxis, path or process of mission. Attention to mission spirituality helps to make the means of mission consistent with its end and to ensure that the medium or messenger embodies the gospel message. Mission spirituality is a lifestyle that integrates inward experience of God with desire to see Jesus Christ glorified in church and society, passion for God's glory with outgoing compassion for the poor and oppressed. This and any missionary spirituality is, by definition, a kind of spirituality which is oriented to the world. It is not individualistic or otherworldly but an engaged spirituality that is lived out in mission, a 'spirituality of the road'.[65]

In theological terms, mission spirituality connects the human spirit in mission with the Spirit of God sent into the world. It sets the church's witness since Pentecost within the work of the Spirit of God since creation, shifting interest from the Spirit of mission or missionary Spirit to the mission of the Spirit. This broadens the scope of mission to include the whole creation and encourages the co-operation of Christian mission with other movements for justice and peace. It suggests that Christian mission begins with the spiritual activity of discerning the spirits (according to the revelation of Jesus Christ) in order to discover the movement of the Spirit of God in the world and join with it. Thus mission spirituality becomes mission 'in the Spirit'.[66]

Notes

1 Jyoti Sahi, 'Healing the Blind: Vision and Reconciliation in a Multi-faith world', in Kirsteen Kim (ed.), *Reconciling Mission: The Ministry of Healing and Reconciliation in the Church Worldwide* (Delhi: SPCK, 2005), pp. 118–37, at p. 120.

2 Samuel Rayan, *Come, Holy Spirit* (Delhi: Media House, 1998), pp. 43, 102.

3 Walter Brueggemann, *The Prophetic Imagination* (London: SCM Press, 1992).

4 Christopher Rowland, *The Open Heaven: A Study of Apocalyptic in Judaism and Early Christianity* (London: SPCK, 1985).

5 Addresses by W. P. Paterson and Henry Sloan Coffin at the World Mission Conference, Edinburgh, 1910. See World Missionary Conference (WMC), *World Missionary Conference 1910, Vol. 9: The History and Records of the Conference* (Edinburgh: Oliphant, Anderson and Ferrier / New York: Fleming H. Revell Co., 1910), pp. 156–72. Archbishop of York, 'The Duty of the Christian Nations', in WMC, *World Missionary Conference 1910, Vol. 9*, pp. 272–7, see p. 272. John R. Mott, 'Closing Address', in WMC, *World Missionary Conference 1910, Vol. 9*, pp. 347–52, p. 347.

6 R. Gary Tiedemann, 'China and Its Neighbours', in Adrian Hastings (ed.), *A World History of Christianity* (London: Cassell, 1999), pp. 369–415; Samuel Hugh Moffett, *A History of Christianity in Asia* (Maryknoll, NY: Orbis Books): Vol. I, 2nd edn (1998), *Beginnings to 1500*; Vol. II (2005), *1500–1900*; Ka-Lun Leung, 'China', in Scott W. Sunquist (ed.), *A Dictionary of Asian Christianity* (Grand Rapids, MI: Wm B. Eerdmans, 2001), pp. 139–46; Tony Lambert, *China's Christian Millions*, rvsd edn (Oxford: Monarch, 2006); Daniel H. Bays (ed.), *Christianity in China, from the Eighteenth Century to the Present* (Stanford, CA: Stanford University Press, 1996).

7 See China Study Centre of Churches Together in Britain and Ireland <www.chinaonlinecentre.org>; David B. Barrett, George T. Kurian and Todd M. Johnson (eds), *World Christian Encyclopedia* (Oxford: Oxford University Press, 2001), p. 191.

8 Centre for Multireligious Studies, *Christian Theology and Intellectuals in China*, Occasional Paper (Aarhus: University of Aarhus, 2003): Jørgen Skov Sørensen, 'Christian Theology and Intellectuals in China: A Historical and Theological Introduction', pp. 7–25; Guanghu He, 'Some Causes and Features of the "Christian Upsurge" among Chinese Intellectuals', pp. 43–9.

9 James M. Phillips, *From the Rising of the Sun: Christians and Society in Contemporary Japan* (Maryknoll, NY: Orbis Books, 1981); Moffett, *History of Christianity in Asia: Vol. II*, pp. 68–104, 502–27; Mark

R. Mullins, *Christianity Made in Japan: A Study of Indigenous Movements* (Honolulu: University of Hawai'i Press, 1998).

10 Chai-shin Yu (ed.), *The Founding of Catholic Tradition in Korea* (Mississauga, Ontario: Korea and Related Studies Press, 1996); Chai-shin Yu (ed.), *Korea and Christianity* (Fremont, CA: Asian Humanities Press, 2004); Donald N. Clark, *Christianity in Modern Korea* (Lanham, MD: University Press of America, 1986); Robert E. Buswell Jr and Timothy S. Lee (eds), *Christianity in Korea* (Honolulu: University of Hawaii, 2006).

11 James Huntley Grayson, *Korea – a Religious History*, rvsd edn (Abingdon, Oxon: RoutledgeCurzon, 2002), p. 2.

12 Kirsteen Kim, 'Christianity's Role in the Modernization and Revitalization of Korean Society in the Twentieth Century', *International Journal of Public Theology* (forthcoming); Kenneth M. Wells, *New God, New Nation: Protestants and Self-reconstruction Nationalism in Korea, 1896–1937* (Honolulu: University of Hawaii Press, 1990).

13 Yi, Wŏn-sun, 'The Sirhak Scholars' Perspectives of Sŏhak in the Late Chosŏn Society', in Yu, *Founding of Catholic Tradition in Korea*, pp. 45–102, at p. 99.

14 Yi, Mahn-yŏl, 'The Birth of the National Spirit of the Christians in the Late Chosŏn Period', in Yu, *Korea and Christianity*, pp. 39–72, at pp. 41, 42.

15 For further discussion, see David Kwang-sun Suh, *The Korean Minjung in Christ* (Kowloon: Commission on Theological Concerns, Christian Conference of Asia, 1991), p. 112.

16 Kim, Yong-Bock, 'Korean Christianity as a Messianic Movement of the People', in Commission on Theological Concerns of the Christian Conference of Asia (CTCCCA) (ed.), *Minjung Theology: People as the Subjects of History* (London: Zed Press, 1981), pp. 80–119, at pp. 113–16.

17 Sebastian C. H. Kim, 'The Word and the Spirit: Overcoming Poverty, Injustice and Division in Korea', in Sebastian C. H. Kim (ed.), *Christian Theology in Asia* (Cambridge: Cambridge University Press, 2008), pp. 129–53; Kim, 'Korean Christianity as a Messianic Movement', p. 110.

18 Cho, Kwang, 'The Meaning of Catholicism in Korean History', in Yu, *Founding of Catholic Tradition in Korea*, pp. 115–40; Mahn-yŏl Yi, 'The Birth of the National Spirit'.

19 David Kwang-sun Suh, 'A Biographical Sketch of an Asian Theological Consultation', in CTCCCA, *Minjung Theology*, pp. 15–37, at p. 22; Jong Chun Park, *Crawl with God, Dance in the Spirit! A Creative Formulation of Korean Theology of the Spirit* (Nashville, TN: Abingdon Press, 1998), p. 23.

20 Park, *Crawl with God*, pp. 61, 64–72; Suh, *Korean Minjung in Christ*, p. 56.

21 Kim, Yang-sŏn, 'Compulsory Shinto Shrine Worship and Persecution', in Yu, *Korea and Christianity*, pp. 87–120, at pp. 87–92, 103–16; Suh, *Korean Minjung in Christ*, p. 55.

22 Kim, Yong-Bock, 'Messiah and Minjung: Discerning Messianic Politics over against Political Messianism', in CTCCCA, *Minjung Theology*, pp. 183–93.

23 Adrian Buzo, *The Making of Modern Korea* (London: Routledge, 2002), p. 110; Keith Pratt, *Everlasting Flower: A History of Korea* (London: Reaktion Books, 2006), pp. 260, 290.

24 David Martin, *Pentecostalism: The World Their Parish* (Oxford: Blackwell Publishers, 2002), pp. 14–16.

25 Cf. Djun Kil Kim, *The History of Korea* (London: Greenwood Press, 2005), p. 123.

26 For a leading example see Rev. Kyung-Chik Han Memorial Foundation, *Just Three More Years to Live* (Seoul: Rev. Kyung-Chik Han Memorial Foundation, 2005), pp. 178–81.

27 Kim, 'Christianity's Role in the Modernization and Revitalization of Korean Society in the Twentieth Century'.

28 See the following in Bong Rin Ro and Marlin L. Nelson (eds), *Korean Church Growth Explosion*, 2nd edn (Seoul: Word of Life Press, 1995): Bong Rin Ro, 'The Korean Church: God's Chosen People for Evangelism', pp. 11–44, at p. 26; Kim, Joon-Gon, 'Korea's Total Evangelization Movement', pp. 45–73, at pp. 45–9; Han, Chul-Ha, 'Involvement of the Korean Church in the Evangelization of Asia', pp. 74–95, at pp. 74–7; Kim, Sam-Hwan and Kim Yoon-Su, 'Church Growth through Early Dawn Prayer Meetings', pp. 96–110, at pp. 97–8.

29 Nam-dong Suh, 'Towards a Theology of *Han*', in CTCCCA, *Minjung Theology*, pp. 55–69; Suh, 'Biographical Sketch of an Asian Theological Consultation', p. 33; Kim, 'Korean Christianity as a Messianic Movement', p. 98; Sok Hon Ham, *Queen of Suffering: A Spiritual History of Korea*, trans. E. Sang Yu, ed. and abridged John A. Sullivan (London: Friends World Committee for Consultation, 1985); Suh, *Korean Minjung in Christ*, p. 141.

30 Pratt, *Everlasting Flower*, p. 290; Bruce Cumings, 'Cold War Structures and Korea's Regional and Global Security', in Jang Jip Choi (ed.), *Post-Cold War and Peace: Experiences, Conditions and Choices* (Seoul: Asiatic Research Centre, 2003), pp. 129–50, at p. 141.

31 <www.opendoorsuk.org>.

32 See Sebastian C. H. Kim, 'Reconciliation Possible? The Churches' Efforts toward the Peace and Reconciliation of North and South Korea', in Sebastian C. H. Kim, Pauline Kollontai and Greg Hoyland (eds), *Peace and Reconciliation: In Search of Shared Identity* (Aldershot, Hants: Ashgate, 2008), pp. 161–78; Kirsteen Kim, 'Reconciliation in Korea: Models from Korean Christian Theology: Humanization,

Healing, Harmonization, *hanpuri*', *Missionalia* (South African Missiological Society) 35/1 (April 2008), pp. 15–33.

33 See Cumings, 'Cold War Structures', pp. 141–4; Samuel S. Kim, *The Two Koreas and the Great Powers* (Cambridge: Cambridge University Press, 2006), pp. 302–7.

34 Suh, *Korean Minjung in Christ*, p. 185. Rev. Han Kyung Chik donated all his Templeton prize money for the cause of reunification – see Memorial Foundation, *Just Three More Years to Live*, p. 196.

35 Suh, 'Towards a Theology of *Han*'; Kyung Chung Hyun, '"Han-pu-ri": Doing Theology from a Korean Woman's Perspective', *Ecumenical Review* 40/1 (January 2008), pp. 27–36.

36 National Council of Churches in Korea, 'Declaration of the Churches of Korea on National Reunification and Peace', unanimously adopted at the thirty-seventh general meeting of the National Council of Churches in Korea held in the Yondong Presbyterian Church, Seoul on 29 February 1988 – available at <www.warc.ch>.

37 Cumings, 'Cold War Structures', p. 132; Dae-Jung Kim, Nobel Laureate Lecture, 10 December 2000, Oslo – available at <http://nobelpeaceprize.org/>.

38 Sebastian C. H. Kim, 'The Problem of Poverty in Post-war Korean Christianity', *Transformation: An International Journal of Holistic Mission Studies* 24/1 (January–March 2007), pp. 43–50.

39 Robert J. Schreiter, 'The Theology of Reconciliation and Peacemaking for Mission', in Howard Mellor and Timothy Yates (eds), *Mission, Violence and Reconciliation* (Sheffield: Cliff College Publishing, 2004), pp. 11–28.

40 Cecelia Clegg, 'From Violence to Peace: Reflections from Northern Ireland', in Mellor and Yates, *Mission, Violence and Reconciliation*, pp. 61–71. See also Joseph Liechty and Cecelia Clegg, *Moving beyond Sectarianism: Religion, Conflict and Reconciliation in Northern Ireland* (Blackrock: Columba Press, 2001). Cf. Miroslav Volf, *Exclusion and Embrace: A Theological Exploration of Identity, Otherness, and Reconciliation* (Nashville, TN: Abingdon Press, 1996), pp. 36–7.

41 Schreiter, 'Theology of Reconciliation and Peacemaking for Mission', pp. 11–15.

42 Jonathan Sacks, *The Dignity of Difference: How to Avoid the Clash of Civilizations* (London: Continuum, 2002), pp. 53–4.

43 Kirsteen Kim, 'Reconciliation as the Ministry of the Spirit: Neither Jew nor Gentile', in Kim, *Reconciling Mission*, pp. 62–82.

44 Robert J. Schreiter, *The Ministry of Reconciliation: Spirituality and Strategies* (Maryknoll, NY: Orbis Books, 1998).

45 Israel Selvanayagam, 'Gal-ed versus Peniel: True Reconciliation in the Esau–Jacob/Israel Story', in Kim, *Reconciling Mission*, pp. 1–22, see p. 22.

46 Donal Dorr, *Mission in Today's World* (Blackrock, Co. Dublin: The Columba Press, 2000), p. 128.

47 Pervaiz Sultan, 'Healing the Nations: Mission and Development', in Kim, *Reconciling Mission*, pp. 103–17, quote from p. 110.

48 Ruth Tetlow, 'Interreligious Reconciliation: Lessons from Interfaith Dialogue', in Kim, *Reconciling Mission*, pp. 138–54.

49 Robert J. Schreiter, 'The Spirituality of Reconciliation and Peacemaking in Mission Today', in Mellor and Yates, *Mission, Violence and Reconciliation*, pp. 29–43, at pp. 26–7.

50 Lap Yan Kung, 'Reconciliation as Trust-building: An Exploration of Christian Mission in Hong Kong', in Kim, *Reconciling Mission*, pp. 176–200, quotes from pp. 197, 198.

51 See, for example, Chad N. Gandiya, 'Mission as Healing: Reconciling Spirit and Body', in Kim, *Reconciling Mission*, pp. 23–42.

52 Sahi, 'Healing the Blind', pp. 118, 137.

53 Colin Marsh, 'Reconciliation: An Ecumenical Mission Paradigm', in Kim, *Reconciling Mission*, pp. 43–61, at p. 58.

54 John Corrie, 'Anglican Perspectives on Reconciliation and Mission: Resonances from the Communion', in Kim, *Reconciling Mission*, pp. 155–75.

55 Val Ogden, 'Communicating the Message of Reconciliation: Speaking the Truth in Love', in Kim, *Reconciling Mission*, pp. 83–102.

56 Dorr, *Mission in Today's World*, p. 133.

57 For the World Council of Churches' Decade to Overcome Violence, see <www.overcomingviolence.org>.

58 Jacques Matthey, 'Reconciliation, *missio Dei* and the church's mission', in Mellor and Yates, *Mission, Violence and Reconciliation*, pp. 113–37, see pp. 116–17.

59 For background papers, see Jacques Matthey (ed.), *'You Are the Light of the World': Statements on Mission by the World Council of Churches 1980–2005* (Geneva: WCC Publications, 2005): 'Mission as Ministry of Reconciliation' (2005), pp. 90–126; 'The Healing Mission of the Church' (2005), pp. 62–89 – also available at <www.mission2005.org> and in Jacques Matthey (ed.), *'Come, Holy Spirit, Heal and Reconcile!' Report of the WCC Conference on World Mission and Evangelism, Athens, Greece, May 2005* (Geneva: WCC Publications, 2008).

60 Ogden, 'Communicating the Message of Reconciliation'.

61 Volf, *Exclusion and Embrace*; David Porter, 'Bearing Witness to the Overcomer of Violence: Reflections from a Practitioner Theologian in Northern Ireland', in Mellor and Yates, *Mission, Violence and Reconciliation*, pp. 73–89, at p. 88.

62 Schreiter, 'Spirituality of Reconciliation and Peacemaking in Mission Today'.

63 Gustavo Gutiérrez, *We Drink from Our Own Wells: The Spiritual Journey of a People* (Maryknoll, NY: Orbis Books, 1984).

64 Dorr, *Mission in Today's World*, p. 128; cf. Volf, *Exclusion and Embrace*, p. 105.

65 David J. Bosch, *A Spirituality of the Road* (Scottdale, PA: Herald Press, 1979).

66 Jürgen Moltmann, *The Church in the Power of the Spirit*, 2nd edn (London: SCM Press, 1992 [1977]); Kirsteen Kim, *Mission in the Spirit: The Holy Spirit in Indian Christian Theologies* (Delhi: ISPCK, 2003).

10

THE MISSION OF THE SPIRIT

Connecting World Church and Local Mission

> All too often statements about what 'modern Christians accept' or 'what Catholics today believe' refer only to what that ever-shrinking remnant of *Western* Christians and Catholics believe. Such assertions are outrageous today, and as time goes by they will become ever further removed from reality.[1]
> Philip Jenkins

The Bible is a multicultural, inter-cultural and cross-cultural book.[2] The Bible is a multicultural book because different books of the Bible were written in different places, sometimes in different languages, and often in very different cultural contexts from other parts. Knowledge of the cultural context from which the biblical books emerged can be an important aid to understanding their meaning. The Bible is an inter-cultural book because its present form is the result of ecumenical – or inter-cultural – discussion. The compliers of the canon did not attempt to reconcile the different books of the Bible – such as the four Gospels – into one authoritative account but allowed them to stand side-by-side as equally authoritative accounts of the life and work of Jesus Christ which inform one another. Recognition that the Bible does not speak with one voice but contains within it inter-cultural debate is also highly significant for biblical interpretation. The Bible is a cross-cultural book. Whereas the Old Testament is mainly concerned with the faith experience of one particular ethnic group, the New Testament shows how the faith of Israel as fulfilled in Jesus Christ transcended an ethnic boundary, and became the faith of Gentiles as well as Jews. This became the archetypal model for the way the Christian gospel has become the faith of many different cultural groups across the world.[3] Since then the gospel has been, and is now, at home in many different cultures of the world – from China to Spain, from Russia to South Africa.[4]

Today the reality of world Christianity, to which the Bible testifies, has come home to us in a new way as Europeans find themselves a minority among the Christians of the world, and no longer the global standard by which local adaptations of Christianity should be measured.[5] In *The Next Christendom*, Philip Jenkins was one of the first to shock Western Christians by showing just what a different perspective Christians may have who live in other continents where churches are fast growing. Some of the differences he highlighted were: different ways of reading the Bible; belief in spiritual forces affecting daily life; different priorities for faith due to economic factors; optimistic expectations of the future of Christianity; and different theologies of religion due to their proximity to other growing faiths.[6] In Britain we have responded to 'the resurgence of religions' and the presence of people of many different faiths within our own society by a widespread process of education designed to help us appreciate one another, through revised religious education curricula, informational and inspirational television programmes, and forums for people of other faiths to meet one another. But we have not made the same effort in the case of 'the strangely unfamiliar world of the new Christianity',[7] and this in spite of the fact that Christians from around the world live among us in Britain too. As I have tried to show in this book, gaining such awareness is immensely enriching in terms of new relationships, and also in terms of our own self-understanding and appreciation of Christian faith. In order to do so, we are in need of a new ecumenism or catholicity which will help us rethink and reshape our beliefs and practice.

10.1 Ecumenism and churches together

The Spirit in which we do mission is the spirit of unity but the form of that unity has been a matter of considerable debate, especially since Edinburgh 1910. Christian unity was not a new theme even then. According to John, Jesus prayed that his disciples might be one and experience the love he shared with the Father so 'that the world may believe' in Jesus as Son of God (John 17.21). The Apostle Paul pleaded with the Corinthian Christians not to behave according to the flesh but to live in the Spirit of love into which they were baptized as a sign to the world of Jesus' resurrection (1 Cor. 1.12–15). Through centuries of division Christians have entertained the idea of visible Christian unity and searched for ways to achieve it. At, and after, Edinburgh 1910, the 'ecumenical movement' laid particular emphasis on achieving organic or organizational unity by reaching agreement on matters of doctrine and ministry. National councils of Protestant churches were formed beginning in the USA in 1908. The British Council of Churches was formed in 1942 after the pattern projected for the World Council of Churches. Ecumenical initiatives in different parts of the world resulted in a number of unions of Protestant denominations. The most outstanding was the formation of the Church of South India (CSI) in 1947 by the union of Congregational, Presbyterian, Methodist and Anglican churches.[8] The CSI was a model and inspiration for many united and uniting churches across Asia and around the world, including the United Reformed Church in England and Wales, in 1972.

In India the chief impetus for unity was the damage perceived to be done to Christian witness in India by the spectre of the denominational divisions imported from the West. In Europe itself, however, the strength of the ecumenical movement among Protestant churches in the twentieth century had more to do with the peace of Europe. The reconciliation of the European churches was a step toward the unity of the whole continent after the devastating wars of the twentieth century and, given that European nations exercised colonial power, toward the unity of the world. In 1948 most of the Protestant churches represented at Edinburgh 1910, and some Orthodox churches, came together to form the World Council of Churches. For the Orthodox, unity was of supreme theological and missiological importance (see Chapter 4) and also a practical means of preventing the proselytizing activities of Western churches in what they regarded as Orthodox lands. Through the World Council of Churches, efforts were made to overcome all divisions between the historic denominations. Orthodox, Protestant and Roman Catholic leaders worked together in the preparation of the *Baptism, Eucharist and Ministry* document of 1982, and reached a remarkable degree of consensus on justification by faith, the two natures of Christ and other key areas of doctrinal debate.[9]

In the later twentieth century, however, efforts to achieve organic unity have foundered. This is partly a reflection of a shift in the world political climate. In the years after 1945, there were strong centripetal forces in international affairs which encouraged the unity of humanity in a shared modernity but since about 1968 the forces have been centrifugal, with increasing fragmentation and insistence on diversity.[10] At the level of world communions of churches, although considerable doctrinal progress was made to the early 1970s, disagreement about ministry has now led to an impasse. At the same time the church scene has become much more complex with many new churches and movements arising in different parts of the world and appreciation of the need for inculturation of faith in local contexts. Furthermore, in the post-colonial era, the emphasis on peace is often seen to be in tension with the prophetic ministry of justice. The result of these developments is that organic union and agreement are no longer so significant in the aims of ecumenical activity because at present a commitment to continuing dialogue is perhaps the most that can be achieved.[11]

Since the 1960s the word 'ecumenism', which originally referred to the Church and its mission of proclamation, has taken on a wider meaning. In view of the *missio Dei* and the purpose of God to create a new humanity and renew the whole creation, ecumenism extends beyond church structures and overlaps to a large extent with mission concerns.[12] The paradigm of mission as reconciliation affirms the close connection between the unity of the church and the mission of God. Authentic mission of reconciliation requires a reconciled community, and the reconciliation in Christ is extended to the whole universe.[13] In ecumenical mission, the model for reconciliation and unity in church and mission is the Trinity. In other words, it is 'diversity in unity' or 'unity in diversity' which is envisaged. This was grasped at the mission conference in 1952 in Willingen, Germany, which stated:

> Out of the depths of His love for us, the Father has sent forth His own Son to reconcile all things to Himself, that we and all men [*sic*] might through the Spirit, be made one in Him with the Father in that perfect love which is the very nature of God.[14]

Since the persons of the Trinity retain their own distinctiveness in unity, the emphasis in the ecumenical movement has shifted from 'a fellowship based on agreement' to 'a fellowship of those who are unlike and not necessarily agreed' but who come together for a missionary purpose.[15] There are biblical precedents for this: when James, Peter and John gave Paul and Barnabas the right hand of fellowship (Gal. 2.7–9), this signified mutual respect of one another's distinctive missions. The fellowship or communion of the Holy Spirit (2 Cor. 13.13) is expressed in the apportioning by the Holy Spirit of a variety of gifts, ministries and expressions of faith exercised in love which respects the contribution of each (1 Cor. 12—14). So God's mission is a co-operative effort and the Apostle Paul could say, 'I planted, Apollos watered, but God gave the growth' (1 Cor. 3.6).

Many of the same forces have been at play in the ecumenical movement in Britain, where in the early 1960s there were high hopes of visible unity by 1980. A great deal of effort was put into working for unity but this became detached from mission as a result of post-colonial criticism and the pressures of secularization, which militated against explicit Christian confession on grounds of tolerance. But, 'Unity pursued only for unity's sake becomes empty and sterile, limiting the ecumenical journey to dry doctrinal negotiations and the production of texts for ecumenical academics', and to the danger that these are imposed on local congregations rather than connecting with grass-root realities.[16] The situation is now significantly different for two main reasons: first, with the appreciation of diversity in postmodernity, the need for a uniform Christian confession and united organization is no longer appreciated; second, the importance of mission and witness has been recovered. Although successful schemes of union have been few, considerable progress toward unity has been made at the grass-roots level in over 800 'local ecumenical partnerships' and in shared projects and mission events.

Since the 1960s relationships between churches have been improving and, considering the depths of division, the level of co-operation between the historic churches achieved in just 50 years is quite remarkable in many ways. What is more, ecumenical co-operation has broadened considerably. It is no longer just Protestant churches but also the Roman Catholic Church and many newer churches which are represented in the ecumenical instruments. The background to this lies in discussions between the Roman Catholic Church and the World Council of Churches on mission and unity, which resulted in a commitment in 1984 to 'common witness'.[17] In Britain this led to the winding up of the former British Council of (Protestant) Churches and the creation of what became in 1999 Churches Together in Britain and Ireland (CTBI). The new body included the Roman Catholic Church as a full member and widened geographically to include Ireland as well. It also allowed for the participation of black-majority churches and other new groups in ecumenical activities. The processes of the late 1980s, which initiated this change, were exercises in reconciliation at local as well as national level and emphasized common mission and service in society as the aim. 'Churches Together' was intended to release energy from efforts to achieve structural unity, corporate action and agreed statements, and to direct it instead into sharing of resources and co-operation in the mission and ministry in which the churches were already engaged.[18] Despite the new vision, CTBI continues to have to adjust to low levels of financial support and the changing landscape of UK politics, especially in view of devolution.

Britain is unusual among nations in not having a 'council of churches' but its model of 'churches together' is a model studied with interest by others worldwide. In the interests of widening participation, the World Council of Churches has also been re-thinking its nature and purpose in the light of the proliferation in new churches since 1948. The World Council of Churches process towards Common Understanding and Vision (CUV) took a broad understanding of the term 'ecumenical' to include both 'the unity and renewal of the church and the healing and destiny of the human community'. It concluded in 1997 by encouraging 'the search for new forms of relationships at all levels between World Council of Churches member churches, other churches and other ecumenical organizations'.[19] With this in mind, at the Athens conference on world mission and evangelism in 2005 a quarter of those invited were from non-member bodies. In Nairobi in 2007 an even broader gathering was sponsored but deliberately not owned by the World Council of Churches. The Global Christian Forum is about 'bringing into conversation with one another Christians and churches from very different traditions' who have rarely or never talked to each other with a view to the rebirth of ecumenism.[20] Pentecostal input has been particularly significant in this initiative.

10.2 Together with migrant churches

The face of British church life has been changing considerably not only because of the decline of older denominations and the rise of new forms of church such as Pentecostalism, but also because of the growing numbers of 'migrant churches'. 'Migrant churches' has become a common designation for churches which are founded and run by and for (recent) migrants to this country. The term is not satisfactory because in one sense, since

Christians are pilgrims, all churches are migrant churches.[21] Furthermore, churches of migrants to Britain may prove to be in many cases 'settler churches'. However, for the purposes of our discussion we will stick to what has become the convention. Migrant churches have existed in Britain for many centuries. After the end of World War Two, for example, there were many Germans who settled here and wished to retain their language and traditions of worship in their own churches. Very few now remain as the young people have integrated into British society and the original members are passing away.[22] The migrants from the Caribbean in the 1950s and 1960s did not necessarily face a language or denominational barrier to worshipping in British churches but the racial and cultural obstacles were huge and they were not made welcome, so they founded their own Afro-Caribbean churches.[23] Today there are many newer African churches, together with churches serving recently arrived communities from different parts of Asia, from Latin America, the Middle East, the former Soviet bloc and the Pacific.

Migrants and their communities vary greatly, as do the reasons they are here. Some feel themselves forced out of their countries of origin and see themselves as unwilling exiles here – a little like the Israelites in Babylon. Others have struggled to get here to make a better life for themselves and their families in what they see as a kind of 'promised land'. Some come for political, some for economic, some for educational, and others for almost accidental reasons, or a combination of these.[24] Relations between indigenous British churches and newer migrant churches are complicated by the fact that each may regard themselves as having a mission toward the other. While some British churches feel they should minister among what they believe to be needy migrants, migrants who are aware of a great outpouring of the Holy Spirit on their own nation believe that British churches also need such a revival. Although most foreign clergy are pastoring congregations predominantly of their own community, some actively work for the conversion of the local people or the revival of British churches. This tendency is particularly marked in some West African churches which engage in 'reverse mission'. African Christians may liken European churches to the valley of dry bones waiting for the prophet to tell them to listen to the word of God (cf. Ezek. 37).[25]

In order to consider how indigenous churches can relate to migrant churches, we will look at a particular example: the Korean diaspora in Britain, first considering its social profile and then its churches.[26] The Korean community in the UK is more than 40,000 strong. The overwhelming majority have come from South Korea over the past 40 years for reasons of study or business. About 15,000 are estimated to live in Kingston Borough, where the first Korean company was based, making them the largest minority in this small area. There are now more than 100 Korean companies operating in the UK, and there are many other small businesses, mostly in the London area. Many of these serve the Korean community primarily, providing food, accommodation, travel, news and schooling. Koreans are also in Britain as students, and may be found at different levels of the education system from language students, to postgraduates (including many theological students). Apart from specific business and study opportunities, Britain may be attractive to South Koreans for other reasons: it is an opportunity to improve English language skills, and Britain is an English-speaking gateway to the rest of Europe. The UK offers a more relaxed and comfortable lifestyle than South Korea where competition is very intense. Children especially can escape the cut-throat education system of Korea. Some are attracted by English/British culture and heritage. Others relish the golf, which is a prestige game but for which opportunities are severely limited and very expensive in mountainous Korea.

As well as immigrants from South Korea, there are smaller numbers from North Korea and from Korean communities in China and Central Asia. These are more likely to be poor, alone, less well prepared for British life (especially in knowledge of the English language), and may even be the victims of trafficking. Many of them are restaurant or sweatshop workers, probably employed by South Koreans. South Korean Christian missionaries are working with North Koreans, who are often here illegally. So the Korean community is not one but several. However, taken as a whole it has a distinctive profile compared to other migrant communities in the UK. A much larger proportion of Koreans in Britain are temporary residents, who return to Korea after a short stay. About 90 per cent of Koreans have temporary resident status, and perhaps 80 per cent return home within five years. This gives them little need or incentive to get involved in British society. Current economic conditions make it perfectly possible and acceptable to move around the world on this basis, however hurtful this is to the resident community. Koreans who wish to experience British life, and wish to build relationships, find a significant language barrier to more active participation in British society. South Koreans are relatively well off, often receiving generous support from home. Social problems are less apparent in this community, most are well behaved and law abiding, and their presence has not provoked significant opposition from or conflict with other groups. Another respect in which the Korean community is different from many others is that most South Koreans in the UK are Christians, or gravitate to Korean Christian churches as focal points of their society. This presents problems for local authorities who liaise with migrant groups through a council of faiths, seemingly unaware that there are Asian Christians.

From the perspective of local government, the most significant characteristic of the Korean community is its 'self-sufficiency'. Koreans have a very strong ethic of self-help and a desire not to lose face as a nation, so communities overseas offer a great deal of mutual support, and rarely articulate problems to outsiders. Apart from community isolation, there is the difficulty that Koreans are ignorant of government services available, especially because they are not used to a welfare state and tend not to see government officials in a friendly way. This is compounded by government and social services' lack of awareness of Korean identity and culture, and poor communication with the community. The local government and the churches tend to approach migrant communities from a needs-based perspective. This is problematic because Koreans would not wish to be perceived as needy or as asking for help.

Korean churches in the UK were first established more than 30 years ago. There may now be 25 or more churches in Kingston Borough alone, and 100 or more across the UK. Many British Christians, especially those brought up in the ecumenical movement, find it difficult to understand why Korean Protestant churches are split into so many different groups. There are a number of reasons for this. The first is the practice of the first Protestant missionaries in Korea to encourage independent local churches which were self-supporting, self-governing and self-propagating. Second, Korean churches tend to operate as businesses rather than societies or social service organizations. In this context, competition between churches is seen as a good thing because it is good for growth. Furthermore, ministers' salaries are usually linked to the size of their congregations. Third, divisions from Korea may be exported to the UK – although there are also examples of where divisions have been overcome abroad. A further reason for the establishment of separate churches overseas is that to obtain a long-term visa an individual (almost always a married man) may start a congregation for which to work as pastor. In this case, as far as his home church in Korea is concerned, he is likely to be designated a missionary.

British Christians also wonder why Koreans tend not to join the existing local churches. Apart from the obvious language problem, there are several other reasons for this. Most Korean Christians abroad wish to be sustained by the spirituality they are familiar with from Korea, especially if, as in most cases, they are here only temporarily. Some may also be convinced of its superiority by the evidence of spectacular church growth and vibrant church life in Korea. For Korean Christians, national loyalty and peer pressure makes it very difficult to absent themselves from Korean community activities and churches. The churches are often the first port of call for new arrivals, whether practising Christians in Korea or not, because of the network of support and contacts they offer. Nevertheless there are Korean Christians who, for a variety of reasons, choose to make the effort to integrate into local English-speaking churches.

British churches operate with broadly three models of ministry to ethnic minorities. One is the common practice of renting out church premises for use by migrant churches. This could be seen as a ministry of hospitality on the part of the host church but often it is a source of revenue, especially from communities like Koreans who can afford a market rent. The level of contact between the congregation of the host church and that of the migrant church can vary greatly in this situation. Examples include regular leadership meetings, occasional shared worship, a shared flower rota, shared meals (with contributions from both communities), children's clubs, equipment, DIY, and swapping of preaching and choirs. In the second model a chaplain is appointed to minister to and represent the minority group, liaise with local churches, support incumbents and relate to the churches in the group's homeland. The chaplain organizes regular services (say monthly) for the community, who otherwise attend local British churches. This model is quite varied in practice, there being no uniformity in sources of funding for chaplains, a lack of clarity about the accountability of chaplains, and ambiguity about the status and structure of congregations formed. Making such a chaplaincy arrangement is complex but the London diocese of the Church of England, for example, has several. The Anglican sense of responsibility to everyone in the parish is strange to most Koreans, who would be surprised that the church should think of appointing a priest/minister to serve them, at least not in any other way than to make them into Anglicans. Since they expect to be self-sufficient, Koreans may experience the offer of help as patronizing or interfering.

The third model is a local church attempting to reach out to a migrant community and encouraging them to join. In the case of the Korean community, some of the ways this is done include: acting as buddies or mentors to students; Anglo-Korean study groups looking at Korea and its culture; social activities, including meals and cross-cultural evenings; translation of service and information sheets; interpretation, particularly of sermons; hosting Korean-led events and meetings; including Korean-style music and prayer in services; providing Korean-style refreshments at shared lunches; running English classes or English conversation practice sessions; and hosting after-school activities for schoolchildren. Several churches have gone further in employing Korean ministers; teaching Korean forms of spirituality; inviting Korean mega-church leaders to address mixed audiences; inviting police and other community organizations to meet Koreans on church premises; and even arranging visits by members of the British congregation to South Korea. The churches that have been successful in integration with the Korean community – either at an individual level or church-to-church – seem to be those which have developed reciprocal relations of mutual help and learning. They do not see Koreans as necessarily in need but genuinely believe Koreans have something to offer the church here and draw out their gifts.

A fourth model is not much used in Britain but is common in the United States. That is to encourage the growth of ethnic minority congregations within a denomination. So, for example, the Presbyterian Church of the USA and the Episcopal Church of the USA have Korean congregations, among many other ethnic churches. Such an arrangement poses obvious challenges to the traditional parish systems of the established churches in Britain.

Working cross-culturally is fraught with misunderstanding and confusion. This is compounded by differences of church tradition and spirituality. In particular, confusion arises because the same denomination may appear very different in different countries. For example, as a minority church in Korea, the Anglican Church of Korea upholds the Anglo-Catholic tradition that it originally received and has appropriated. The Church of England, in contrast, as the established church in England is obliged to encompass many streams within it. A particular local British Anglican church may not appear to Korean Anglicans to be faithful to Anglicanism. Moreover, the 'mainstream' way of being Christian varies between countries and so those who prefer to worship in a church they consider to be 'mainstream' may have to switch denominations if they change countries. Mainstream churches in Korea – which are also popular churches – are mainly Presbyterian, conservative evangelical and charismatic – all in a distinctively Korean way. A Korean Presbyterian coming to Scotland might feel at home in the Church of Scotland because it is the mainstream church but they may not appreciate its spirituality. In England s/he might pass by the United Reformed Church, which represents his/her tradition in England and Wales, and prefer to join the Church of England because it is the major denomination.

Not having been colonized by Europe (but by Japan), Korean Christians do not tend to defer to European norms – or to react against them – but present a distinctive and confident form of Christian witness in Europe. Interaction between Korean and British Christians can help both to gain new perspectives on the Christian faith, but this will only be possible if there is mutual respect and openness between the two groups.

10.3 The new catholicity: worldwide fellowship of the Spirit

The experience of the historic churches of Europe today is not dissimilar to that which befell the first Christians in Jerusalem. The witness of the first disciples to Jesus Christ did not result in the expansion of Judaism from Jerusalem to Samaria and the ends of the earth exactly as was envisaged at the beginning of the book of Acts (Acts 1.8). Such a pattern would have retained Jerusalem as its centre, with Christianity encompassing the rest of the world in ever-increasing concentric circles. In fact what happened was the creation of a largely Gentile church with multiple centres in Antioch, Rome, Alexandria, Edessa and so on. The 'mother church' in Jerusalem then struggled to redefine itself in relation to these new centres, and to see itself as a local hub of a worldwide network rather than the centre of an ever-spreading circle. Luke, the writer of Acts, is aware of this and gradually shifts the attention in the narrative from Jerusalem to Rome. Furthermore he lays foundations for this outcome by his theology of the Spirit in two stages. First, the story of Pentecost justifies an ecumenical and global understanding of the church and salvation brought about by the work of Christ and the outpouring of the Spirit. Amos Yong has argued that Pentecost provides a new agenda for ecumenism, healing the fragmentation of the church and gathering people 'from every nation under heaven' (Acts 2.5) as the Spirit continues to be 'poured out on all flesh'.[27]

Second, the work of the Spirit affirms the experience of Gentiles and allows Jews to transcend their exclusivity to include other nations. According to Luke, when a shocked Apostle Peter discovered that Gentiles received the Holy Spirit in just the same way as the Jewish disciples had done at Pentecost (Acts 11.15), he concluded that, although they might be ignorant of the Scriptures, they could not be considered second-class Christians in any way and were to be baptized and received on an equal footing with Jews (Acts 10.47). But 'Judaizers', who held that being a Christian was not possible outside the Jewish tradition, tried to enforce uniformity to it by sending out envoys to other churches and condemning those – in one famous case Peter himself – who compromised the purity of the Hebrew law (Gal. 2.12). According to Luke, at least one attempt was made to work out a compromise that would protect Jewish sensibilities and allow them to eat with their Gentile brothers and sisters in Christ (Jerusalem Council, Acts 15). As the Gentile churches grew in size and in locations further and further away from Jerusalem, fewer Christians visited the temple and, though the Hebrew Scriptures were retained as the Old Testament, contact with actual Jews lessened and the Jewish perspective carried less importance. Although the mother church continued to be accorded special respect by the Apostle Paul, leader of the main Gentile mission (e.g. Rom. 15.25–31), his view, which came to prevail, was that Christian allegiance was not to the earthly Jerusalem but to 'Jerusalem above', who is 'our mother' (Gal. 4.26). And even those documents in the

New Testament which were most obviously addressed to believers from a Jewish background encourage the idea that in the light of the new situation, the old is relativized, and those who were first could now be last. The Evangelist Matthew emphasizes time and time again in his Gospel Jesus' teaching that it is not those schooled in the law who will inherit the kingdom of heaven but only those who, by grace, are obedient to the Lord's ethical commands, from whatever nation they come (e.g. Matt. 7.21; 28.19–20). The writer to the Hebrews explains that Jesus Christ's priesthood, covenant and sacrifice transcend the priesthood, covenant and sacrifice of Israel and are part of a kingdom above (Heb. 3—10; 13.10–14). And James reminds his rich and wise readers that God has 'chosen the poor in the world to be rich in faith' and that true wisdom 'comes down from above' (Jas 2.5; 3.17).

In the Western tradition, however, the model of concentric circles persists, in particular where Rome is seen to replace Jerusalem as the centre of the faith, as if the pneumatology of Luke is not fully understood. Writing from a Roman Catholic perspective, Robert Schreiter has suggested that the context of the church in a globalized world calls for a rethinking of the theological notion of catholicity. Schreiter points out that, whereas in the West, 'Catholic' came to mean 'in communion with Rome', in the Eastern church – and in the churches of the Reformation – Catholicity meant 'the fullness of the Church that would be achieved only at the end of time'. This eschatological view was affirmed by the Roman Catholic Church also at the Second Vatican Council (1962–5) but even this Schreiter does not find satisfactory. He goes on to argue that in a globalized world the eschatological understanding needs to be broadened to include 'wholeness', referring to 'the physical extension of the Church throughout the world' and 'fullness of faith', referring to orthodox belief. 'Wholeness' recognizes the variety of forms faith takes in different cultures and includes the faith of the poor and marginalized, whose experience of culture is fragmented, and of both those who benefit from globalization and those excluded by it. Fullness of faith requires true communication of the message along with recognition of the indeterminacy that allows the message to have multiple meanings and a number of, rather than one single, guiding visions for humanity inspired by Scripture. This 'new catholicity', writes Schreiter, can only be achieved by intense inter-cultural exchange and communication in an attitude of generosity and respect toward other Christians from whom we may differ.[28]

Schreiter's vision of catholicity is of a church which encompasses the whole of time and space, and celebrates the variety of Christian expression and experience within them, while also encouraging mutual sharing and close interaction between different parts of the church catholic. He is critical of present policies of the Roman Catholic Church which attempt to force conformity of Christians in different parts of the world to models developed in Rome and a spirit which is quick to criticize as 'syncretistic' genuine attempts to re-express the Christian message locally. There are considerable strains associated with this centralized model in a globalized world that may not be solved by a simple extension of catholicity from Rome, and this calls for a more receptive learning attitude as part of an 'individual, communal and structural conversion' of the church to its contemporary ecumenical context.[29] Now that Europe is no longer the most Catholic continent – Latin America has 44 per cent of all Roman Catholic believers worldwide[30] – it may be that the church will be forced to adopt a more devolved and decentred model in order to maintain its catholicity.

If mission means incorporating people into a world church which has an overarching Christian culture, then it is a very similar project to the globalizing plans of modernity.[31] But, using the resources of the Bible and theology, US Catholic theologian William T. Cavanaugh strongly denies that catholicity means globalization. In contemporary globalization the universal is dominant and the world is fragmented so that localities are detached from one another and each locality is seen as 'an administrative division of a larger whole'. But each local church, he argues, is not a part but 'a concentration of the whole'. Diverse local churches identify with one another not by the compulsion of the head but because, participating in the one body and sharing one Spirit, they suffer and rejoice together. Unlike the modern state constructed by social contract, which is made up of citizens each individually subject to the state, the church is a true body, originally one, in which the parts relate to each other as well as to the head. For Cavanaugh, the chief expression of this is the Eucharist, which is celebrated in diaspora, 'in the multitude of local churches scattered throughout the world', but 'nevertheless gathered up into one'. In each local action the whole body of Christ, the whole church, is present.[32]

The letter to the Ephesians comes out of a period in the life of the early church when memories of the origins of Christianity in the Jewish community were fading. The Apostle Paul (or his representative) reminds his hearers how the Lord Jesus Christ, by his death on the cross, broke down the wall that had once divided Jew from Gentile and established a single new community, the household of God, a spiritual temple (2.11–22). This new, resurrected body of Christ, the church, which Paul had once persecuted but now serves, is indwelt by one Spirit, which unites the whole body in the 'bond of peace' (4.3–6). At the same time, Paul recognizes that the same Spirit inspires a diversity of gifts for building up the Christian community and a number of different stages of maturity among members (4.7, 11–13). Paul is writing not to the church universal but to a particular Christian community in Ephesus whose expression of Christianity is but one of many. The final result that Paul envisages is not a human institution or earthly project, a particular form of church, spirituality or theology but the participation of this local church in something over and above it, the body of Christ, now enthroned in heaven (Eph. 1.20–3; 3.15–16).

Baptism into the body of Christ is not just a personal or family affair, it involves the local congregation, and they are representatives not only of the particular church denomination within the nation-state but of the universal Church. By baptism, therefore Christians become part of a worldwide fellowship, while also rooted in a local congregation. National governments may feel threatened by transnational churches. For example, at a time when the church in Europe was being fragmented into nation-states, the transnational wandering of the Anabaptists annoyed the established churches and unsettled national governments. In later centuries in England, baptism as a Roman Catholic frightened the government because it suggested an ultimate loyalty outside the country. Similarly, in the twentieth century the Chinese government expelled all foreign missionaries and insisted the churches cut all foreign links. But, problematic though this may be politically, Christian baptism in the one Spirit leads to a global connectedness. Christians are members of local congregations but also global people with membership in one of the world's largest transnational bodies.

While Christian transnationalism may be threatening to governments, it is also something Christians have to offer society. So, for instance, in China today when nationalism is rising very strongly, the upsurge in Christianity could be seen as having a constructive effect politically in encouraging transnationalism against a background of rampant nationalism.[33] As we become aware that we all inhabit one planet with its delicate environment and finely balanced ecology which sustains us, and that we are increasingly bound together by one global economy with shared markets and global migration, governments are calling for 'global citizenship', 'cross-cultural capability', and 'internationalization' to produce a sustainable future. In this scenario Christians, as world people with some of the largest and strongest global networks, have an important role to play. After 2,000 years of being a global community, the Christian church can lead the way toward a globalized world in which each local community is treated with respect and honoured as integral parts of the whole body. Christianity may be said to encourage global citizenship and responsible participation in the international community because Christians are part of a worldwide fellowship in the one Spirit.

10.4 Together in mission – local and global

The Spirit which binds Christians together is the missionary Spirit, the Spirit sent into the world. This is the theological basis of the missionary nature of the church. To say that the church is always and everywhere missionary is not only to say that the local church has a mission but also to say that the church participates in God's mission, which is prior to and wider than the institutions we call church. A mission theology of the church may start from the local church and its context but it also shares the divine concern for the world as a whole.

God's initiative in the world, the *missio Dei*, is prior to the church. The church has not always existed but, both theologically and empirically, comes into being as a result of mission. The church was conceived in the context of the mission of Jesus Christ, in which his disciples and the early Christians were called to take part. If the earliest church is the community of the disciples, then they were those called to follow Jesus as he fulfilled the mission entrusted to him. If the church was born at Pentecost then the coming into being of the church was at the same time the disciples' empowering for participation in God's mission in the world without the physical presence of Christ but accompanied by the Paraclete, the Holy Spirit (Acts 1.8; 2; John 20.19–23). In either case, the church is a missionary movement before it is an institution. The apostles are, by the etymology of the word, those who are sent, the messengers going into the world. The notion that they are also static pillars guarding the message (cf. Gal. 2.9) can only be secondary.

As we have seen in this book, many churches in different parts of the world have a recent memory of their founding as a result of mission initiative and popular response. The churches of Europe may have long forgotten it but there was also a time before the Christian gospel was brought to them, when there was no local church. The missionaries who brought the gospel to the churches of Europe are known in English as 'patron saints', and the local people who led the response as 'founding fathers'. In the interests of establishment and as a result of a long-settled existence, the churches' origins in missionary movements tend to be obscured. As a society is Christianized, evangelism and mission gradually become education and social welfare. We see ourselves as the guardians of the message, not the receivers of it. But any history of any church begins with mission activity and, if the church is alive and growing (whether in wisdom or in numbers), it continues with mission activity. It is not possible to separate the church from mission in either theological or historical origin. Nor is it possible to separate church and mission in terms of their purpose. The church came into being as a result of the mission of God to bring salvation to the world. The church remains faithful in so far as it continues in that purpose of salvation.

Church leaders, whose responsibility is for the institution, may sometimes lose the larger picture of God's mission and the sense that they are part of a movement. Mission activity by its nature transcends the structures of local churches. While churches are usually pleased to take the credit for mission activity, such as increased membership, global links and greater social credibility, they are sometimes less willing to recognize and support the process. Mission – especially mission in its global connectedness – is not yet accepted as essential to the life of the mainline churches in the way that faith-and-order concerns and public policy issues are. Our theology of mission is underdeveloped. We may have recognized the missionary context of the local church but we have not yet understood that in mission we are linked into the worldwide movement of the Spirit, and therefore with other churches worldwide. As Jesus' commission to his disciples and the story of Pentecost show, worldwide vision and global links are not secondary but of the essence of church. Without them we are inclined forget that we are not the whole church but only part of a much wider movement of God's grace. Without them we are frightened and doubtful (Matt. 28.17; John 20.19, 29; Luke 24.38–49). Without maintaining them we will cut ourselves off from what God is doing in the world and be marginal to the movement of the Spirit.

God's mission is greater than any church, and it is in this wider movement of the Spirit that all the churches in the world participate. It is within the greater purposes of God that we find our unity. The *missio Dei* is not confined to any locality; it spills over, crosses boundaries and is carried across the world by the wind of the Spirit. It does not have a single origin or one direction but comes and goes as the Spirit wills. However, it is one movement because the Spirit witnesses to a unique person, Jesus Christ of Nazareth, crucified and raised, who reveals the Father in heaven, source of all things. We have yet to realize that the cosmic Christ is manifested in the unity of local churches in the mission of the Spirit. When we do, we will connect world church with local mission. We will be able to join with the Spirit who moves over the earth sustaining our world and our life – the Spirit of Jesus Christ, who is given to bring about good news in the whole creation.

Notes

1 Philip Jenkins, *The Next Christendom: The Coming of Global Christianity* (Oxford: Oxford University Press, 2002), p. 3.

2 The inspiration for this paragraph is from Donald Senior and Carroll Stuhlmueller, *The Biblical Foundations for Mission* (London: SCM Press, 1983).

3 Kwame Bediako, *Theology and Identity: The Impact of Culture upon Christian Thought in the Second Century and Modern Africa* (Oxford: Regnum Books, 1992).

4 Jaroslav Pelikan, *Jesus through the Centuries: His Place in the History of Culture* (Yale: Yale University Press, 1999); Andrew F. Walls, *The Missionary Movement in Christian History: Studies in the Transmission of Faith* (Maryknoll, NY: Orbis Books, 1996), pp. 16–25.

5 Jenkins, *Next Christendom*, pp. 24, 109, 119.

6 Jenkins, *Next Christendom*, pp. 217–20, 123, 160–2, 9, 171.

7 Jenkins, *Next Christendom*, p. 214.

8 Harold E. Fey (ed.), *A History of the Ecumenical Movement, Vol. II: 1948–68*, 4th edn (Geneva: WCC Publications, 1993); Stephen Charles Neill, 'Plans of Union and Reunion 1910–1948', in Ruth Rouse and Stephen C. Neill (eds), *A History of the Ecumenical Movement*, Vol. 1: 1517–1948, 4th edn (Geneva: WCC Publications, 1993), pp. 445–505; T. V. Philip, *Ecumenism in Asia* (Delhi: ISPCK, 1994).

9 World Council of Churches, *Baptism, Eucharist and Ministry* (1982) – available at <www.oikoumene.org>. Michael Kinnamon, 'Assessing the Ecumenical Movement', in John Briggs, Mercy Amba Oduyoye and Georges Tsetsis (eds), *A History of the Ecumenical Movement, Vol. 3: 1968–2000* (Geneva: WCC Publications, 2004), pp. 51–81, at p. 51.

10 Martin E. Marty, 'The Global context of Ecumenism 1968–2000', in Briggs, Oduyoye and Tsetsis, *History of the Ecumenical Movement, Vol. 3*, pp. 3–22.

11 Kinnamon, 'Assessing the Ecumenical Movement'. Melanie A. May, 'The Unity We Share, the Unity We Seek', in Briggs, Oduyoye and Tsetsis, *History of the Ecumenical Movement, Vol. 3*, pp. 83–102.

12 Kinnamon, 'Assessing the Ecumenical Movement', pp. 53–4.

13 Jacques Matthey, 'Reconciliation, *Missio Dei* and the Church's Mission', in Howard Mellor and Timothy Yates (eds), *Mission, Violence and Reconciliation* (Sheffield: Cliff College Publishing, 2004), pp. 113–37.

14 Quoted in Matthey, 'Reconciliation, *Missio Dei* and the Church's Mission', p. 115.

15 Kinnamon, 'Assessing the Ecumenical Movement', p. 79.

16 Colin Marsh, 'Reconciliation: An Ecumenical Mission Paradigm', in Kirsteen Kim (ed.), *Reconciling Mission: The Ministry of Healing and Reconciliation in the Church Worldwide* (Delhi: ISPCK, 2005), pp. 43–61, p. 53.

17 Joint Working Group of the Roman Catholic Church and the World Council of Churches, *Common Witness* (Geneva: WCC Publications /Rome: SPCU, 1984).

18 Not Strangers but Pilgrims Inter-Church Process, *The Next Steps for Churches Together in Pilgrimage* (London: British Council of Churches and the Catholic Truth Society, 1989); see p. 3. See also David Butler, *Dying to Be One – English Ecumenism: History, Theology and the Future* (London: SCM Press, 1996).

19 World Council of Churches, *Towards a Common Understanding and Vision of the World Council of Churches* (1997) – available at <www.oikoumene.org>.

20 <http://<www.globalchristianforum.org/>.

21 Tim Naish, 'Mission, Migration and the Stranger in Our Midst', in Stephen Spencer (ed.), *Mission and Migration* (Sheffield: Cliff College Publishing, 2008), pp. 7–30.

22 For the experiences of Germans here, see Walther Bindemann (ed.), *'Strange Home Britain' – Memories and Experiences of Germans in Britain* (Edinburgh: Alpha Books, 2001).

23 Leon Murray, *Being Black in Britain: Challenge and Hope* (London: Chester House, 1995).

24 Gerrie Ter Haar, *Halfway to Paradise: African Christians in Europe* (Cardiff: Cardiff Academic Press, 1998); Afe Adogame and Cordula Weissköppel, *Religion in the Context of African Migration* (Bayreuth: Pia Thielmann and Eckhard Breitinger, 2005).

25 Gerrie ter Haar, 'African Christians in Europe', in Spencer, *Mission and Migration*, pp. 31–52.

26 The basis of this section is my personal experience of Korea and the Korean diaspora, and also the research carried out for a report I prepared on Anglican ministry to Koreans in Kingston Deanery in 2006. For this project I was helped by church leaders and members (especially Revd Canon Stewart Downey, Mr Seok Hee Lee and Mrs Suk Kyung Lee, Revd Mandy Beck, Revd Dr Paul Cho, Venerable Bill Jacob, Revd Luke Lee) and also by personnel of the London Borough of Kingston, where I had access to a recently compiled internal report on the Korean community.

27 Amos Yong, *The Spirit Poured Out on All Flesh: Pentecostalism and the Possibility of Global Theology* (Grand Rapids, MI: Baker Academic, 2005), p. 168.

28 Robert J. Schreiter, *The New Catholicity: Theology between the Global and the Local* (Maryknoll, NY: Orbis Books, 1997), pp. 116–33.

29 Paul D. Murray, *Receptive Ecumenism and the Call to Catholic Learning: Exploring a Way for Contemporary Ecumenism* (Oxford: Oxford University Press, 2008).

30 David B. Barrett, George T. Kurian and Todd M. Johnson (eds), *World Christian Encyclopedia* (Oxford: Oxford University Press, 2001), p. 12.

31 Bert Hoedemaker, 'Mission beyond Modernity: A Global Perspective', in Simon Barrow and Graeme Smith (eds), *Christian Mission in Western Society* (London: CTBI, 2001), pp. 212–33; see pp. 214–16.

32 William T. Cavanaugh, *Theopolitical Imagination: Discovering the Liturgy as a Political Act in an Age of Global Consumerism* (London: T&T Clark, 2002), pp. 97–121.

33 Guanghu He, 'A Religious Spirit: The Hope for Transnationalism in China Today', in Centre for Multireligious Studies, *Christian Theology and Intellectuals in China*, Occasional Paper (Aarhus: University of Aarhus, 2003), pp. 73–83.

SELECT BIBLIOGRAPHY

Websites

Anglican Communion, <www.anglicancommunion.org>.

CAFOD, <www.cafod.org.uk>.

China Study Centre of Churches Together in Britain and Ireland, <www.chinaonlinecentre.org>.

Christian Aid, <www.christian-aid.org.uk>.

Church in a Spiritual Age, The Group for Evangelization (Churches Together in England), <www.churchinaspiritualage.org.uk>.

Church Mission Society (CMS), <www.cms-uk.org>.

Church of England, <www.cofe.anglican.org>.

Conference on World Mission and Evangelism, Athens, 2005, <www.mission2005.org>.

Decade to Overcome Violence, World Council of Churches, <www.overcomingviolence.org>.

Dictionary of African Christian Biography website, <www.dacb.org>.

Edinburgh 2010, <www.edinburgh2010.org>.

Episcopal Church of the United States of America, http://ecusa.anglican.org/>.

Fresh Expressions, <www.freshexpressions.org.uk>.

Global Christian Forum, <www.globalchristianforum.org>.

Gospel and Our Culture Network, <www.gospel-culture.org.uk>.

Joshua Project, <www.joshuaproject.net>.

Kendal Project, <www.kendalproject.org.uk>.

Kingsway International Christian Church (KICC), London, <www.kicc.org.uk>.

Lausanne Movement, <www.lausanne.org>.

Methodist Church, <www.methodist.org.uk>.

Methodist Missionary Society History Project at the University of Edinburgh, <www.div.ed.ac.uk>.

Missional Church Network, <missionalchurchnetwork.com>.

OMF International, <www.omf.org>.
Open Doors, <www.opendoorsuk.org>.
Re:jesus, <www.rejesus.co.uk>.
'Religion and development' conference, Free University of Amsterdam, 14–15 June 2007, <www.religionanddevelopment.nl>.
Religions and Development Programme, University of Birmingham, <www.rad.bham.ac.uk>.
Rethinking Mission online journal, <www.rethinkingmission.org>.
Southern Baptist Convention, <www.sbc.net>.
Spiritual Journeys, The Mission Theological Advisory Group, <www.spiritualjourneys.org.uk>.
Tearfund, <www.tearfund.org>.
Vatican (The Holy See), <www.vatican.va>.
World Council of Churches, <www.oikoumene.org>.
World Values Survey, <www.worldvaluessurvey.org>.
Yoido Full Gospel Church, Seoul, <www.fgtv.org>.

Publications

Mission and world Christianity

Adogame, Afe, Roswith Gerloff and Klaus Hock (eds), *Christianity in Africa and the African Diaspora: The Appropriation of a Scattered Heritage* (London: Continuum, 2008).
_____ and Cordula Weissköppel, *Religion in the Context of African Migration* (Bayreuth: Bayreuth University, 2005).
Allen, Roland, *Missionary Methods: St Paul's or Ours?* (Grand Rapids, MI: Wm B. Eerdmans, 1962 [1912]).
Anderson, Allan, *An Introduction to Pentecostalism* (Cambridge: Cambridge University Press, 2004).
_____ *Zion and Pentecost: The Spirituality and Experience of Pentecostal and Zionist/Apostolic Churches in South Africa* (Pretoria: UNISA, 2000).
_____, and Walter J. Hollenweger (eds), *Pentecostals after a Century: Global Perspectives on a Movement in Transition* (Sheffield: Sheffield Academic Press, 1999).
Barrett, David B., George T. Kurian and Todd M. Johnson (eds), *World Christian Encyclopedia* (Oxford: Oxford University Press, 2001).
Bevans, Stephen B. and Roger P. Schroeder, *Constants in Context: A Theology of Mission for Today* (Maryknoll, NY: Orbis Books, 2004).
Bria, Ion (ed.), *Go Forth in Peace: Orthodox Perspectives on Mission* (Geneva: WCC Publications, 1986).

_____ *The Liturgy after the Liturgy: Mission and Witness from an Orthodox Perspective* (Geneva: WCC Publications, 1996).

Bosch, David J., *A Spirituality of the Road* (Scottdale, PA: Herald Press, 1979).

_____ *Transforming Mission: Paradigm Shifts in Theology of Mission* (Maryknoll, NY: Orbis Books, 1991).

_____ *Witness to the World: The Christian Mission in Theological Perspective* (London: Marshall, Morgan and Scott, 1980).

Cox, Harvey, *Fire From Heaven: The Rise of Pentecostal Spirituality and the Reshaping of Religion in the Twenty-first Century* (London: Cassell, 1996).

Daneel, Inus, *Quest for Belonging: Introduction to the Study of African Independent Churches* (Harare: Mambo Press, 1987).

Dempster, Murray W., Byron D. Klaus and Douglas Petersen (eds), *The Globalization of Pentecostalism: A Religion Made to Travel* (Oxford: Regnum, 1999).

Dorr, Donal, *Mission in Today's World* (Blackrock, Co. Dublin: The Columba Press, 2000).

Goheen, Michael W., *As the Father Has Sent Me* (Zoetermeer: Boekencentrum, 2000).

Goodall, Norman (ed.), *Missions under the Cross* (London: Edinburgh House Press, 1953).

Guder, Darrel L. (ed.), *Missional Church: A Vision for the Sending of the Church in North America* (Grand Rapids, MI: Eerdmans, 1998).

Hocking, William Ernest, *Re-thinking Missions: A Laymen's Inquiry after One Hundred Years* (New York: Harper and Brothers, 1932).

Hrangkhuma, F. (ed.), *Christianity in India: Search for Liberation and Identity* (Delhi: ISPCK, 1998).

Hunter, Harold D. and Peter D. Hocken (eds), *All Together in One Place: Theological Papers from the Brighton Conference on World Evangelization* (Sheffield: Sheffield Academic Press, 1990).

Jenkins, Philip, *The Next Christendom: The Coming of Global Christianity* (Oxford: Oxford University Press, 2002).

_____ (ed.), *The New Faces of Christianity: Believing the Bible in the Global South* (Oxford: Oxford University Press, 2006).

John Paul II, *Redemptoris Missio* ('On the Permanent Validity of the Church's Missionary Mandate') (1990) – available at <www.vatican.va>.

Johnson, Eleanor and John Clark (eds), *Anglicans in Mission: A Transforming Journey* (London: SPCK, 2000).

Kim, Kirsteen, *The Holy Spirit in the World: A Global Conversation* (Maryknoll, NY: Orbis Books, 2007).

_____ *Mission in the Spirit: The Holy Spirit in Indian Christian Theologies* (Delhi: ISPCK, 2003).

Kim, Sebastian and Kirsteen Kim, *Christianity as a World Religion* (London: Continuum, 2008).

Kirk, J. Andrew, *What Is Mission? Theological Explorations* (London: Darton, Longman and Todd, 1999).

Lambert, Tony, *China's Christian Millions*, rvsd edn (Oxford: Monarch, 2006).

Langmead, Ross, *The Word Made Flesh: Towards an Incarnational Missiology* (Lanham, MD: University Press of America, 2004).

Lausanne Committee for World Evangelization, *The Lausanne Covenant* (1974) – available at <www.lausanne.org>.

Lord, Andrew, *Spirit-shaped Mission: A Holistic Charismatic Missiology* (Milton Keynes: Paternoster, 2005).

Martin, David, *Pentecostalism: The World Their Parish* (Oxford: Blackwell, 2002).

Matthey, Jacques (ed.), *'Come, Holy Spirit, heal and reconcile': Report of the World Council of Churches Conference on Mission and Evangelism, Athens, May 2005* (Geneva: WCC Publications, 2008).

_____ *'You are the light of the world': Statements on Mission by the World Council of Churches 1980–2005* (Geneva: WCC Publications, 2005).

Moltmann, Jürgen, *The Church in the Power of the Spirit*, 2nd edn, trans. Margaret Kohl (London: SCM Press, 1992 [1977]).

_____ *The Spirit of Life: A Universal Affirmation*, trans. Margaret Kohl (London: SCM Press, 1992).

Nazir-Ali, Michael, *From Everywhere to Everywhere: A World View of Christian Mission* (London: Collins, 1991).

Nessan, Craig L., *Beyond Maintenance to Mission: A Theology of the Congregation* (Minneapolis, MN: Fortress Press, 1999).

Newbigin, Lesslie, *The Open Secret: An Introduction to the Theology of Mission*, rvsd edn (Grand Rapids, MI: Wm B. Eerdmans, 1995).

Oduyoye, Mercy Amba, *Hearing and Knowing: Theological Reflections on Christianity in Africa* (Maryknoll, NY: Orbis Books, 1986).

Okure, Teresa, *The Johannine Approach to Mission: A Contextual Study of John 4.1–42* (Tübingen: J. C. B. Mohr, 1988).

Pobee, John S. and Gabriel Ositelu II, *African Initiatives in Christianity* (Geneva: WCC Publications, 1998).

Rayan, Samuel, *Come Holy Spirit* (Delhi: Media House, 1998).

Rivers, Robert S., *From Maintenance to Mission: Evangelization and the Revitalization of the Parish* (New York: Paulist Press, 2005).

Saayman, Willem and Klippies Kritzinger (eds), *Mission in Bold Humility: David Bosch's Work Considered* (Maryknoll, NY: Orbis Books, 1996).

Sanneh, Lamin, and Joel A. Carpenter (eds), *The Changing Face of Christianity: Africa, the West and the World* (Oxford: Oxford University Press, 2005).

Senior, Donald and Carroll Stuhlmueller, *The Biblical Foundations for Mission* (London: SCM Press, 1983).

Smith, Christian and Joshua Pokopy (eds), *Latin American Religion in Motion* (New York: Routledge, 1999).

Spencer, Stephen (ed.), *Mission and Migration* (Sheffield: Cliff College Publishing, 2008).

Sunquist, Scott W. (ed.), *Dictionary of Asian Christianity* (Grand Rapids, MI: Wm B. Eerdmans, 2001).

Taylor, John V., *The Go-between God: The Holy Spirit and the Christian Mission* (London: SCM Press, 1972).

Ter Haar, Gerrie, *Halfway to Paradise: African Christians in Europe* (Cardiff: Cardiff Academic Press, 1998).

Thomas, Norman E. (ed.), *Classic Texts in Mission and World Christianity* (Maryknoll, NY: Orbis Books, 1995).

Vähäkangas, Mika, and Andrew A. Kyomo (eds), *Charismatic Renewal in Africa: A Challenge to African Christianity* (Nairobi: Acton Publishers, 2003).

Van der Veer, Peter (ed.), *Conversion to Modernities: The Globalization of Christianity* (New York: Routledge, 1996).

Van Gelder, Craig, *The Ministry of the Missional Church: A Community Led by the Spirit* (Grand Rapids: Baker Books, 2007).

Vatican II, *Ad Gentes* ('Decree on the mission activity of the Church') (1965) – available at <www.vatican.va>.

Walls, Andrew and Cathy Ross (eds), *Mission in the 21st Century: Exploring the Five Marks of Mission* (London: Darton, Longman and Todd, 2008).

Wild-Wood, Emma, *Migration and Christian Identity in Congo (DRC)* (Leiden: Brill, 2008).

World Council of Churches (Faith and Order Commission), *The Nature and Mission of the Church* (Geneva: WCC Publications, 2005).

Yates, Timothy, *Christian Mission in the Twentieth Century* (Cambridge: Cambridge University Press, 1994).

_____ (ed.), *Mission – an Invitation to God's Future* (Sheffield: Cliff College Press, 2000).

_____ (ed.), *Mission and the Next Christendom* (Sheffield: Cliff College, 2005).

History of the world Christian movement

Anderson, Allan H., *African Reformation: African Initiated Christianity in the Twentieth Century* (Trenton, NJ: Africa World Press, 2001).

_____ *Spreading Fires: The Missionary Nature of Early Pentecostalism* (London: SCM Press, 2007).

Anderson, Gerald H., Robert T. Coote, Norman A. Horner and James M.

Phillips (eds), *Mission Legacies: Biographical Studies of Leaders of the Modern Missionary Movement* (Maryknoll, NY: Orbis Books, 1994).

Armour, Rollin, *Islam, Christianity, and the West: A Troubled History* (Maryknoll, NY: Orbis Books, 2002).

Ayegboyin, Deji and S. Ademola Ishola, *African Indigenous Churches: An Historical Perspective* (Lagos: Greater Heights Publications, 1997).

Bays, Daniel H. (ed.), *Christianity in China, from the Eighteenth Century to the Present* (Stanford, CA: Stanford University Press, 1996).

Beaver, R. Pierce, *American Protestant Women in World Mission* (Grand Rapids, MI: Wm B. Eerdmans, 1980).

Bebbington, D. W., *Evangelicalism in Modern Britain: A History from the 1730s to the 1980s* (London: Routledge, 1989).

Broomhall, Alfred, *Hudson Taylor and China's Open Century*, 7 vols (London: Hodder and Stoughton, 1982–89).

Buswell Jr, Robert E. and Timothy S. Lee (eds), *Christianity in Korea* (Honolulu: University of Hawaii, 2006).

Chaillot, Christine, *The Ethiopian Orthodox Tewahedo Church Tradition: A Brief Introduction to Its Life and Spirituality* (Paris: Inter-Orthodox Dialogue, 2002).

Chapman, Colin, *Whose Promised Land? The Continuing Crisis Over Israel and Palestine* (Oxford: Lion, 2002).

Clark, Donald N., *Christianity in Modern Korea* (Lanham, MD: University Press of America, 1986).

Dussel, Enrique, *A History of the Church in Latin America*, trans. Alan Neely (Grand Rapids, MI: Wm B. Eerdmans, 1981).

England, John C., *The Hidden History of Christianity in Asia: The Churches of the East before 1500* (Delhi: ISPCK, 1996).

Fey, Harold E. (ed.), *A History of the Ecumenical Movement, Vol. II: 1948–68*, 4th edn (Geneva: WCC Publications, 1993).

Fiedler, Klaus, *The Story of Faith Missions* (Oxford: Regnum, 1994).

Fiorenza, Elisabeth Schüssler, *In Memory of Her: A Feminist Theological Reconstruction of Christian Origins* (London: SCM Press, 1983).

Gausted, Edwin S. and Leigh E. Schmidt, *The Religious History of America*, rvsd edn (New York: HarperCollins, 2002).

Gutiérrez, Gustavo, *Las Casas: In Search of the Poor of Jesus Christ*, trans. Robert R. Barr (Maryknoll, NY: Orbis Books, 1993 [1992]).

Hastings, Adrian (ed.), *A World History of Christianity* (London: Cassell, 1999).

Hollenweger, Walter J., *Pentecostalism: Origins and Developments Worldwide* (Peabody, MA: Hendrickson Publishers, 1997).

Irvin, Dale T., and Scott W. Sunquist, *History of the World Christian Movement, Vol I: Earliest Christianity to 1453* (Maryknoll, NY: Orbis Books, 2001).

Isichei, Elizabeth, *A History of Christianity in Africa, from Antiquity to the Present* (Grand Rapids, MI: Wm B. Eerdmans, 1995).

McManners, John (ed.), *The Oxford History of Christianity*, 2nd edn (Oxford: Oxford University Press, 2002).

Moffett, Samuel Hugh, *A History of Christianity in Asia, Vol. I: Beginnings to 1500* (Maryknoll, NY: Orbis Books, 2001).

_____ *A History of Christianity in Asia, Vol. II: 1500–1900* (Maryknoll, NY: Orbis Books, 2005).

Mullins, Mark R., *Christianity Made in Japan: A Study of Indigenous Movements* (Honolulu: University of Hawaii Press, 1998).

Myung, Sung-Hoon and Hong Young-Gi (eds), *Charis and Charisma: David Yonggi Cho and the Growth of Yoido Full Gospel Church* (Oxford: Regnum Books, 2003).

Noll, Mark A., *American Evangelical Christianity: An Introduction* (Oxford: Blackwell, 2001).

Norris, Frederick W., *Christianity: A Short Global History* (Oxford: Oneworld, 2002).

O'Connor, Daniel, and others, *Three Centuries of Mission: The United Society for the Propagation of the Gospel, 1701–2000* (London: Continuum, 2002).

O'Mahony, Anthony (ed.), *Eastern Christianity: Studies in Modern History, Religion and Politics* (London: Melisende, 2004).

Pirouet, Louise, *Black Evangelists: The Spread of Christianity in Uganda, 1891–1914* (London: Collings, 1978).

Robert, Dana Lee, *American Women in Mission*, 2nd edn (Macon GA: Mercer University Press, 1997).

Ross, Cathy Rae, *Women with a Mission: Rediscovering Missionary Wives in Early New Zealand* (Auckland, NZ: Penguin, 2006).

Rouse, Ruth and Stephen C. Neill (eds), *A History of the Ecumenical Movement, Vol. I: 1517–1948*, 4th edn (Geneva: WCC Publications, 1993).

Semple, Rhonda, *Missionary Women: Gender, Professionalism, and the Victorian Idea of Christian Mission* (Rochester, NY : Boydell Press, 2003).

Spickard, Paul R. and Kevin M. Cragg, *A Global History of Christians: How Everyday Believers Experienced Their World* (Grand Rapids, MI: Baker Academic, 1994).

Stanley, Brian, *The Bible and the Flag: Protestant Missions and British Imperialism in the Nineteenth and Twentieth Centuries* (Leicester: Apollos, 1990).

_____ *The History of the Baptist Missionary Society, 1792–1992* (Edinburgh: T&T Clark, 1992).

_____ *The World Missionary Conference: Edinburgh 1910* (Grand Rapids, MI: Wm B. Eerdmans, 2009).

Sunquist, Scott W. (ed.), *A Dictionary of Asian Christianity* (Grand Rapids, MI: Wm B. Eerdmans, 2001), pp. 139–46.

Thorogood, Bernard, *Gales of Change: Responding to a Shifting Missionary Context: The Story of the London Missionary Society, 1945–1977* (Geneva: WCC Publications, 1994).

Tucker, Ruth A., *From Jerusalem to Irian Jaya: A Biographical History of Christian Missions* (Grand Rapids, MI: Zondervan, 1983).

_____ and Walter Liefeld, *Daughters of the Church: Women and Ministry from New Testament Times to the Present* (Grand Rapids, MI: Zondervan, 1987).

Walls, Andrew F., *The Missionary Movement in Christian History: Studies in the Transmission of Faith* (Maryknoll, NY: Orbis Books, 1996).

_____ *The Cross-cultural Process in Christian History: Studies in the Transmission and Appropriation of Faith* (Maryknoll, NY: Orbis Books, 2002).

Ward, Kevin and Brian Stanley (eds), *The Church Mission Society and World Christianity, 1799–1999* (Grand Rapids, MI: Wm B. Eerdmans, 2000).

Williams, Peter, *America's Religions: Traditions and Cultures* (New York: Macmillan, 1990).

Yates, Timothy, *The Expansion of Christianity* (Oxford: Lion Publishing, 2004).

Yu, Chai-shin (ed.), *The Founding of Catholic Tradition in Korea* (Mississauga, Ontario: Korea and Related Studies Press, 1996).

_____ *Korea and Christianity* (Fremont, CA: Asian Humanities Press, 2004).

Gospel, cultures, religions and spirituality

Abhishiktananda, *Hindu-Christian Meeting Point: Within the Cave of the Heart*, rvsd edn (Delhi: ISPCK, 1976 [1965]).

Anderson, Allan, *Moya: The Holy Spirit in an African Context* (Pretoria: UNISA, 1991).

Arbuckle, Gerald A., *Earthing the Gospel: An Inculturation Handbook for the Pastoral Worker* (Maryknoll, NY: Orbis Books, 1990).

Barrow, Simon and Graeme Smith (eds), *Christian Mission in Western Society* (London: CTBI, 2001).

Beckford, Robert, *Jesus Is Dread: Black Theology and Black Culture in Britain* (London: Darton, Longman and Todd, 1998).

Bediako, Kwame, *Theology and Identity: The Impact of Culture upon Christian Thought in the Second Century and Modern Africa* (Oxford: Regnum Books, 1992).

Berger, Peter L., *A Rumour of Angels: Modern Society and the Rediscovery of the Supernatural* (London: Penguin, 1970).

Bevans, Stephen B., *Models of Contextual Theology* (Maryknoll, NY: Orbis Books, 1992).

Braybrooke, Marcus, *Pilgrimage of Hope: One Hundred Years of Global Interfaith Dialogue* (London: SCM Press, 1992).

Burrows, William R. (ed.), *Redemption and Dialogue: Reading* Redemptoris Missio *and Dialogue and Proclamation* (Maryknoll, NY: Orbis Books, 1993).

Conn, Joann Wolski, *Women's Spirituality: Resources for Christian Development*, 2nd edn (Mahwah, NJ: Paulist Press, November 1996).

Cray, Graham (ed.), *Mission-shaped Church: Church Planting and Fresh Expressions of Church in a Changing Context* (London: Church House Publishing, 2004) – available at <www.cofe.anglican.org>.

Davie, Grace, *Europe: The Exceptional Case. Parameters of Faith in the Modern World* (London: Darton, Longman and Todd, 2002).

_____ *Religion in Britain since 1945: Believing without Belonging* (Oxford: Blackwell, 1994).

_____ *Religion in Modern Europe: A Memory Mutates* (Oxford: Oxford University Press, 2000).

Donovan, Vincent J., *Christianity Rediscovered: An Epistle from the Masai*, 3rd edn (London: SCM Press, 2001).

Drane, John, *The McDonaldization of the Church: Spirituality, Creativity, and the Future of the Church* (London: Darton, Longman and Todd, 2000).

Dupuis, Jacques, *Jesus Christ and His Spirit* (Bangalore: Theological Publications in India, 1977).

_____ *Toward a Christian Theology of Religious Pluralism* (Maryknoll, NY: Orbis Books, 1999 [1997]).

Duraisingh, Christopher (ed.), *Called to One Hope: The Gospel in Diverse Cultures: Report of the Conference of the CWME, Salvador, Brazil, 1996* (Geneva: WCC Publications, 1998).

Ford, David F., *Shaping Theology: Engagements in a Religious and Secular World* (Oxford: Blackwell, 2007).

Foust, Thomas F., George R. Hunsberger, J. Andrew Kirk and Werner Ustorf (eds), *A Scandalous Prophet: The Way of Mission after Newbigin* (Grand Rapids, MI: Wm B. Eerdmans, 2001).

Gilliland, Dean S. (ed.), *The Word among Us: Contextualizing Theology for Mission Today* (Dallas, TX: Word Publishers, 1989).

Gnanakan, Ken R., *The Pluralistic Predicament* (Bangalore: Theological Book Trust, 1992).

Gorringe, Timothy J., *Discerning Spirit: A Theology of Revelation* (London: SCM Press, 1990).

_____ *Furthering Humanity: A Theology of Culture* (Aldershot: Ashgate, 2004).

Gossai, Hemchand and Nathaniel Samuel Murrell (eds), *Religion, Culture, and Tradition in the Caribbean* (London: Macmillan, 2000).

Guder, Darrel L. (ed.), *Missional Church: A Vision for the Sending of the Church in North America* (Grand Rapids, MI: Wm B. Eerdmans, 1998).

Hedlund, Roger E. (ed.), *Christianity Is Indian: The Emergence of an Indigenous Community* (Delhi: ISPCK, 2000).

Heelas, Paul and Linda Woodhead, *The Spiritual Revolution: Why Religion is Giving Way to Spirituality* (Oxford: Blackwell 2004).

Heim, S. Mark, *Salvations: Truth and Difference in Religion* (Maryknoll, NY: Orbis Books, 1995).

Hesselgrave, David J., *Communicating Christ Cross-culturally* (Grand Rapids, MI: Zondervan, 1991).

Hick, John, *God and the Universe of Faiths* (Basingstoke: Macmillan, now Palgrave Macmillan, 1988).

____ and Paul F. Knitter (eds), *The Myth of Christian Uniqueness: Toward a Pluralistic Theology of Religions* (Maryknoll, NY: Orbis Books, 1987).

Hiebert, Paul G., *Anthropological Insights for Missionaries* (Grand Rapids, MI: Baker Book House, 1985).

Hollinghurst, Steve, Yvonne Richmond and Roger Whitehead, with Janice Price and Tina Adams, *Equipping Your Church in a Spiritual Age* (London: Church House Publishing, 2005).

Hull, John, *Mission-shaped Church: A Theological Response* (London: SCM Press, 2006).

Hunsberger, George R., *Bearing the Witness of the Spirit: Lesslie Newbigin's Theology of Cultural Plurality* (Grand Rapids, MI: Wm B. Eerdmans, 1998).

____ and Craig Van Gelder (eds), *The Church between Gospel and Culture: The Emerging Mission in North America* (Grand Rapids, MI: Eerdmans, 1996).

Job, G. V., P. Chenchiah, V. Chakkarai, D. M. Devasahayam, S. Jesudason, Eddy Asirvatham and A. N. Sudarisanam, *Rethinking Christianity in India* (Madras: A. N. Sudarisanam, 1938).

Jongeneel, Jan A. B., *Pentecost, Mission and Ecumenism: Essays on Intercultural Theology* (Frankfurt am Main: Peter Lang, 1992).

Kim, Sebastian C. H., *In Search of Identity: Debates on Religious Conversion in India* (Delhi: Oxford University Press, 2003).

Kinnamon, Michael (ed.), *Signs of the Spirit: Official Report of the Seventh Assembly of the World Council of Churches, Canberra, 1991* (Geneva: WCC Publications, 1991).

Kirk, J. Andrew and Kevin J. Vanhoozer (eds), *To Stake a Claim: Mission and the Western Crisis of Knowledge* (Maryknoll, NY: Orbis Books, 1999).

Knitter, Paul F., *No Other Name? A Critical Survey of Christian Attitudes toward the World Religions* (Maryknoll, NY: Orbis Books, 1985).

_____ *One Earth Many Religions: Multifaith Dialogue and Global Responsibility* (Maryknoll, NY: Orbis Books, 1995).

Kraemer, Hendrik, *The Christian Message in a Non-Christian World* (London: Edinburgh House, 1938).

Kraft, Charles H., *Anthropology for Christian Witness* (Maryknoll, NY: Orbis Books, 1996).

_____ *Christianity in Culture: A Study in Dynamic Biblical Theologizing in Cross-Cultural Perspective* (Maryknoll, NY: Orbis Books, 1979).

_____ *Communication Theory for Christian Witness* (Maryknoll, NY: Orbis Books, 1991).

Lausanne Committee for World Evangelization, *The Willowbank Report: Consultation on Gospel and Culture*, Lausanne Occasional Paper 2 (1978) – available at <www.lausanne.org>.

Luzbetak, Louis J., *The Church and Cultures: New Perspectives in Missiological Anthropology* (Maryknoll, NY: Orbis Books, 1988).

Lynch, Gordon, *Understanding Theology and Popular Culture* (Oxford: Blackwell, 2005).

Marsden, George M., *Fundamentalism and American Culture*, 2nd edn (Oxford: Oxford University Press, 2006).

Martin, David, *On Secularization: Towards a Revised General Theory* (Burlington, VT: Ashgate, 2005).

Mbiti, John, *Bible and Theology in African Christianity* (Nairobi: Oxford University Press, 1986).

Mellor, Howard and Timothy Yates, *Mission and Spirituality: Creative Ways of Being Church* (Sheffield: Cliff College Publishing, 2002).

Middleton, J. Richard and Brian J. Walsh, *Truth Is Stranger than It Used to Be: Biblical Faith in a Postmodern Age* (Downers Grove, IL: InterVarsity Press, 1995).

Mojzes, Paul and Leonard Swidler (eds), *Christian Mission and Interreligious Dialogue* (Lewiston: Edwin Mellen Press, 1990).

Mugambi, J. N. K., *Christianity and African Culture* (Nairobi: Acton Publishers, 2002).

Newbigin, Lesslie, *Foolishness to the Greeks: The Gospel and Western Culture* (London: SPCK, 1986).

_____ *The Gospel in a Pluralist Society* (London: SPCK, 1989).

_____ *The Other Side of 1984: Questions for the Churches* (Geneva: WCC Publications, 1983).

_____ *Proper Confidence: Faith, Doubt, and Certainty in Christian Discipleship* (Grand Rapids, MI: Eerdmans, 1995).

Niebuhr, H. Richard, *Christ and Culture* (New York: Harper and Row, 1951).

Panikkar, Raimundo, *The Unknown Christ of Hinduism: Towards an Ecumenical Christophany* rvsd edn (London: Darton, Longman and Todd, 1981).

Park, Jong Chun, *Crawl with God, Dance in the Spirit! A Creative Formation of Korean Theology of the Spirit* (Nashville, TN: Abingdon Press 1998).

Parratt, John, *Reinventing Christianity: African Theology Today* (Grand Rapids, MI: Wm B. Eerdmans, 1995).

Pelikan, Jaroslav, *Jesus through the Centuries: His Place in the History of Culture* (Yale: Yale University Press, 1999).

Pinnock, Clark H., *A Wideness in God's Mercy: The Finality of Jesus Christ in a World of Religions* (Grand Rapids, MI: Zondervan, 1992).

Race, Alan, *Christians and Religious Pluralism: Patterns in the Christian Theology of Religions* (London: SCM Press, 1983).

Ramachandra, Vinoth, *The Recovery of Mission: Beyond the Pluralist Paradigm* (Carlisle: Paternoster, 1996).

Richards, Anne (ed.), *Sense Making Faith: Body, Spirit, Journey* (London: Churches Together In Britain and Ireland, 2008).

Samartha, Stanley J., *Between Two Cultures: Ecumenical Ministry in a Pluralist World* (Geneva: WCC Publications, 1996).

_____ *The Hindu Response to the Unbound Christ: Towards a Christology in India* (Bangalore: CISRS, 1974).

_____ *One Christ – Many Religions: Towards a Revised Christology* (Maryknoll, NY: Orbis Books, 1991).

Samuel, Vinay and Christopher Sugden (eds), *Mission as Transformation: A Theology of the Whole Gospel* (Oxford: Regnum Books, 1999).

Sanders, John, *No Other Name: Can Only Christians Be Saved?* (London: SPCK, 1994).

Sanneh, Lamin, *Translating the Message: The Missionary Impact on Culture* (Maryknoll, NY: Orbis Books, 1989).

_____ *West African Christianity: The Religious Impact* (London: C. Hurst, 1983).

Scherer, James A. and Stephen B. Bevans (eds), *New Directions in Mission and Evangelization 3: Faith and Culture* (Maryknoll, NY: Orbis Books, 1999).

Schreiter, Robert, *Constructing Local Theologies* (Maryknoll, NY: Orbis Books, 1985).

Selvanayagam, Israel, *A Dialogue on Dialogue: Reflections on Interfaith Encounters* (Madras: CLS, 1995).

_____ *A Second Call: Ministry and Mission in a Multifaith Milieu* (Madras: CLS, 2000).

Shorter, Aylward, *Evangelization and Culture* (London: Geoffrey Chapman, 1994).

Shourie, Arun, *Missionaries in India: Continuities, Changes, Dilemmas* (New Delhi: ASA Publications, 1994).

Singh, David Emmanuel and Bernard Farr (eds), *Christianity and Cultures: Shaping Christian Thinking in Context* (Oxford: Regnum Books, 2008).

Stark, Rodney and Roger Finke, *Acts of Faith: Explaining the Human Side of Religion* (Berkeley, CA: University of California Press, 2000).

Stinton, Diane B., *Jesus of Africa: Voices of Contemporary African Christology* (Maryknoll, NY: Orbis Books, 2004).

Sugirtharajah, R. S., *Postcolonial Biblical Reader* (Oxford: Blackwell Publishing, 2006).

_____ *A Postcolonial Commentary on the New Testament Writings* (London: Continuum, 2007).

_____ (ed.), *Frontiers in Asian Christian Theology: Emerging Trends* (Maryknoll, NY: Orbis Books, 1994).

_____ (ed.), *Postcolonial Bible* (Sheffield: Sheffield Academic Press, 1998).

_____ (ed.), *Vernacular Hermeneutics* (Sheffield: Sheffield Academic Press, 1999).

Sumithra, Sunand (ed.), *Doing Theology in Context* (Bangalore: Theological Book Trust, 1992).

Tacey, David, *The Spirituality Revolution: The Emergence of Contemporary Spirituality* (New York: Brunner-Routledge, 2004).

Thomas, M. M., *The Acknowledged Christ of the Indian Renaissance*, 3rd edn (Madras: CLS, 1991 [1970]).

Tippett, Alan R., *Introduction to Missiology* (Pasadena, CA: William Carey Library, 1987).

Ustorf, Werner, *Sailing on the Next Tide: Missions, Missiology, and the Third Reich* (Oxford: Peter Lang, 2000).

Vandana, *And the Mother of Jesus Was There: Mary in the Light of Indian Spirituality* (Garhwal, UP: Jeevan Dhara Ashram Society, 1991).

_____ *Waters of Fire* (Bangalore: Asia Trading Corporation, 1989).

_____ (ed.), *Christian Ashrams: A Movement with a Future?* (Delhi: ISPCK, 1993).

_____ *Shabda, Shakti Sangam* (Bangalore: NBCLC, 1995).

Vanhoozer, Kevin J. (ed.), *Postmodern Theology* (Cambridge: Cambridge University Press, 2003).

Vatican II, *Nostra Aetate* ('Declaration on the relation of the Church to non-Christian religions') (1965) – available at <www.vatican.va>.

Ward, Graham (ed.), *The Postmodern God* (Oxford: Blackwell, 1997).

_____ (ed.), *Postmodern Theology* (Oxford: Blackwell, 2001).

Ward, Pete, *Liquid Church* (Carlisle: Paternoster Press, 2002).

Welker, Michael, *God the Spirit*, trans. John F. Hoffmeyer (Minneapolis, MN: Fortress Press, 1994).
Wiarda, Howard J., *The Soul of Latin America: The Cultural and Political Tradition* (New Haven: Yale Divinity Press, 2001).
Wilson, F. R. (ed.), *The San Antonio Report* (Geneva: WCC Publications, 1990).
World Council of Churches, *Guidelines for Dialogue* (1979) – available at <www.oikoumene.org>.
Yong, Amos, *Discerning the Spirit(s): A Pentecostal-charismatic Contribution to Christian Theology of Religions* (Sheffield: Sheffield Academic Press, 2000).

Mission, power, justice and development

Anderson, Gerald H. and Thomas F. Stransky (eds), *Mission Trends 3: Third World Theologies* (New York: Paulist Press/Grand Rapids, MI: Wm B. Eerdmans, 1976).
Armstrong, Karen, *The Battle for God* (New York: Alfred A. Knopf, 2000).
Barton, Mukti, *Scripture as Empowerment for Liberation and Justice: The Experience of Christian and Muslim Women in Bangladesh* (Bristol: University of Bristol, 1999).
Belshaw, Deryke and Robert Calderisi (eds), *Faith in Development* (Oxford: Regnum, 2001).
Boesak, Allan Aubrey, *Farewell to Innocence: A Socio-ethical Study on Black Theology and Power* (Maryknoll, NY: Orbis Books, 1977).
Boff, Leonardo, *Ecclesiogenesis: The Base Communities Reinvent the Church* trans. Robert R. Barr (London: Collins, 1986).
____ and Virgil Elizondo (eds), *1492–1992: The Voice of the Victims* (London: SCM Press, 1990).
Bonino, José Miguez, *Doing Theology in a Revolutionary Situation* (Philadelphia, PA: Fortress Press, 1975).
Brown, Terry (ed.), *Other Voices, Other Worlds: The Global Church Speaks Out on Homosexuality* (London: Darton, Longman and Todd, 2006).
Bruce, Steve, *Fundamentalism* (Cambridge: Polity, 2000).
Brueggemann, Walter, *The Prophetic Imagination* (London: SCM Press, 1992).
Caipora Women's Group, *Women in Brazil* (London: Latin America Bureau, 1993).
Cavanaugh, William T., *Theopolitical Imagination: Discovering the Liturgy As a Political Act in an Age of Global Consumerism* (London: T&T Clark, 2002).
Charles, Rodger, *Christian Social Witness and Teaching: The Catholic*

Tradition from Genesis to Centesimus Annus (Leominster: Gracewing, 1998).

Cleary, Edward L. and Hannah W. Stewart-Gambino (eds), *Power, Politics and Pentecostals in Latin America* (Boulder, CO: Westview, 1998).

Comblin, José, *The Holy Spirit and Liberation* (Maryknoll, NY: Orbis Books, 1989).

Commission on Theological Concerns of the Christian Conference of Asia (ed.), *Minjung Theology: People as the Subjects of History* (London: Zed Press, 1981).

Cone, James H., *A Black Theology of Liberation*, 3rd edn (Maryknoll, NY: Orbis Books, 1990 [1970]).

Curran, Charles E., *Catholic Social Teaching, 1891–Present* (Washington DC: Georgetown University Press, 2002).

Daly, Mary, *Beyond God the Father: Toward a Philosophy of Women's Liberation* (London: The Women's Press, 1973).

Davis, Kortright, *Emancipation Still Comin': Explorations in Caribbean Emancipatory Theology* (Maryknoll, NY: Orbis Books, 1990).

De Gruchy, John W., *The Church Struggle in South Africa* 3rd edn (London: SCM Press, 2004).

Deberri, E. P. and J. E. Hug, with P. J. Henriot and M. J. Schultheis, *Catholic Social Teaching: Our Best Kept Secret*, 4th edn (Maryknoll, NY: Orbis Books, 2003).

Devasahayam, V., *Frontiers of Dalit Theology* (Delhi: ISPCK, 1997).

Dorr, Donal, *Option for the Poor: A Hundred Years of Vatican Social Teaching*, rvsd edn (Maryknoll, NY: Orbis Books, 1992).

Ela, Jean-Marc, *My Faith as an African* (Maryknoll, NY: Orbis Books, 1988).

Elizondo, Virgil, *Guadalupe, Mother of a New Creation* (Maryknoll, NY: Orbis Books, 1997).

Ellingsen, Mark, *The Cutting Edge: The Churches Speak on Social Issues* (Geneva, WCC Publications, 1993).

Fabella, Virginia and R. S. Sugirtharajah (eds), *Dictionary of Third World Theologies* (Maryknoll, NY: Orbis Books, 2000).

Forrester, Duncan B., *Caste and Christianity: Attitudes and Policies on Caste of Anglo-Saxon Protestant Missions in India* (London: Curzon Press, 1980).

Freston, Paul, *Evangelicals and Politics in Asia, Africa and Latin America* (Cambridge: Cambridge University Press, 2001).

Gill, David (ed.), *Gathered for Life: Report of the 6th Assembly of the World Council of Churches, Canada, 24 July–10 August 1983* (Geneva: WCC Publications, 1983).

Gutiérrez, Gustavo, *A Theology of Liberation*, trans. Caridad Inda and John Eagleson (Maryknoll, NY: Orbis Books, 1973 [1971]).

Gutiérrez, Gustavo, *We Drink from Our Own Wells: The Spiritual Journey of a People* (Maryknoll, NY: Orbis Books, 1984).

Hennelly, A. T., *Liberation Theology: A Documentary History* (Maryknoll, Orbis Books, 1990).

Hopkins, Dwight N., *Introducing Black Theology of Liberation* (Maryknoll, NY: Orbis Books, 1999).

Hughes, Dewi A. with M. Bennett, *God of the Poor: A Biblical Vision of God's Present Rule* (Carlisle: OM Publishing, 1998).

Isasi-Díaz, Ada María, *Mujerista Theology: A Theology for the Twenty-first Century* (Maryknoll, NY: Orbis Books, 1996).

Jagessar, Michael N. and Anthony C. Reddie (eds), *Postcolonial Black British Theology: New Textures and Themes* (Peterborough: Epworth, 2007).

John Paul II, *Centesimus Annus* ('On the hundredth anniversary') (1991) – available at <www.vatican.va>.

_____ *Sollicitudo Rei Socialis* ('On social concern') (1987) – available at <www.vatican.va>.

Juergensmeyer, Mark, *Terror in the Mind of God: The Global Rise of Religious Violence*, 3rd edn (Berkeley, CA: University of California Press, 2003).

Kappen, Sebastian (ed.), *Jesus Today* (Madras: AICUF, 1985).

Katoppo, Marianne, *Compassionate and Free: An Asian Woman's Theology* (Geneva: WCC Publications, 1979).

Keller, Catherine, Michael Nausner and Mayra Riviera (eds), *Postcolonial Theologies: Divinity and Empire* (St Louis, MO: Chalice Press, 2004).

Kim, Sebastian C. H. (ed.), *Christian Theology in Asia* (Cambridge: Cambridge University Press, 2008).

Kinnamon, Michael (ed.), *Signs of the Spirit: Official Report of the Seventh Assembly of the World Council of Churches, Canberra, 1991* (Geneva: WCC Publications, 1991).

Kirk, J. Andrew, *Loosing the Chains: Religion as Opium and Liberation* (London: Hodder & Stoughton, 1992).

Klaiber, Jeffrey, *The Church, Dictatorships, and Democracy in Latin America* (Maryknoll, NY: Orbis Books, 1998).

Küng, Hans and Jürgen Moltmann, *Fundamentalism as an Ecumenical Challenge* (London: SCM Press, 1992).

Kwok, Pui-Lan, *Introducing Asian Feminist Theology* (Sheffield: Sheffield Academic Press, 2000).

Land, Steven J., *Pentecostal Spirituality: A Passion for the Kingdom* (Sheffield: Sheffield Academic Press, 1993).

Lausanne Committee for World Evangelization and the World Evangelical Fellowship, *Evangelism and Social Responsibility: An Evangelical Commitment*, Lausanne Occasional Paper 21 (1982), pp. 24–5 – available at <www.lausanne.org>.

Lowe, Chuck, *Territorial Spirits and World Evangelization? A Biblical, Historical and Missiological Critique of 'Strategic Level Spiritual Warfare'* (Sevenoaks, UK: Mentor, 1998).

McGavran, Donald A. and C. Peter C. Wagner, *Understanding Church Growth*, 3rd edn (Grand Rapids, MI: Wm B. Eerdmans, 1990).

Mathew, C. V., *The Saffron Mission: A Historical Analysis of Modern Hindu Missionary Ideologies and Practices* (Delhi: ISPCK, 1999).

_____ and Charles Corwin, *Area of Light: The Indian Church and Modernization* (Delhi: ISPCK, 1994).

Moltmann, Jürgen, *God for a Secular Society* (London: SCM Press, 1999).

Müller-Fahrenholz, Geiko, *God's Spirit: Transforming a World in Crisis* (Geneva: WCC Publications, 1995).

Oduyoye, Mercy Amba, *Beads and Strands: Reflections of an African Woman on Christianity in Africa* (Oxford: Regnum, 2002).

_____ *Introducing African Women's Theology* (Sheffield: Sheffield Academic Press, 2001).

Parratt, John (ed.), *A Reader in African Christian Theology*, 2nd edn (London: SPCK, 1997).

Parsons, Susan Frank (ed.), *The Cambridge Companion to Feminist Theology* (Cambridge: Cambridge University Press, 2002).

Paul VI, *Populorum progressio* ('On the development of peoples') (1967) – available at <www.vatican.va>.

Percy, Martyn, *Words, Wonders and Power: Understanding Contemporary Christian Fundamentalism and Revivalism* (London: SPCK, 1996).

Phillips, James M., *From the Rising of the Sun: Christians and Society in Contemporary Japan* (Maryknoll, NY: Orbis Books, 1981).

Pieris, Aloysius, *An Asian Theology of Liberation* (Maryknoll, NY: Orbis Books, 1988).

Ro, Bong Rin and Marlin L. Nelson (eds), *Korean Church Growth Explosion*, 2nd edn (Seoul: Word of Life Press, 1995).

Rowland, Christopher, *The Open Heaven: A Study of Apocalyptic in Judaism and Early Christianity* (London: SPCK, 1985).

Scott, Peter and William T. Cavanaugh (eds), *The Blackwell Companion to Political Theology* (Oxford: Blackwell, 2004).

Segundo, Juan Luis, *The Liberation of Theology*, trans John Drury (Maryknoll, NY: Orbis Books, 1976 [1975]).

Storrar, W. F. and A. R. Morton, *Public Theology for the 21st Century* (Edinburgh: T&T Clark, 2004).

Stott, John, *Christian Mission in the Modern World* (London: Church Pastoral Aid Society, 1975).

Sugirtharajah, R. S. *Asian Biblical Hermeneutics and Post Colonialism: Contesting the Interpretations* (Maryknoll, NY: Orbis Books, 1998).

Sugirtharajah, R. S. *The Bible and Empire: Postcolonial Explorations* (Cambridge: Cambridge University Press, 2005).

_____ *The Bible and the Third World: Precolonial, Colonial and Postcolonial Encounters* (Cambridge: Cambridge University Press, 2001).

_____ *Postcolonial Criticism and Biblical Interpretation* (Oxford: Oxford University Press, 2002).

_____ *Postcolonial Reconfigurations: An Alternative Way of Reading the Bible and Doing Theology* (London: SCM Press, 2003).

_____ (ed.), *Voices from the Margin: Interpreting the Bible from the Third World*, rvsd edn (Maryknoll, NY: Orbis Books, 1995).

Suh, David Kwang-sun, *The Korean Minjung in Christ* (Kowloon: Commission on Theological Concerns, Christian Conference of Asia, 1991).

Taylor, Michael, *Not Angels But Agencies* (London: SCM Press, 1995).

_____ *Poverty and Christianity* (London: SCM Press, 2000).

Thomas, Scott M., *The Global Resurgence of Religion and the Transformation of International Relations: The Struggle for the Soul of the Twenty-first Century* (New York: Palgrave Macmillan, 2005).

Wallis, Jim, *God's Politics: Why the Right Gets It Wrong and the Left Doesn't Get It* (New York: HarperCollins, 2005).

Wamue, Grace and Matthew M. Theuri (eds), *Quests for Integrity in Africa* (Nairobi: Acton Publishers, 2003).

Webster, John C. B., *The Dalit Christians: A History*, 2nd edn (Delhi: ISPCK, 1994).

Wells, Kenneth M., *New God, New Nation: Protestants and Self-reconstruction Nationalism in Korea, 1896–1937* (Honolulu: University of Hawaii Press, 1990).

West, Gerald and Musa Dube (eds), *The Bible in Africa: Transactions, Trajectories and Trends* (Leiden: Brill, 2000).

Williams, Lewin L., *Caribbean Theology* (Frankfurt: Peter Lang, 1994).

Wimber, John, *Power Evangelism* (New York: Harper and Row, 1985).

Wink, Walter, *Engaging the Powers: Discernment and Resistance in a World of Domination* (Minneapolis, MN: Fortress Press, 1992).

_____ *Naming the Powers: The Language of Power in the New Testament* (Minneapolis, MN: Fortress Press, 1984).

_____ *The Powers That Be: Theology for a New Millennium* (New York and London: Doubleday, 1998).

_____ *Unmasking the Powers: The Invisible Forces that Determine Human Existence* (Minneapolis, MN: Fortress Press, 1986).

Mission as healing, reconciliation and unity

Bookless, Dave, *Planetwise* (Leicester: Inter Varsity Press, 2008).

Briggs, John, Mercy Amba Oduyoye and Georges Tsetsis (eds), *A History of the Ecumenical Movement, Vol. 3: 1968–2000* (Geneva: WCC Publications, 2004).

Butler, David, *Dying to be One – English Ecumenism: History, Theology and the Future* (London: SCM Press 1996).

Deane-Drummond, Celia E., *Creation through Wisdom: Theology after the New Biology* (Edinburgh: T&T Clark, 2000).

____ *The Ethics of Nature* (Oxford: Blackwell, 2004).

____ *A Handbook in Theology and Ecology* (London: SCM Press, 1996).

Hallman, David G. (ed.), *Ecotheology: Voices from South and North* (Geneva: WCC Publications, 1994).

Ham, Sok Hon, *Queen of Suffering: A Spiritual History of Korea*, trans. E. Sang Yu; edited and abridged by John A. Sullivan (London: Friends World Committee for Consultation, 1985).

Joint Working Group of the Roman Catholic Church and the World Council of Churches, *Common Witness* (Geneva: WCC Publications /Rome: SPCU, 1984).

Kim, Kirsteen (ed.), *Reconciling Mission: The Ministry of Healing and Reconciliation in the Church Worldwide* (Delhi: SPCK, 2005).

Kim, Sebastian C. H., Pauline Kollontai and Greg Hoyland (eds), *Peace and Reconciliation: In Search of Shared Identity* (Aldershot, Hants: Ashgate, 2008).

Liechty, Joseph and Cecelia Clegg, *Moving beyond Sectarianism: Religion, Conflict and Reconciliation in Northern Ireland* (Blackrock, Co. Dublin: Columba Press, 2001).

Marak, Krickwin C. and Atul Y. Aghamkar (eds), *Ecological Challenge and Christian Mission* (Delhi: ISPCK, 1998).

Matthey, Jacques (ed.), *'Come, Holy Spirit, heal and reconcile': Report of the World Council of Churches Conference on Mission and Evangelism, Athens, May 2005* (Geneva: WCC Publications, 2008).

____ *'You are the light of the world': Statements on Mission by the World Council of Churches 1980-2005* (Geneva: WCC Publications, 2005).

Mellor, Howard and Timothy Yates (eds), *Mission, Violence and Reconciliation* (Sheffield: Cliff College Publishing, 2004).

Murray, Paul D., *Receptive Ecumenism and the Call to Catholic Learning: Exploring a Way for Contemporary Ecumenism* (Oxford: Oxford University Press, 2008).

Newbigin, Lesslie, *The Household of God*, 2nd edn (London: SCM Press, 1964).

Not Strangers but Pilgrims Inter-Church Process, *The Next Steps for Churches Together in Pilgrimage* (London: British Council of Churches and the Catholic Truth Society, 1989).
Philip, T. V., *Ecumenism in Asia* (Delhi: ISPCK, 1994).
Rayan, Samuel, *Renew the Face of the Earth* (Delhi: Media House, 1998).
Sacks, Jonathan, *The Dignity of Difference: How to Avoid the Clash of Civilizations* (London: Continnum, 2002).
Schreiter, Robert J., *The Ministry of Reconciliation: Spirituality and Strategies* (Maryknoll, NY: Orbis Books, 1998).
_____ *The New Catholicity: Theology between the Global and the Local* (Maryknoll, NY: Orbis Books, 1997).
Volf, Miroslav, *Exclusion and Embrace: A Theological Exploration of Identity, Otherness, and Reconciliation* (Nashville, TN: Abingdon Press, 1996).
World Council of Churches, *Towards a Common Understanding and Vision of the World Council of Churches* (1997) – available at <www.oikoumene.org>.
Yong, Amos, *The Spirit Poured Out on All Flesh: Pentecostalism and the Possibility of Global Theology* (Grand Rapids, MI: Baker Academic, 2005).

INDEX OF MODERN AUTHORS